P9-CMX-298

Cosby
The Life of a Comedy Legend

Ronald L. Smith

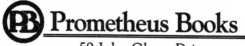 Prometheus Books

59 John Glenn Drive
Amherst, New York 14228-2197

Published 1997 by Prometheus Books

01 00 99 98 97   5 4

Library of Congress Cataloging-in-Publication Data

Smith, Ronald L., 1952–
      Cosby : the life of a comedy legend / Ronald L. Smith. — [Rev. ed.]
          p.   cm.
      Discography: p.
      Filmography: p.
      Includes bibliographical references.
      ISBN 1–57392–126–2 (hardcover : alk. paper)
      1. Cosby, Bill, 1937–   . 2. Comedians—United States—Biography.
I. Title.
PN2287.C632S63   1997
792.7'028'092—dc21
[B]   96–48075
                                                                    CIP

Printed in the United States of America on acid-free paper

Preface

This is an updated edition of the biography of Bill Cosby, titled *Cosby*, which was originally published in 1986. A Literary Guild selection upon its release, *Cosby* got front-page attention in the *New York Daily News* (April 6, 1986), and was warmly received by both reviewers and readers.

Cosby: The Life of a Comedy Legend contains expanded information and fresh interview material. It's a whole new Cosby.

Ronald L. Smith

Chapter One

"The only thing I had to give him," his mother said, "was plenty of love, and oh, dear God, I gave him all I had. But success comes from within, and Bill was determined to be something."

Born to Anna and William Cosby on July 12, 1937, William Henry Cosby, Jr., arrived at three A.M., just to make sure he had everyone's attention.

He was born in the Germantown district of Philadelphia. The people who lived there, like the Cosby family, sometimes called it "the Jungle." At first, William Cosby, Sr., made a fairly decent living as a welder, and his family lived comfortably on Beechwood Street. But with an expanding family, ever more pressure, and no way out of long sweaty days and exhausted nights, the elder Cosby began to drink. The family was washed down to Steward Street and less pleasant accommodations.

There was no bathtub in the house. Instead there was a half-size metal tub that had to be hoisted atop the stove and heated, then lugged back down for bathing. Faced with an arduous procedure like that, young Cos figured there had to be an easier way out. On the nightclub stage, Cosby would talk about bathing in the toilet instead. Of course, he'd warm up the water first—by dumping his brother in it.

As William Cosby, Sr., became more of an absentee father, the family drifted still deeper into "the Jungle," ending up in a first-floor apartment at 919A Parish Place in the Richard Allen Homes, a series of squat buildings that housed the poor. The people who lived in them called the place by a less fancy name: "the projects." The homes were among the first experiments in such housing for the poor in Philly.

Some kids in the projects had a tough time making it home, not because of crime, but because the barracks all looked alike. Every building was the same dirty beige with a stripe of red brick along the first floor. But as Bill remembered it, as bad as the projects were, they could be appreciated as an almost "upper-class place in a lower-class district."

He grew up with the sound of the trains roaring by night and day, shaking the hollow walls and flooring of the Cosby home. "There was a railroad bridge and when Mother would hang clothes the trains would go by and dirty them. But it wasn't a life of poverty. We always had plenty of hot water and heat."

Three more children arrived, one of them an epileptic, and the Cosby household was soon a crowded one. Bill and his young brother James slept in the same bed. He and James shared many of the childhood pranks and jokes that would later turn up in Bill's monologues, from giggling late at night to feuding over who'd roll over on the cold spot when the younger boy wet the bed.

Bill had less time to share with his parents. His mother had to work as a cleaning lady. By the time he was able to say "Dad," he was hardly able to find him anymore.

Squeezed with wife and kids into the cramped quarters at the Richard Allen Homes, William Cosby, Sr., wasn't too thrilled with his new job in the navy. Home didn't offer much relief, either. He stayed away as much as possible and when he returned he was often drunk. For young Bill, who thought of his father as "the Giant," and who would later create brilliant humor about the frightening presence of a grumbling parental behemoth, real life was more nightmare than fairy tale.

Cos told the story in nightclubs of how he and his brother would wait for their father to come home. He "would go out and really booze it up, 'cause my mother'd give him an allowance of about five dollars and he'd go down to the tavern . . . he'd come home around nine o'clock really loaded." Breathing heavily, struggling with his clothes, he'd drop his pants and the boys would hear the sound of coins.

"Clink! The Giant . . . has money!" And they'd sneak into his room and steal it.

It made a suspenseful story, filled with conspiratorial whispers, the wide-eyed look of fear at being caught, and the glee in counting out eighty-five cents. In the routine, it was even funny when the Giant woke up and said, "Fee, fie, foe, fum, who stole my dough! Was it the kids? I'll beat the kids!" To which Cosby's mom answered, "Leave the children alone." The Giant stormed, "Why? You in it with them?" She said, "Yes, I get twenty percent!"

Bill Cosby's creative story, told years later in a nightclub, is more than selective amnesia. It's a magical transformation of pain into laughter. For one thing, Bill's dad rarely came home with any money left over from his nights shooting darts and drinking at the bar. Even on payday, there was somehow no money.

Bill's father may not have been serious when he shouted, "I'll beat the kids." But, when his wife pressed too hard for spending money, he didn't threaten her. He hit.

A more accurate bedtime scene would show a young, frightened Cos listening with mounting fear and confusion to the strained and pleading female voice and the loud rumbling male voice coming from the other room.

"But, Bill, you got paid today!"

"Take this, because that's all I have."

"But, Bill—'

"Well, this is all I have, so don't ask me for any more."

Some nights the loud voices would subside. But other nights, Bill's mom tried desperately to get a share of the paycheck, for the rent, for food, for the kids. And there was the sudden sound of sickening violence, followed by the softer sound of sobbing. Too young to understand and too old to ever forgive, Bill could do nothing about these scenes of anger and tears except hope for the Giant to stay away a little longer the next time he disappeared

Who was this drunk, violent man named *Bill Cosby*? For the other Bill Cosby in the house, this grown-up image was a source of confusion and pain. *Father.* "The word still spells disappointment to my brothers and me."

Anna Cosby couldn't make it without taking matters into her own hands. With her husband disappearing more and more, she ended up working twelve-hour days cleaning other people's homes, and it still wasn't enough. "Many's the time I saw her come home from work exhausted and hungry and give her supper to one of my brothers who was still hungry after he'd eaten his own."

The family ended up on relief. "We needed those checks on the fifteenth and thirtieth," Cos adds. The Cosby boys tried to make things easier for their mom, but inevitably there would be squabbles, homework problems, or maybe just a game of indoor basketball that left a lamp broken. When there was trouble, poor Mrs. Cosby couldn't help but burst into tears.

"Her tears alone would shake us up," Bill recalls. "No spankings. No beatings. She'd start crying and you'd start crying."

In the midst of the frustration and heartache, Cos couldn't quite understand what was happening. His father was always gone, but now even his brother James was disappearing. For long periods the boy was gone, and when he'd come back, he'd be sick. Little James was only two years younger than Bill. At six, the child died of rheumatic fever.

The family tragedy only worsened the situation at the house. A few more years, and the Giant was gone for good. He had simply stepped out, abandoned his home and family, and left it to William Henry Cosby, Jr., to take his place

"My first job," Bill recalled, "was to make a shoeshine box out of orange crates. Then go out and buy shoe polish and washrags and go downtown and shine shoes. When I was eleven, I worked summer vacation at a grocery store. Hauling boxes and stuff, from six in the morning until six at night, nine on Saturday nights. For eight dollars a week. That was 1948."

Not yet into his teens, Cos had three jobs in the fall. First, he had to make money for the family, getting up at sunrise to sell fruit over on Marshall Street, or shining shoes. Then he had school. And then he had to take care of his younger brothers Russell and Robert till his mom came home. He learned to deal with all their familiar childhood arguments, ranging from who got the extra piece of cake left over from last night to when it was time to do homework.

"He kept us in line and whipped us when we got out of line," Russell remembers.

Sometimes it was part of Bill's responsibility to make breakfast. He evidently inherited some skill from his father, who could work wonders with whatever leftovers were lying around—but in the case of the son, there was the unique Cos touch to it. He liked to put food coloring into everything, something his dad never tried in the navy.

"I liked purple waffles, green, orange, red waffles. I loved them and I couldn't understand why my mother never dug them. Nobody seemed to want to eat them. But food coloring is cool. Take scrambled eggs. Put some food coloring in, scramble 'em up, cook 'em, and they look like green or blue sponges."

It was one thing not to eat one of Cos's masterpieces. But not to help clean up? That was something else again. Russell recalls: "I tried to be smart one day when my little brother came out and said, 'Bill wants you to come in and wash the dishes.' I was with a couple of my friends and was going to be real brave and so I said, 'If Bill wants me tell him to come out here and get me.' And he did. It was in the summertime and he put me in this room with no fan, with the windows closed, and he closed the door, and that was my punishment."

Russell would grow into a 250-pound man, and he was big for his age even in childhood, but he never tried to push around his older brother Bill. "I never tried to lick him. I had that father respect for him."

When Cos went to the Mary Channing Wister Elementary School, he found himself in the midst of some pretty confusing adults, but at least none of them was as threatening—or as disappointing—as his father. School was weird, though. A curious kid, Cos wondered why, when he was wide awake at eleven in the morning, the teacher would clap her hands and announce that everybody had to go take a nap. He also wondered why the teacher had to know whether he was going to the bathroom for a "number one" or a "number two."

School was a place not to take too seriously, and Cos didn't. Later on, Cosby would look back at ghetto schools and remember them as places of "trouble and turmoil, where the teachers look on it as a stepping-stone to somewhere else and nobody really cares and the kids look up to the wrong people." But at the time Cos was doing his best to make it as painless as possible, so there'd be more time for play.

Sometimes Cos would con his mom and get to take the day off pretending he was sick. He found that a little charm could go a long way: "You start out at about three or four conning your mother out of a cookie. You know that she'll say no the first time you ask, but you know that if you can get her laughing you can get around her." Soon he was able to con the teachers and, with a little joking around, con his classmates, too.

Nicknamed "Shorty," shy little Cos "got to feeling that as long as people were laughing, they were my friends. So to get myself across and to be an important person, I made them laugh. Through humor I gained acceptance."

Some of the humor came from the unfailing spirits of his mother. Sometimes she would share the humor by spending an hour or two reading funny stories about mischievous boys named Huck and Tom who lived down in Missouri.

"My mother used to read Mark Twain to us," Bill remembers. "She scared us half to death with those kids going down into that cave."

To interviewers, who would often ask him about his comic influences, he'd simply say, "Read Twain." He was confident that they would learn something if they did, and even more confident that they hadn't read Twain in the first place.

When young Bill helped his mom to raise baby James, baby Russell, and baby Robert, he probably would've enjoyed the description of a newborn in Twain's *Pudd'nhead Wilson*. It's easy to imagine Cosby delivering Twain's lines:

"The baby would claw anybody who came within reach of his nails and pound anybody he could reach with his rattle. He would scream for water until he got it, and then throw cup and all on the floor and scream for more. He was allowed to eat anything he wanted, particularly things that would give him a stomach-ache."

As Langston Hughes wrote, "Mark Twain, in his presentation of Negroes as human beings, stands head and shoulders above the other Southern writers of his times."

But in the public schools of Bill Cosby's childhood, the idea of Negroes as human beings was a novelty. Few teachers sought to instill pride in their black students. However, Cosby remembered one of his teachers, Mrs. McKinney, being very agitated one day. The children at the racially mixed school he attended had just come back from assembly, where they had sung, in about ten different keys, a bunch of songs starting with "My Country 'Tis of Thee." Mrs. McKinney asked the kids if they knew what the lyrics to one of the songs was all about— the one that was called "Old Black Joe."

"She said we were never, ever to sing that song again. She said none of us had any business singing that song. And it brought an awareness to us, because we were just little children and didn't think about what we were singing. But we were absorbing something from that song which said we were second-class citizens."

Cos was learning fast to separate the truth and the lies, and learning even faster how to make his own lies pass for truth. But sometimes he could still get taken in by those adults. Like Mom. Talking about fright and bewilderment onstage, Cos did a riff about the time he was playing with his navel:

"My mother said, 'All right, keep playin' with your navel, pretty soon you're gonna break it wide open and the air's gonna come right out of your body, you'll fly around the room backwards for thirty seconds, land and be flat as a piece of paper, nothin' but your little eyes buggin' out.' "

Cos said he was so shaken he used to carry Band-Aids in case he had an accident.

Cosby's feelings toward adults in general, and teachers in particular, might best be summed up in a few lines from one of the Twain books his mom read to him. Huckleberry Finn talks about prissy Miss Watson:

"Miss Watson would say, 'Don't put your feet up, don't scrunch like that, don't stretch, set up straight, why don't you behave?' Then she told me all about the 'bad place' and I said I wished I was there."

At the Wister School, Cos finally found a teacher who wasn't the typical "Miss Watson." Her name was Miss Mary Forchic. She did her job seriously yet joyfully. She knew that the little kids had big problems. They were often hungry, they had to go about in torn clothes and flapping-soled shoes. And they were lost. Lost among all the other kids at school, lost in a crowd of other brothers and sisters at home. And when these little kids were overlooked by adults who considered themselves too big and powerful to give them time or attention, they were not only lost—they were alone.

Miss Forchic's class was for the "unreachable and unteachable." However, she felt many of the kids' problems came from their own sense of smallness, helplessness, and lack of self-worth, and this problem wasn't "unsolvable." They needed desperately to have a sense of pride. The first thing she used to do when she set up a classroom was to spread the tables around as much as possible, so each child could have "his own space" and a little breathing room.

Most public school teachers were biding their time, waiting for something better, or simply acting like paid baby-sitters. They weren't about to put in any extra effort to reach out and risk getting kicked by some rowdy brat, or getting yelled at by some obstinate, angry parent who didn't want to listen to someone else's advice. But Miss Forchic gave her time, and even her money. She offered prizes of toys and treated some kids to after-school snacks at the local luncheonette. In order to meet with parents, she would invite herself over after dinner, bringing something for the whole family—dessert.

Cos remembered the time she gave him a special treat. She took him to the movies, giving him a chance to get out of the neighborhood for the first time and see a gaudier, dreamier district of town. "I was so happy to be downtown. After the movie, my teacher took me to dinner and then she rode me home in a taxicab. This was a big thing because in my neighborhood if you rode in a taxicab, something bad or something wonderful had happened to you."

"Every child is interested in something," Miss Forchic once said. "The teacher's job is to find out what that something is. If it's baseball or football, for example, you can build math around that." If a kid wanted to know how to compute his batting average, he went to Miss Forchic.

When a child turned in a hastily scrawled little homework assignment, she didn't scream or yell. She said, "I'll accept this—if you tell me it's the best you can do." And her techniques for teaching, her dedication and inspiration, impressed Cos enough to make him think about becoming a teacher—a thought traitorously abhorrent to the minds of most kids doing time in elementary prison.

Bill got his first taste of show business in Miss Forchic's class. He'd cut up for the other kids in the class. But doing that didn't seem to amuse his teacher. She'd warn, "In this classroom, there is one comedian and it is I. If you want to be one, grow up, get your own stage, and get paid for it."

She had a more constructive idea for Cos. She figured that if Bill was such a natural entertainer, why not channel that talent the right way? Bill turned up in such immortal class plays as *Tom Tit Tot* and *King Koko from Kookoo Island.* He loved to perform, but he was still a shy boy needing to be drawn out. "If somebody would pick me for the play I would go ahead and do it, but if they said, 'We want a volunteer' I never volunteered."

In 1972, Bill was reunited with his favorite teacher, now the retired Mrs. Paul Nagle of Washington, D.C. At a convention of the American Association of School Administrators, she received an award for her many years of teaching. In an interview for the *NEA Journal*, she shared her advice for teachers, advice that Cos seems to have used in reaching a new generation of kids.

"Learn understatement," she said. "Talk less. Speak quietly. Listen to the children . . . never belittle anything the child says or embarrass him in front of his peers. Instead, help each student to shine in his group."

Cos began to shine a little. Miss Forchic did write on his sixth-grade report card, "He would rather be a clown than a student and feels it is his mission to amuse his classmates in and out of school," but she also noted he was "a boy's boy, an all-around fellow, and he should grow up to do great things."

But how was he supposed to do that, growing up in one of the ghettos of Philadelphia?

Chapter Two

Cosby has tended to sidestep detailed questions about his childhood. Even with close friends, many aspects are "too painful to even think about." Instead, he's created a mythical childhood of laughter with his monologues.

Once, asked if his childhood was a happy one, he answered, "It will be, onstage."

Bill's youngest brother Robert put it this way: "Bill could turn painful situations around and make them funny. You laughed to keep from crying."

Christmas was the worst time of the year. It taxed even Cosby's ability to conquer misery with mirth. The stores were swollen with glittering toys, and kids talked about it with narcotic obsession, figuring up the take. In school, Christmas stories and songs painted fantasy pictures of mommy and daddy and the kids having a feast of a dinner and dozens of gaily wrapped presents to give and get.

Some ghetto families risked it all around Christmastime, scrimping and saving to chisel a little piece of that perfect Christmas ice sculpture. But at the Cosby house, with three growing boys, an absentee father, and a mother struggling to keep her family in the projects, some years there was hardly even wishful thinking. The boys knew better than to ask.

At school the teacher would ask if the kids were hanging their stockings on the fireplace. Well, Cos had no fireplace, of course. "We didn't have enough socks for our feet let alone any spare ones to hang."

Christmas was the season when want and need were felt more sharply than ever in the midst of plenty and greed. Only numbing December winds could put a freeze on the feeling of helplessness and rage. It was up to Bill to do something about the emptiness at the Cosby house.

"I wanted to cheer everybody up," Cos remembers. Since they couldn't afford a Christmas tree, "I took an orange crate and painted it with watercolors. We had a little Santa that lit up and I put that on top."

Mrs. Cosby had been working hard all day, as usual. When she got home, there in the corner of the bare apartment was the little painted crate, and the Santa Claus plugged in, the one red light in it throwing off a small reddish glow.

"When my mother saw it—about 9:00 P.M. on Christmas Eve—she put on her coat and went out. She must have borrowed money from the neighbors, but she came back with a kind of scrawny Christmas tree, and the next morning we all had a few presents."

For decades thereafter Christmas would remain one of the most important holidays at the Cosby home, and Bill would try every way possible to avoid nightclub or TV commitments that would keep him away. When Cosby's kids were small, and the family was living in Beverly Hills, the center of attention in the living room was a giant tree, some eighteen feet high, with more presents than its huge, fluffy green branches could hide. It beat out the displays of most of the neighbors, although the tree of silent film comic Harold Lloyd was something special. It was a foot shorter than Cosby's, but Lloyd kept it up—and fully decorated—all year long.

Discussing Christmas now, Cosby's wife, Camille, says: "I am inclined to give [the children] many gifts because I was given many gifts as a child. Bill is inclined to give them less. He feels that other things are more important. That's probably because he never really celebrated Christmas in that way, because of the circumstances."

What was important was to make every gift meaningful. Once Bill cried because his mom had given him money instead of a real gift. It was just paper to him.

In his adult life, sometimes the simplest gifts have given him the greatest joy. One year, his young daughter Ensa gave him a pair of tennis sweatbands. "He loved it," Camille recalled, "because he knew she had thought 'My daddy plays tennis and likes these. . . .' "

As a child, Cos was especially sensitive to gag gifts, or presents that could have been given to anyone. He believed a gift showed how much one person knows about the other, and how much that person cares.

And then there was the black-white problem. Cos remembered the time at Fitz-Simons Junior High when his racially mixed class was celebrating Christmas. As he's often said, he was propelled toward white middle-class values. The radio stars were white, the movie stars were white, and the culture was white. For Christmas, the kids were told to bring in holiday records. One white kid brought a Bing Crosby album. One black girl brought a Mahalia Jackson record.

The class seemed to enjoy Bing Crosby and his "traditional" sound of Christmas. But when the gospel style of Mahalia Jackson was heard, some of the kids giggled, and some of the black kids felt shame. Black wasn't beautiful then, not to see and not to listen to.

Assimilation was as much a battle for Bill as it was for kids of other minority groups. Bill's generation of blacks wanted to be like their radio and movie heroes, and developed the all-American way of talking and walking. Accents, ethnic foods, and unusual styles of music were frowned upon. Cosby remembered being embarrassed by his grandparents' accents, where a word like *gentlemen* came out a drawling *jemmen*. (Later Cos would celebrate that word when he made his first movie and formed Jemmin Incorporated.) Ethnic accents were funny, the kind of thing you'd hear on Fred Allen's radio sketches for "Allen's Alley."

For his junior high friends, Cos would imitate some of the radio comedians, doing a pretty fair squealing Jerry Lewis, and a blustery Senator Claghorn. Radio was a source of wonder for Cos. He was impressed with the way storytellers spun their tales, with the different sound effects and dialects, with shows that had the power to enthrall just with a few vivid lines of dialogue. He loved "Suspense," and "Inner Sanctum," and "Lights Out."

The monsters were special fun. For kids scared by adults and treated like "little monsters," there was a special bond with creatures like Frankenstein's—awkward, ungainly beings who seemed to cause harm no matter what their intentions, and who really only wanted a friend. Their rampages of frustration appeared only natural to the child's mind. They were just tantrums.

In the ghetto real-life crime and fear could be distorted, confronted, and conquered when the villain was something like "The Chicken Heart," the amazing, constantly growing load of pulsating flesh that, in a "Lights Out" radio show episode, engulfed the world and became a vivid memory for Cos. He imitated the show for his friends, adding the sound effects, building up the terror, and then blowing it apart with laugh-making excess. Later, on stage, he went through the process all over again, describing how he listened to the show and got so scared he threw Jell-O all over the floor so the monster would slip if he came through the door.

Hanging out at the apartment of one of the kids who was lucky enough to have a TV set, Cosby saw the comedians up close. He could do their moves and make funny faces. He used to watch Sid Caesar and Carl Reiner performing on "Your Show of Shows," and the images stayed with him into the night. "I used to dream of being Caesar's second banana," he recalled.

TV in the early fifties was peopled with friendly comics, stars like Jack Benny, George Gobel, Gertrude Berg, George Burns, and Sam Levenson. Levenson was a precursor to Bill Cosby, a guy who simply came out and told anecdotes about his friends and his childhood. Once a teacher of Spanish in Brooklyn public schools, Levenson had joked with his students and prefaced lectures at parent-teacher conferences with anecdotes and quips. He became an after-dinner speaker, and then a TV star, doing a fifteen-minute show that preceded Jack Benny's.

"Good evening, good evening. Relax. It's a warm night and we'll have a lot of fun," Sam would begin, as pleasant as a friendly neighbor. Then on to his observations. "Did you ever try to tell your kid what we went through before anybody gave us a penny? He can't stand it: 'Here we go again. Oh boy, how you suffered.' What's the use of talking to him? Would he believe me if I told him I used to save all week just to weigh myself? And you didn't weigh yourself alone. Who could afford the luxury? Eight kids used to pile on the scale, hold on together, and we weighed ourselves. You divided by eight, each kid got his weight, and we were all happy. I weighed eleven pounds till I was about fourteen. . . ."

Levenson even did jokes about his brothers. "We were eight boys. We were born about three weeks apart, we were so close . . . when my mother hit my brother Albert, I cried. You know why? I knew I was next."

By the time Cos reached junior high, he had bigger worries than getting socked by his mother. He had his hands full with the other kids. Sometimes touch football was tackle. Games with the gang became gang games. There was the time Bill tangled with a lefty named Edward:

"He beat me. I just couldn't get used to a guy with his dukes up on the wrong side. I'd swing to his right and he'd pop me with his old bony left fist. I kept yelling for him to turn around and fight fair."

Kids were restless, sometimes with the kind of restlessness a game of hoops couldn't solve. There were plenty of temptations, and Cos was tempted just like the rest, but he resisted the major schemes and scams because he knew that if he got caught there would be shame and disgrace. If he were put away, there would be Mom, with nobody to look after her except the bill collectors.

Junior high was full of tough kids: "They'd wear the hat sideways, wouldn't stand up straight or nothin', and when they'd talk to ya, they had about twelve toothpicks in the mouth." But they were still just kids. In gym class, half of them didn't know which way they were supposed to wear their jocks.

Some of their favorite pastimes had a ghetto twist to them. Like having fun going on rat hunts in the junkyard. Almost as much fun as swimming was outwitting the lifeguard at the public swimming pool and sneaking in for more than the one-hour swim limit. And it was a barrel of laughs to play "buck buck" and have kids jumping on each other, moaning and groaning under the weight as more and more kids would pile aboard.

Cos would later sublimely capture in comedy the childhood glee of rough sport—like his "Revenge" routine where Junior Barnes smacks him in the face with a slushball. The audience is in tears of laughter watching Cosby, his face a sorrowful pout, cry out, "What you want to hit somebody in the face with a slushball for?" Obviously, for laughs!

Sometimes the laughs were definitely too cruel to be appreciated. In their kid way, some of Cosby's pals couldn't help but be chillingly mean. "Man, you're *really* poor," they'd tell him. They weren't talking about the scuffed, resoled shoes he wore or the faded pants. They were pointing to the eviction notices pinned to his door. And they were glad it wasn't them. Sure, everybody was poor, but look at Shorty Cosby! His family was just this close to getting thrown out into the street.

Even with all the odd jobs he was doing, Cos never quite had pocket money. There were times when he couldn't get dates because of his clothes. The girls took one look at him with his mismatched jacket and pants and didn't look again. He nearly didn't make it to the junior high prom, ashamed as he was of his clothes. To make matters worse, he didn't have money for any transportation except a trolley car. His date's parents took pity on him and slipped him a few bucks for cab fare.

Some of Cosby's friends could make more in sixty seconds of shoplifting than he did in an entire morning of shoe-shining. Even so, Bill felt that he was smart enough to be an honest "con man." He liked conning the teachers, charming the girls now and then, and using some easy jokes and ingratiating gab to coax a bigger tip from the men who asked for a shine.

Mixed with the smile, there was also some resentment about shoe-shining. Bill would call out, "How about a shine . . . fifteen cents." And there would be no response. Then, seeing the guy heading back his way, he'd try again. "How about a shine? Your shoes are really filthy . . . a nickel."

As Cos recalled, the bargain salesmanship worked: "He'd say go. Then he'd give me a thirty-cent tip. . . . It's still the same shine, now what difference does that make? He'd rather have it for a nickel and figure he tipped me a quarter than tip me fifteen cents. How generous of him to do that."

In school he could coax a B-minus out of a C-plus tipping the balance with the Cosby smile. Teachers would just shake their heads. One said, "William, you should be a politician. You lie so well." Some recognized that he was bright, talented, and something special. An IQ test proved it on paper. He ended up with the tag "gifted," and that meant he could go to a school for "gifted students," Central High School.

Central High had a football team. That was definitely a step in the right direction. Cos remembered how he used to play football out on the street: "We used to wad up newspapers and put 'em inside our sweaters to look like shoulder pads. . . . My uniform was an old pair of corduroys with the torn cuff on the right leg and the shoes with the loose sole. . . ."

Now he had his own uniform: good old number 32. He got a chance to learn some real plays, too, on a real field. Out on the street, as described in one of his classic bits, football was pretty messy. The quarterback might offer a play that went: "Arnie, go down ten steps, and cut left behind the black Chevy. Philbert, you run down to my house and wait in the living room. Cosby, you go down to Third Street, catch the J bus, have him open the doors at Nineteenth Street—I'll fake it to ya."

At Central High, it was football the way it should be played, with referees and rules and a uniform with protection and padding. What a great environment! Within the first week of practice, Cosby broke his arm.

As for the scholastic end of the deal, Cosby was stifled by the atmosphere of the school, where "gifted" meant cliques of smug, self-assured, and disdainful kids. Cos was out of his depth, and the only thing he could do was demonstrate class-clown bravado, showing the miniature Brainiacs the difference between uptight and cool.

Cos would be sitting in class, swapping the textbook for a comic book. The teacher would come over, take it, and utter an archly meaningful "You'll get this back at the end of the school year." And Cos would say, "Why? Does it take you that long to read it?"

Cos put it mildly: "I wasn't having any fun and I wasn't passing." He decided it would be best to get out of the place. He went to Germantown High, which had a slightly more even racial mix (fifty-fifty), and also kids who were definitely not allowed at Central High: "Germantown had some girls at least!"

Germantown High was significantly more comfortable, but by this time Cosby was already way behind in his studies, and he'd lost interest. When he finished tenth grade, he discovered something that he hadn't expected. The teachers didn't think he was finished with tenth grade. Left back, Cos found insult added to injury. He was surrounded by babies, kids a full year younger.

Cosby figured he could do better by dropping out and learning a trade. Things weren't quite so bad for the Cosby family by this time. They'd moved to Twenty-first Street, and Cos even had his own room. Now if he took a job, he could keep a little more of the money for himself. Some of his friends were doing all right. They had pocket money, free time, and maybe even a used 1946 DeSoto to tool around in. These drop-outs seemed to have the right idea. Besides, what good was a high school diploma if all you could get with it was a job working in a factory?

Cos apprenticed in a shoemaker's shop, stitching leather soles, tapping on rubber ones. It turned out to be a grind, just a dead-end dream. So were the other menial jobs he found. There were still some slick kids Cos knew who were making money the mysterious way— but every now and then they'd disappear. Like from one to three years. "If I do so-and-so and get caught," Cos reflected, "and they lock me up, who'll look out for Mom?"

What else was there? Those futureless jobs? Cosby could hang out in front of his house in the late evening and see the walking dead trudging home somber and exhausted. Their reward was nothing but a cheap meal and a bed and they thanked the Lord for it, too.

Cos thought about it and figured that maybe, for once, his father had had the right idea. Go navy.

Chapter Three

"I joined the navy because my buddies had all joined the airforce and I didn't want to be like everybody else."

William H. Cosby, Jr., hospital corpsman, 1956.

The navy promised a chance to see the world. Anything outside North Philly was a new world. Cos spent some time aboard ships from Newfoundland to Cuba and served at the Marine base at Quantico, Virginia, and Bethesda Naval Hospital in Maryland. He was given courses in a variety of medical procedures and ended up working in a ward where casualties of the Korean War lay—many of them amputees, some brain-damaged, others with twisted limbs, all with the dream of piecing at least part of their lives back together.

Some of the patients could even make a few jokes on their tragedies, a line or two about being in the wrong place at the wrong time. Cosby swapped stories about his old neighborhood, and heard ones about the war. Some he would later use onstage, in a graceful balance of humor and exciting storytelling that was right on target, even though it was right on the edge.

He was told about "burial at sea," where the dead are draped in the flag they died for and then chucked off the side of the boat and into the sea.

"It seemed like the cheap thing to do," Cos would tell his audience. "I didn't understand it. I thought the flag was supposed to go with the body. And it must be embarrassing for a guy that dies. . . ." The body slides away and the flag is furled back up on deck like some kind of magic trick. Cosby's imagination took a new twist.

"One of the guys died at sea, and as rigor mortis was setting in we clamped his hands around the flag. . . ."

Cos relived the whole scene, complete with the *fudda-dudda dum* of the sober drums, and the *gobby-gobby domini-domini* of the last rites, and *phew*: the body tumbling over the side, with the corpse's hands clamped tight to the flag.

"Hey, leggo of the goddamn thing—"

"He wants to go with his flag, he loves it. . . ."

The stories Cos heard underwent magical changes, and emerged as vivid cartoons that blended comic fantasy with painful reality. He translated battle scenes from the old-fashioned viewpoint of stalwart heroics to the style that would one day become popular with "M*A*S*H." He had medics realizing they were sitting ducks with the red crosses on their helmets. ("Anybody wanna buy a helmet with a red cross on it? For a gun? How about some morphine? Take this helmet for some morphine.") And he peopled the stage with an entire battalion assaulting a beachhead, the men praying for their lives. He even drew on the forbidden thoughts of self-preservation:

"Medic!" a soldier cries to a corpsman safe in a foxhole.

"Waddya want?"

"My leg, my leg—"

"I don't make housecalls! Take two aspirin and mail in the five dollars."

Cos sounded like a seasoned veteran of combat when he told his stories. But during his navy service, his battlefield was a common one for many blacks. It was just the United States.

Members of the navy track squad, Cos and company would travel by bus to compete with other branches of the service as well as at meets with college teams. He wasn't in the back of the bus on those trips, but once the bus stopped . . .

One day the team bus pulled off the hot, dusty road in a small South Carolina town. The guys piled into the roadside diner, appetites whetted for a fine meal. But Cosby knew that he wasn't welcome. While the others joked around with each other, the black track star walked around to the back of the diner, alone.

He had to keep his emotions under control, ignore the insult.

But when he opened the screen door in back, he stopped and stared.

The kitchen was staffed by blacks who greeted him with smiles.

They sat Cos down and unveiled the entire well-stocked refrigerator in the white man's diner. The young athlete saw his place of honor crowned with a royal feast of cold cuts all piled high in a giant hero sandwich.

When Cos got back on the bus, his teammates noticed he was nonchalantly munching on the tail end of a giant hero. Some of them kidded with Cos over his "special treatment," and begged him to let them hang out with him back in the kitchen the next time.

There was special treatment in the navy. It didn't have to do with the color of a man's skin as much as what kind of little insignia was on his shirt. One stripe made all the difference between an even look into a man's eyes and a forced salute to his power.

He looked in the mirror and he saw a man with more tools than most, an athlete with discipline, a man with the brains to be an honor student. Out on the quad he saw the hustlers moving up in rank, moving up in pay, turning around and expecting his salute for their achievement.

By guts and guile, he was determined to change his life. By practice, raw practice, he was getting faster and faster out on the track, reaching higher and higher with his jumps. At work, he was finding ways of reaching the dispirited and beaten soldiers lying in the wards. He decided to "stop fighting things I couldn't change and use the intelligence I was born with." He learned from the men in the wards, and from the guys who were not only bucking for promotions, but getting them.

"I was meeting navy men who really worked at bettering themselves," Cosby recalls, "guys taking college and high school correspondence courses. They were having difficulty with courses that I could do after reading through once. I thought about how these guys were suffering to learn and how much of a sin it was for me, who had a better intelligence, to be doing nothing. I was committing a sin, a mental sin, by not using my brains. So I applied for a special high school program, and got my diploma."

When Cos visited home, he was happy to see that his younger

brothers were taking care of business, and the family was doing well. His brother Russell was no longer the mischief-making little kid, but Bill still got a kick out of observing him.

Bill recalled the time he wanted to use the phone, "but my brother Russell grabbed it first to call his girlfriend. Fifteen minutes later, I listened in and all I could hear was breathing. Picked it up in another ten minutes and heard more breathing. Finally I yelled into the phone, 'I gotta use this phone.' 'You can't,' said my brother. 'We're talkin.'"

Cosby could be pretty paternal even though his brothers were practically out of school. When brother Bob would send him letters, Cosby would read them, then check them for grammatical and spelling mistakes, and then grade them.

Bob knew better than to question Bill's intentions. "With people I love," says Bill, "if they don't do what I think is right, then I become very sarcastic. And that's hard to take. Most of the folks in my family, I think, have this biting sense of humor. If you're out of line, man, they can just drop it right on you. And it's just as dry as sawdust but it just goes so deep into the wound."

In the service Cosby had ripened into a lean six-footer with a wiry frame. Even through his thirties and forties Cos tried to keep his weight under 190 pounds and usually succeeded. Back then he won track awards for the navy team. At the national AAU competition he hit his all-time high of six feet five inches in the high jump, which landed him a respectable seventeenth place. He could run the hundred-yard dash in 10.2 seconds.

When his four-year hitch was up, he recalled that he was "too ashamed to go back home and live off my mother." He was proud of his diploma and all the honors he'd won for his track feats. He decided to make a pitch for himself at Temple University.

They were impressed. Heading toward twenty-three, Bill Cosby was more of a man than the freshmen just out of high school. He was a seasoned serviceman, a guy with the guts to discipline himself in both mind and body. Those were the qualities Temple University was looking for. The only thing Cos didn't have was money. But, finally, it didn't matter.

On an athletic scholarship, majoring in physical education, Cos wasn't the stereotypical dumb jock wooed by his school to play ball while somebody else did his homework. In addition to joining the football team and getting his letter in track, Cos maintained a B average in his studies.

Cosby was hustling all over. He was on scholarship, but this didn't entitle him to room and board. He had to commute between home and Temple, which got to be pretty arduous. Sometimes he'd crash in somebody's dorm room, and for meals he'd get somebody to loan him a meal card. Before long he became so well known to the cafeteria personnel that they hardly ever questioned him when he'd walk in.

It was more fun to be on campus. He liked to play drums at jam sessions, and he impressed the girls with his music, his athletic prowess, and his sense of humor, which continued to grow sharper and wilder as he became accustomed to college life.

Temple's athletic director, Ernie Casale, remembers that when Cos came in as a freshman he was all business: "He reminded me a little of the students we had after World War II—they were the best because they came out of the service, and they wanted an education, and they were determined. Bill was the same way. He came to do a job, and he did."

When the freshman came out onto the field, it wasn't to clown around. "Oh, he was a real competitor," says Casale. "In fact as a freshman he was a fierce competitor. He got into a couple of fights, and in fact I can remember him almost being thrown out of a game. That's how much of a competitor he was." In the midst of the rough pushing and shoving of college football, Cos could definitely hold his own. "That doesn't mean he was fighting in every game. I don't recall him arguing with officials or anything like that, but against opposing players in the intensity of the game, he would show his toughness."

Losing wasn't funny to Cos. At least, not usually. But there was the time he was out on the track at Franklin Field with over seventy thousand screaming, cheering fans jammed into the stands to watch the guys from Temple compete against teams from neighboring schools. Cos was the ace of the relay squad, the anchor man, the guy with the powerful kick who could make up ground, put on the pressure, and get the job done.

There he was, primed and ready, pumped up by the roar of the crowd, flexing his muscular legs, kicking at the dirt track and getting ready for the stretch run. On the other side of the track, the relay had begun. Four men were running neck and neck, holding their batons, pounding at the cinders so hard Cos could see the flesh on their faces shudder with every stride.

The hand-off to the second team of runners was made, and it was still neck and neck. The runners' eyes burned as they stared straight ahead, arms and legs pumping rhythmically. Now the third hand-off was completed, and, as the runners came around the turn, ready to hand the baton to the anchor men, it looked like it would definitely be up to Bill Cosby to give it the gun and pull out a victory for Temple.

Cos strained on his mark, his arm outstretched just waiting to get the baton. The race was so close the crowd was screaming. In came the Temple runner, chugging furiously. The guy lifted the baton out to Cos and smacked it up against his own thigh, sending the thing hurtling high into the air.

The crowd roared as the rivals got their batons and sped off. Cos stayed on his mark. Ready. But the Temple runner, exhausted and laughing, barely had enough strength to go and get the baton. Chuckling helplessly, he finally picked it up off the dusty track, and handed it to the furious Cosby.

Cos did the only thing he could do: "I took the baton and bopped him right on the head with it, which is when the fans began screaming with laughter. But old Cosby's a team player to the end and I take off after those runners like a madman.

"I'm running and running, and passing one guy and then another, and then I get what you call rigor mortis if you're a runner. It's from the effort. First my face muscles freeze, then my chest, then my legs. I fall down, a beaten man if ever there was one. And while I'm down, the cat I had hit over the head comes up, takes the baton, and bops me back with it. I couldn't dream up a routine that funny."

Cosby got a nickname at Temple: Riggie. And it stood for "rigor mortis." What with his anchor work on the track squad, his high-jumping, his football, freshman basketball, and shot-putting and discus throwing, he'd tell his coach, "Rigor mortis is setting in!"

But Cos kept going. "If I didn't make good at Temple, I knew what waited for me was a lifetime as a busboy in Horn & Hardart, or work in the factory. I was so afraid that I made myself do well."

As Ernie Casale remembers, Bill's best track event was the high jump. He was the Middle Atlantic Conference champion in that event. "Bill was a very valuable athlete, the type of track man who could get you points in several events. He was the top man in the high jump, but in other events he could get you a second place here, a third place there, getting enough points to help the team. He could play all sports."

In addition to his exhausting schedule, Cos was taking a variety of odd jobs to help support himself at Temple. To reward himself for completing a tough, no-nonsense freshman season, Cos decided to stretch his legs and travel. He figured to see the sights in California and get some kind of summer job. Some kind turned to any kind turned to no kind.

"Well, I got some of the worst excuses for not hiring me," he recalled. "I got so tired of riding buses and spending money to hear some guy say 'Well . . .' Finally I just called and said over the phone, "Do you hire Negroes?' 'No.' I wasn't Bill Cosby, famous entertainer, then. I was just a black man trying to get work. And I was ready. If somebody had said 'Burn,' I would have been right there with them. Because the door was being locked. And it was unfair."

Back in Philly, Cos found work, jobs like being a lifeguard at a municipal swimming pool. Returning to Temple in the fall, the sophomore was happy to relax a little, to feel comfortable as a valued, proven asset to the track and football squads. More of the relaxed Cosby humor was showing through.

Most of the coaches had no idea how funny Bill could be. One day Ernie Casale was walking up the tunnel to the stadium for practice when he stopped. He thought he heard his own voice. "And here was Cosby," he recalls with a laugh, "driving these kids wild, imitating me, imitating the football coach, giving a mock lecture, saying things like 'You guys take a good look at this stadium 'cause you'll never see it again.' And this was the first time I'd really heard him in front of a group and he did such a terrific job you could tell that something was gonna happen with that guy. He was great."

There's still a little touch of a blush when the athletic director is reminded that Bill's most famous football routine was about him. In fact, Cos mentions Ernie Casale by name in the extended routine about the Temple squad on his album *Why Is There Air?*

Cosby parodied Casale coming into the locker room before a big game and saying, "We wanna keep our television contract going, so remember that you're on TV. . . . You must not touch . . . certain areas of your body . . . when you're out on the football field. . . . If you're out there diggin' and scratchin' people are gonna turn you right off."

There is a resemblance between Cosby's broad impression of Ernie's voice and his natural speaking voice. But, as Casale insists with a little embarrassed laugh, the resemblance ends there:

"We did have a local TV package, because in those days the NCAA didn't package our division and we could do whatever we chose. And it's true, I did go into the locker room, more than one time, and talk to the players about the fact that we're on TV and we want to make a good showing and do things properly. But never"—Casale laughs again—"did I mention what he was saying. He took it from there, and I've always kidded him about that. But that's Bill Cosby."

Cos made the speech into a memorably hysterical routine, climaxed by the action on the field, where, as number 67, his face a mask of comic pain, he gets kicked in the . . . "'*you must not touch . . . certain areas of your body.*' So I grabbed my head! And just to make it look good they took me off the field and bandaged my head!"

Alas, there was also no "nut squad" filled with players running around naked in snowshoes, putting their helmets on backward, and collapsing in front of a priest to pray before going out to get slaughtered by Hofstra. "Oh no," athletic director Casale says affably, "the nut squad was a bunch of crap. That was all Bill Cosby again. Every football team has a first and second squad and in those days they were interchangeable."

Two positions on the team were not interchangeable, however, and Cosby was not too happy about it. "They made me a fullback," he once complained. "I wanted to be a halfback. I wanted to catch passes. I was never given a chance to do that."

As far as the football coach, Coach Makris, was concerned, those were the breaks of the game. And the same thing was true of Bill's collarbone after one game. It was broken.

While it's true that Temple was in the building stages with their football team in those days—Casale had arrived in 1959 to help turn the athletics program around—the squad wasn't that bad. And neither was Bill Cosby. Cosby has called himself just "a second-string fullback," modestly adding, "That means nothing. But I was great on defense." Actually, he was good enough to attract the attention of Emlen Tunnell, a scout with the New York Giants. It was unlikely that

Bill, several years older than the other college players due to his military service, would have been deemed a youthful enough prospect to be signed, but, as Casale remembers, "He was good. And he could have been a great college football player.

"He had the potential. I think if he'd had nothing to do but play football he could've been a hell of a football player." But he was also studying hard for his classes, working out on the track. And there was something else.

During the summer break after his sophomore year, Bill was restless for still more action: "I decided to do something crazy. You know, so I could go back to college in the fall and write a composition called 'How I Killed Myself during Summer Vacation.'"

He got his chance to do something crazy for five dollars a week. A friend got him a job as a bartender in a joint called the Cellar. He was supposed to mix the drinks and tell some jokes, keep things loose and friendly.

Cos put his "con man" experience to work, and he earned tips as the funniest, most charming bartender the place had ever seen. He wrote down jokes he heard on TV, and gags he picked up from comedy records. There was a young guy out there named Flip Wilson. Flip wasn't a household name at all, but thanks to the comedy record boom, he was one of many club comedians able to get some minor record label interest. Flip sometimes worked a little blue, but Cos only used the few gags, or ideas that were clean.

When he felt comfortable enough, he began to stretch out the jokes, building them into bits. But talk about comfort—the Cellar had no stage, so in order to be seen Cos had to to his act on top of a table. And since the ceiling was too low, Cos couldn't stand up to his full height. He ended up doing stand-up sitting down on a chair on top of a table.

When he graduated from the Cellar to the Underground it wasn't a great leap. Both places were in the same building. But at the Underground he was given more time to tell his little autobiographical stories of life at Temple, and anecdotes about the football team. The Underground had a house comedian, an old-timer who occasionally would skip an evening in favor of an extra bottle of booze. Cosby recalls that the guy "went into the tank" more than he tanked up, deliberately missing shows so that the young comic could get that desperately needed experience—and extra pay for a full night's work.

When he got good enough to stand there and do a solid show, Bill gained even more confidence. His cousin was making a breakthrough of his own, the first black to host a local TV show in Philadelphia. Cos would occasionally go down and try his luck warming up cold sober audiences. They laughed like they were drunk.

Something funny was going on. Not just in Philly, but all over the country. The year before, Shelley Berman had become the first comic to have a best-seller with a comedy album. Mort Sahl was on the cover of *Time* magazine. Hip comedy was the rage, especially if it also bordered on "sick-nik," as with the most controversial star of the day, Lenny Bruce. The "new wave" of stand-up comics was making more money in a season than any football player, college professor, or even the president of the United States.

This was the time to go for it, Bill thought.

But as he began making the trip from the Temple track to the smoky nightclubs, from the little TV studio to the classroom, Cos knew something else. If he left school, and then failed with stand-up comedy, he could be consigning himself to a life in the ghetto forever.

Chapter Four

"Roses are red, violets are blue. Grass is green . . . and dirt is brown."

Bill Cosby, beat poet and hip comedian.

Playing to the college crowd, Cos peppered his routines with stuff like that. He even used bits from Lenny Bruce albums, telling the crowd he was offering a little salute to Lenny.

Bill wasn't the warm, winning teller of tall tales back then, but then many other comics were also off their marks, just starting out. Phyllis Diller wasn't in her housewife persona, she was telling risqué jokes: "I'm a born highbrow, descended from a very long line—my mother once foolishly listened to." Even Jackie Vernon, famous for "dull man" routines, was a hipster back then: "I changed my name to Nefarious and wrote things on the wall: The Little Old Winemaker is a Junkie. . . . I pasted peanuts to the windowsill and watched pigeons go neurotic trying to pick 'em up."

Humor at the time was all hostility and intellect. The hot stars were neurotic virtuosi like Shelley Berman and Nichols and May, with their routines about Freud and Kafka, bleeding alone in a hotel room, or trying to pick a casket for a funeral. And there was the staccato attack on the government from Mort Sahl, spoon-and needle humor from James Komack, reefer gags from Ronny Graham, and racial satire from Dick Gregory.

Cosby tried to fit in. He delivered thought-comedy that cellar bar beatniks could mull over: "A wino drinks from a bottle wrapped in a brown paper bag . . . because he doesn't want to know the end *is* coming."

He took his bits to the local Philly burlesque houses. He remembers being repulsed watching a faded hooker strutting about "throwin' things, her old filthy underwear and stuff," at the old men at ringside. The repulsion was mutual. In between dances, he'd get up there, "telling Ivy League jokes to six sailors and a junkie, doing a routine about how Shakespearean actors talk. They didn't want some college darky talking about Hamlet between bumps and grinds, so I got fired."

Cos worked wherever he could, for whatever audience he could find. Using the Mort Sahl ploy, he'd come onstage with a newspaper, or a copy of *Mad* magazine, which was really just a convenient place to tape crib notes on current events and jokes he could use if things got rough.

Cos tried to work before his peers. The young crowd was the most responsive. "What you fear most is an audience of old people. I think we all turn more bitter the closer we come to our own death. Old people are toughest because you don't know how close to death they are upstairs."

But as he mentioned to Rex Reed, he took jobs anyplace: "I went to a beatnik dive—you know the kind—full of ugly Negro girls and ugly white men—sort of a Lonelyhearts integration. But they laughed. I was getting closer. Finally some cat called and said, 'Aren't you the one who does the funny bit about the guy with Saint Vitus's dance trying to light his own cigarette?' I said, 'Yes.' He said, 'I'll give you sixteen dollars a night.' Big Time. What he really wanted was for me to open the joint at seven-thirty before the regular acts went on at ten. Boy, the things they do to you in this business when you are nobody."

Some club owners asked Cos to throw in some filth. A sexy joke here and there. He simply couldn't do it, even though the money was there. For nearly a decade Nipsey Russell had been making good bread telling whiz-bang rhymes to the bar crowd. They'd roar when Nipsey stood up and recited, "I went to see my girl the other night . . . she came to the door in her nightie . . . she stood between me and the light . . . and good God almighty!"

What Cosby needed to get from "amateur" college work to the big time was a manager. Herb Gart, a student at Temple University . . .

was not exactly a manager. But he was, like Cosby, keenly ambitious about show business and very smart. Gart was learning how to be a manager, getting gigs for some of his folksinger friends.

"Cos and I had some classes in common," Gart recalls, "and I kind of knew him by sight; that was about it. I didn't know he was a comedian." After Herb saw him work as an mc, the two began to get together and plot a strategy. Herb appreciated Bill's natural sense of humor. "One of my favorite moments with Bill was when we were sitting in a breakfast-restaurant with his niece, who had come in from Harrisburg. She was wide-eyed, she said, 'Oh, Philadelphia! It's so exciting!' And Cos paused, and muttered, 'You poor child.' It was a great comment on Philly."

Through the owner of The Underground, Herb and Bill found out that New York's Gaslight Cafe was interested in booking new talent. "It was the middle of winter, and the club was already thinking about the summer. So we figured, summer vacation, maybe we'll be working in Greenwich Village. He'd be the comedian and I'd be the manager. I really honestly knew nothing about managing. I just had a certain intuitive thing, common sense. We went up there for him to audition. He did a guest set, and of course got the gig."

The club owners wanted Cos for the whole summer. As for Herb's two folksinger friends—they got two week bookings.

Cosby could hardly wait for the semester to end: summer in New York City, playing a real New York club!

The bad news: By the time Cosby and Herb Gart arrived, the club had changed hands. The new owner was an old man from Mississippi by the name of Clarence Hood. He'd never heard of Cosby.

The good news, and Herb remembers it well: "Clarence Hood was a very pleasant, very nice old man. When he asked Bill to audition all over again, I started to lecture him about professionalism and commitment. I showed him the booking papers that said that Bill was in for the summer. I'm coming off like I know what I'm talking about, and to Clarence Hood, who didn't know anything, I did. He ended up asking me to help him book the Gaslight! And nobody's heard of me at all. Or Bill Cosby."

Herb persuaded Mr. Hood to dump the two folksingers currently on the bill and give Herb's clients a break. Herb had instantly transformed the Gaslight into an all-Philly talent show. Ironically, Herb's two singers would never attain the fame of the two men he fired—Tom Paxton and Len Chandler.

The Gaslight was a big step up for the two young Temple University students, but this was far from big-time show business. Cosby was required to perform six sets a night, rotating with the two folksingers. "The way it worked, you started to perform as soon as the place opened. People would gradually filter in. This wasn't bad for the singers, but it was a little rough for the comedian. When it was his turn to start the evening, Cos sometimes would begin the first set to no one. Then a couple would sit down, and then somebody else. By the time he's done his first set he's got maybe six people. Some nights much better, but on a Tuesday night you'd be lucky if you got six people. And like the others, Cos had to stay in the club all night, as part of the rotation, until he finished his six sets.

"Cos not only worked there—he slept there. He had a room upstairs above the Gaslight Cafe. The bed, as I remember Cos describing it himself, was a spring and a sheet. He got paid twelve dollars a night plus room and food." Gart usually camped out in the kitchen—his waistline filling out before his wallet.

The important thing for Cosby was to work, to become a seasoned performer in front of a sophisticated audience, to create enough solid material to get him into bigger nightclubs and ultimately records and television.

Cosby was doing it "the hard way," by trying to go with clean routines and observations. As Herb Gart recalled, "Dick Gregory was hot with political material. Flip Wilson and Redd Foxx were not doing clean things. And here was Cosby, doing clean, nonpolitical humor. He was telling stories. He's never been "a stand-up comic," even though he's great a comedian. He's always been a great *storyteller,* and the stories he's chosen to tell come out of experience and they come out of family relationships and friends. Other than Myron Cohen and Sam Levenson who the fuck did that? And they more or less did slightly extended jokes, whereas Cos could literally go on for half an hour about the situation at the dinner table.

"Think about what Cosby was doing. It was against all odds. He was going to come out and make no references to color. He was gonna tell stories about how his father punished him and things like that. He was gonna come out friendly instead of sounding hip. This just wasn't being done. But if he could pull it off—he'd be filling a vacuum, moving into an area that no one else entered—best marketing move anybody could make."

Even though Greenwich Village was, at the time, a great place for both comedians and singers to experiment, audiences (and club owners) did have expectations.

"Bill got a newspaper review that mentioned that he was a black comic. It didn't talk about him in terms of racial humor. He was a storyteller. But they identified him as being black, and that got Bill upset. But there was some good luck in all of this. Dick Gregory was the only black comedian who was happening, and he *was,* at that very moment, happening."

If Bill could be a bit more like Dick Gregory, he'd be able to work all those nightclubs clamoring for another black satirist. "It was fortunate that Bill arrived on the scene when he did, because it made moving along much quicker. He was the other guy they could talk about."

It was impossible to overlook the importance of getting recognized quickly. When liberal white audiences had applauded the political humor of Mort Sahl, the man got on the cover of *Time* magazine. When they pronounced Lenny Bruce the hip social satirist of the age, Lenny began to make records and do TV. And now they were discovering Dick Gregory and the man was getting up there with Mort and Lenny.

They couldn't get enough of Brother Greg's truthful racial humor. "Last time I was down South," he'd say in that quietly conversational voice, "I walked into this restaurant and this white waitress came up to me and said, 'We don't serve colored people here.' I said, 'That's all right, I don't eat colored people. Bring me some fried chicken.' "

And audiences were saying bring on more comedians like Gregory.

It was clear that a concession had to be made. Cos was still determined to ultimately make it as a clean storyteller, but for the moment he would give audiences at least some of the hip, racial humor that they craved. He started working in some Dick Gregory-type observations.

I Passed for White and a few other movies were exploiting racial themes. Cosby parodied those movies. He'd show the light palms of his hands and mimic the actors: "'I passed for white.' Passed for white?" Then he'd turn his hands over: "Didn't anybody look at the other side?"

The crowd ate up the racial stuff. "I used to live in a nice neighborhood," Cos would tell the bohemians and affluent barhoppers. "Then two white families moved in." Laughter. Applause. The new Dick Gregory.

Only there was more to it than that. Cos was really likable, really funny with his voices and his faces. As Ed Wynn said long ago, a comic says funny things—a *comedian* says things funny.

Cosby said things funny. And he was cool. There was no flop sweat for Cos. While other comics fretted, nervous wrecks, rushing their lines and showing the audience their fear, Cosby took his time. When things were going badly, he could even make a joke of it. One night when the new gags weren't working and the ad-lib riffs were off target, Cos simply curled up out of harm's way and did his show from under a piano.

Then he'd talk over the way the shows had gone during lunch at Cafe Figaro, down the street from the Gaslight, or at The Kettle of Fish, which was upstairs. Then he'd go back up to his room. As manager Gart recalls, "with six sets to do each night, he'd use his spare time to think and write."

Herb encouraged Cos by playing him some Lord Buckley records. Buckley was an underground legend, well known for his cool storytelling. Buckley's "hipsomatic" rendition of "Jonah and the Whale" was a classic back in 1950 and audiences were with him when he'd spin away from one-liners and riff through five- and ten-minute tales. The joy was as much in Buckley's delivery and characterizations as in any jokes along the way.

Herb's more unusual choice for Cosby to check out was Anna Russell. Although Russell was the very opposite of Cosby—known for her droll, comically pseudo-pompous lectures on opera—there was something that she could teach him. A comedian needed to listen to the audience, to know when to start speaking again. Gart explains: "If you listen to her pause, you can actually hear the way she waits for the sound of the audience. The sound rolls, and she comes in at the very end of the roll; perfect timing. It's a give and take with her crowd. She gives them all the room they need, and if she says something funny and they don't get it right away, the extra pause she leaves there helps them get it."

Gart did approve of one thing that Cosby always had going for him: clean humor devoid of cheap dirty word laughs:

"Every comedian can carry in his arsenal 'fuck, suck' and a couple of other words that can get him out of trouble any time he's in trouble. But the real challenge is to be basically, genuinely funny without needing to go to the cheap laugh. It's a cheap laugh not because it's a dirty word. It's a cheap laugh because it doesn't take any work to get the laugh."

Also trying to get ahead with solid, clean material were two former comedy writers, Allen Konigsberg and Joanie Molinsky, now known as Woody Allen and Joan Rivers. Joan remembers Cosby as a man of supreme confidence on stage. He got the most out of any piece of material. It wasn't a surprise to her when people began to pick up on him. "Cosby went first," she recalled, "Woody popped out after Cosby, Flip Wilson, then me." Of the Village clubs, she remembered "it wasn't all fun. Struggling isn't. A lot of people who recall that time don't remember it as a funny period. But there was so much talent starting out. It was thrilling. Bobby Dylan was on the same bill with me—six dollars a night. He passed the hat same as me. Barbra Streisand. Simon and Garfunkel. Mama Cass was a hatcheck girl. Mel Brooks was a schlock writer then courting Anne Bancroft. You were just happy and grateful to be working."

Cos was happy to work, and to watch some of the other comics work, like Lenny Bruce. Rivers recalled, "I watched Lenny's act every night for three weeks. I learned from Lenny that you could tell the truth onstage. You name a comedian from that day, and there's probably something they got from Lenny." In Cosby's case, it was watching the way Lenny was able to do characters on stage.

As Cos would later do in routines about his brother Russell and his Philly neighborhood, Lenny was able to make audiences care about fretful Aunt Mima or the attitude at the neighborhood candy store. The truths about human nature came through; personal recollections became universal.

Lenny stayed true to his comedy even when others criticized him and ostracized him. Cosby would soon he blazing his own unique trail of comic style, which also went against traditional "one-liners," and he saw, from Bruce, how difficult it was to be different: "I remember being very, very upset that people would come in to see Lenny knowing that he was going to use four-letter words. At that time in the sixties . . . that was really taboo. And I'm sitting in the Village Vanguard—I went to see Lenny because I had all of his records, and the cuts that I enjoyed most had to do with human behavior—and I'll be darned. Lenny started talking, and in the dialogue of the way the people talked, Lenny used a four-letter word. And four people, as if they had been rehearsing this, stood up and said out loud, 'I've never heard such language in my life.'

"And I remember being very, very angry with these people."

Cos could also get very angry and frustrated with his own audiences at times. Sometimes when Cos tried a silly-funny riff (like a bit on why you should never park your elephant next to a fire hydrant) the crowd reaction was wan. Sometimes they ate and blabbered while he was talking. But he didn't fight them. He knew, even then, one of the basic rules of the comedian: "People have to like you if you're going to be a comic. After a cat establishes the fact that he's funny, forty percent of the pressure is eased up on him because, when he walks out, people already like him."

Herb Gart remembers that Cos was usually even-tempered on stage. "If it didn't go well, he might not be happy but he wasn't about to put his first through a wall, either. But one night, he really had some problems. He had an audience that was really throwing his timing off. He'd tell a joke, and while the audience was laughing, a whole wall of people to stage right would be murmuring among themselves. And then he'd start the next story and they'd start laughing. And this was going on for about ten, fifteen minutes. He really got irritated and said, "Please. Cut it out!" Anyway, they didn't really cut it out. But he finished the set, even though there were these people suddenly laughing while he was trying to set up the next bit.

"He was very upset. When the set was over one of those people came up to Bill and apologized, and explained that these people were students from South America, in town for a special conference. Most of them could not speak English. So Cos would tell a story, someone would translate, and then they'd all laugh. So he put up with shit like that night after night after night."

Cosby learned that, after winning an audience over, "you have to protect" what you've got. "You can become hostile toward a heckler and people wonder what's happened because you're not supposed to get angry in public."

As with most comics, some of the humor Bill was drawing on was the humor of hostility and anger. There was the tension and hostility of a cynical Noah manipulated by God. There was the frustration of parent-child relationships where the parents are confusing, threatening, and amazingly dumb. There was the short tempered put-down of posturing karate stars and their smugness. There were lampoons of irritating commercials. In Cosby's case, he effectively turned much of this anger into such pure laughter that the roots didn't show.

But struggling at the Gaslight, Cosby hadn't found all the keys yet. He wasn't fully able to translate all his personal experiences into effortless-looking comedy. Phyllis Diller, who was going through the same trials, says it best:

"Whether it's Bill Cosby or Woody Allen—whoever it is, there's a period where you have to find out who you really are. It's extremely painful to get there. All along the way people are saying you'll never make it. Practice. Practice is what is so humiliating about becoming a good comic. There's no such thing as a good beginning comic . . . you have a spark and you want to do it, and you have the material and the material isn't that good in the beginning. . . . All of your training is done in front of people and that's what's so humiliating."

Onstage, Cosby would try to free-form like Lenny and offer up some anecdotes, or a riff on an old movie. He'd do his take on a horror movie the way Lenny reenacted a prison picture. But when the audience didn't get it, Bill had to return to set jokes—the Dick Gregory-styled racial humor the audiences in the hip clubs seemed to favor. Then they'd chuckle. They'd even laugh at an ad-libbed threat: "You better laugh. I've got a club that's the opposite of the Ku Klux Klan."

It had been a hot summer, but Cosby had been warmed by the vague promises of higher wages, and the remembered sound of laughter. Coming into the big time and facing big-time competition, he had succeeded. When Bill went back to Temple University, the idea of finishing and getting a degree was now even more remote. He couldn't wait to go back to New York.

Chapter Five

Could you imagine the first black president of the United States? Cos imagined the glorious day—and told his audiences he could just see the response: "For Sale signs in the yards of every home up and down Pennsylvania Avenue."

This was the era when Russia's Nikita Khrushchev was intimidating the entire world—taking off his shoe and pounding on his desk at the United Nations. But could he intimidate Cosby the black president? Bill imagined himself telling his advisors, "What do you mean I shouldn't have pulled the knife? He put the shoe back on, didn't he?"

With barely a few sporadic years of experience, Cosby was attracting the attention of the big shots. The *New York Times* did a piece on the unknown comic, and in bold type they enthused, PHILADELPHIA NEGRO AIMS HIS BARBS AT RACE RELATIONS.

They praised young Bill Cosby for "hurling verbal spears at the relations between whites and Negroes," and for staying in college: "Besides verbal spears, Mr. Cosby throws the discus and javelin, broad-jumps, high-jumps, runs the 200-low hurdles, and plays right half-back on Temple's football team."

The writer weighed in with his assessment of Cosby. "His output thus far is limited, [but] his viewpoint is fresh, slightly ironic, and his best quips are extremely funny."

Cosby became more and more popular. Aside from the Gaslight, he was playing all the clubs in the area, including the Cafe Wha? and The Bitter End.

Earlier, he had studied other people's records: ones by Lenny Bruce, Reiner and Brooks, and Brother Dave Gardner. "Just as some people might learn songs, I'd memorize comedy routines." Now came a more difficult time, when he had to listen to his own stuff over and over; balance the racial gags with the stuff he really wanted to do, like the bit about Noah and the routines about his family. He listened over and over, trying to correct mistakes and move ahead.

"At that time," he admits, "there was no Fat Albert or any of the other characters. I was basically doing sociopolitical material, learning to be a stand-up comic. You cannot learn to do that at home. You have to find an audience to talk to in order to get laughs. That's what I was trying to do. It was at the Gaslight that the 'Noah and the Ark' routine was developed and finished."

Cosby's salary hit two hundred dollars a week. His confidence and drive were at an all-time high. To reporter Hans Knight, Cos was very specific about his goals. "If you asked me why I'm in this, I'd have to tell you honestly—for the money. Yes, sure, I like the work. But I'm not fooling myself or anybody else. I don't consider myself an artist who has to do this because he can't help himself. I think I am funny. I see things funny and I talk about the way I see them. I try to project a family atmosphere—intimate, like sharing a joke with your friends or relatives in your home." And, cautiously he added, "If I fail I can always go back to Philadelphia. . . ."

With his natural cool, and his collection of racial quips, Cosby was more comfortable onstage than ever. He'd learned by trial and error how to handle the crowds. Once, when a table of ringsiders were distracting him by their double-O staring eyes and stony expressions, he simply slid down off the stage, sat at the table with them, and told his jokes from there. He coaxed the smiles out of them, and developed one more weapon. Years later, it would become standard Cosby procedure to warm up the crowd with ringsider conversation.

Cosby was progressing farther as a comedian than his pal Herb Gart was as a manager. Herb realized it. "I was not equipped to do the right job, to do the right thing for Bill." Herb shared office space with a more seasoned and connected manager, Len Rosenfeld. Rosenfeld, whose artist roster included folk acts the Clancy Brothers and Josh White, was able to use some muscle in getting Cosby bookings. Gart worked with other young talent on the "twelve dollars a night" scene, such as Buffy Sainte-Marie and Tim Hardin—and would eventually manage Janis Ian and Don McLean during their heydays in the 1970s.

Cosby found success at The Bitter End (where he would eventually record his first Warner Bros. album). Eventually the club owner, Fred Weintraub, signed up Cos and one of Fred's staff managers, young Roy Silver, began to work exclusively with the young comedian.

Silver would finish the job of grooming Cosby for big time success. It was Silver who got him the glowing review in the *New York Times*. Roy recalled pumping the *Times* writer so full of drinks he could hardly slosh out of the club. He recalled that he even helped the guy come up with such a positive (and coherent) review the following day.

Twenty-nine, just a few years older than Cosby, Roy Silver seemed like any other Ivy Leaguer, with his studious black glasses and close-cropped hair. He looked like somebody's accountant. In fact, before The Bitter End he had worked as director of research for the Scientific Design Company.

Roy had worked with some promising talent—but he was willing to drop the others in favor of Cosby. This included a scruffy but intriguing young folkie by the name of Dylan.

Roy went over Bill's routines—and the two realized there was still a lot of work to be done before he could really be "big time." Silver recalls, "People are always saying to me today that Bill is where he is because he's lucky. There's some kind of magic . . . you've got it and that's it, people laugh. Oh, boy! Bill would do six shows a night, and I'd sit at each one with a tape recorder, getting down every word and every reaction from the audience. After the last show, we'd go up to my dump or his and spend all night sweating about every line. Thus and such was funny in the first two shows, but not the others. Why not? Didn't you punch it right? Was your timing off? Was it just a dead audience? Line by line like this for weeks, till we knew we had a thirty-minute set that was working."

It was tedious work, to "go over every single line, edit and cut, edit and cut," paying attention to a phrase, to a misplaced adjective, making the lines flow like poetry. The two men had fights. Long nights brought tension. Being "almost there" brought frustration.

There was yet another problem, one that both Bill and Roy Silver recognized. Bill was rebelling against the "Negro comedian" tag. He didn't like doing all those race jokes. It wasn't him. It wasn't the kind of comedy he was best at, even if it seemed to go over well in the hard, hip Village clubs.

"I found that, to be a success," Cos recalled, "I'd have to jump over Dick Gregory. I had the shadow of Gregory in everything I did."

Together, he and Silver tried to find a way out. At the time Cos said, "We decided between us that I didn't have to trade on my being a Negro to succeed. I feel that I have no right to speak for all Negroes any more than a Jewish comedian can speak for all Jews, or, for that matter, any American can speak for all other Americans. . . . I still speak out for equal rights, but I do it as an American, not as an entertainer."

Cos's point of view was simple enough. There was no room for another Dick Gregory. Bill Cosby was a comedian in the Twain mold, observing all aspects of human nature, a comedian who just happened to be black. Dick Gregory's inspiration and cause was that he was a black comedian.

Some nights, Cos would try to stay away from the easy racial one-liners. He would do his "Noah and the Ark" bit, stray into ad-libs, riff and ramble on the things he observed riding the subway, the things that happened to him in college. A friend from high school, Ed Weinberger, would occasionally be in the audience, flinching at the mumbling, stumbling words, sharing the pain. Weinberger knew that it was tough creating comedy. He was doing it himself, writing material for Dick Gregory.

Roy Silver would be in the wings watching the trial and error, and error. Sometimes Cosby's was one lone voice in a dead-quiet room. "He'd listen to the loud absence of laughs for a couple of minutes, panic, and blam!" Cos would spit out a racial gag and save himself. And glare over at Silver, the manager who was encouraging him to slide right down the drain with the "straight" stuff.

Coming offstage in a rage, Cosby would push past Silver, barking out a quick "Up yours!"

The men would shout at each other, fight, and Cos would ball up his fist and shove it at Silver's face, ready to punch some sense into him

"Next morning, after we'd both cooled off a little, we'd get together and maybe develop another minute or two of material. It would be painful and hard. . . ."

Fortunately for Cosby, other comedians were in the same boat, trying to do something new besides the scatter-fire one-liners that had made Bob Hope and Henny Youngman popular. Bob Newhart and Shelley Berman used telephone monologues. Audiences were beginning to accept this new form of humor—the "routine" rather than steady patter, a story that was so good, so true, so real, it could be heard over and over again. Audiences wanted Newhart to do his "driving instructor" bit. They wanted to hear Berman talk about the drunk who was suffering through "The Morning after the Night Before."

And for Cos, there was "Noah and the Ark." More than anything else, it established that Bill Cosby was a very funny fellow, in the Mark Twain tradition. Newspaper articles on the rising young comic began to describe the bit, quoting whole segments of it. Cos started it out in the traditional "what if" fashion. He wondered what if Noah were like any skeptical modern cat? And suddenly he heard the voice of God?

"NOAH."

"Who is that?"

"It's the Lord, Noah."

"Right!"

When Noah finally believes he's actually talking to the Lord, he wonders why.

"I want you to build an ark."

"Ri-ight. What's an ark?"

"Get some wood. Build it three hundred cubits by eighty cubits by forty cubits."

"Right. What's a cubit?"

When the Lord tells him he plans to destroy the world, Noah can't believe it: "Am I on 'Candid Camera'?"

"I'm gonna make it rain four thousand days and drown them right out!"

"Ri-ight. Listen, do this and you'll save water. Let it rain for forty days and forty nights and wait for the sewers to back up."

"RIGHT!"

Cosby's comedy had a classic feel to it. More than a hundred years before, Mark Twain had produced comic literature hailed as the work of a genius. A look at a Twain biblical satire, "The Diary of Adam and Eve," shows just how close to the heart Cosby had come. Twain's Adam is also a modern skeptic, grumbling about Eve: "This new creature with the long hair is . . . always hanging around, in the way, following me about. . . . I get no chance to name anything myself. The new creature names everything that comes along . . . and always that same pretext is offered: it looks like the thing. There is the dodo, for instance . . . it 'looks like a dodo.' It looks no more like a dodo than I do!"

Twain's Adam grumbles that Eve eats too much, puts up crazy signs like THIS WAY TO THE WHIRLPOOL and THIS WAY TO GOAT ISLAND, and starts coming up with wacky stories like being a part of his rib. "I have not missed any rib," he challenges. But what do you expect from a crazy creature? "She has taken up with a snake now."

Roy Silver recalls the time Danny Kaye came down to the Village, looking for new talent. A showcase was assembled featuring some of Roy's stars, including Cass Elliot and Bill Cosby, and some from another manager, Jack Rollins.

"I don't have to tell you what a major event this was in our lives. Okay? Now Danny came down with an entourage, in a limousine. And Bill was gonna close the show. "The first act came on, Cass Elliot and the Big Three. Danny saw them, and leaped up and said, 'They're on the show!' and we all applauded. Another act came on and he said, 'They're on the show!'

"Then Jack Rollins's act came on and Danny said, 'He's on the show!' Bill was about to go on, and Danny said, 'Well, that's enough . . .' and left. Cosby never got to go on. And he and I in the middle of the street had a screaming argument."

Setbacks like that happened all too frequently. Worse than that were the weeks when there wasn't any work, or anything to look forward to. But, while things were still very sporadic, with several months going by without a significant gig, he was getting a few bookings at prestigious clubs, like Chicago's Gate of Horn. He and his manager were still not above riding out and staying in a cheap hotel together—and all for a seventy-five-dollar date—but it was getting better.

Cosby was getting close, so close. It was time to make a decision: finish school or become a full-time comedian.

Chapter Six

One weekend Temple had a football game scheduled against an Ohio team. And Cosby had managed to get himself a two-hundred-and-fifty-dollar booking at Town Hall. The coach, George Makris, was worried.

At a meeting with Temple's athletic director, Ernie Casale, George shook his head and said, "You know Cosby, he's involved with this comedy thing. Well, the team's supposed to go out to Toledo on Friday, but he doesn't want to go out.

"He said he can make a couple hundred bucks Friday night being a comedian. He wants to come out Saturday, alone."

"I'll talk to him, George," Casale said.

A short time later, Cos and Casale met. The director looked over Bill's transcripts while the Temple junior waited.

"Bill," Casale said at last, "look at this. You started out, you were an outstanding student, a B student, and now you're in your junior year and your grades are going down. You're trying to do too much. You're participating in track, and football, and you're working nights with all this outside activity . . . you can't do all these things."

"Mr. Casale, do you really mean it would be impossible to do this Friday-night show?"

"Bill," Ernie said apologetically, "I can't permit it. I can't let you go out to Ohio alone, the rules don't allow it. Something might happen to you and all kinds of problems could occur. Besides, they need you first thing Saturday morning."

Ernie Casale can still remember Bill's reaction. Cosby looked up at him and gave him a little smile.

"You know," he told the athletic director, "I think you just made up my mind. I can't pass up that job. I'm gonna turn in my uniform. I'm gonna make it as a comedian."

Recalling it now, Casale adds, "It took a lot of guts to do what he did, but his competitive spirit was such that he thought he could do it."

At the time, one person wasn't sure about it at all: Cosby's mom.

"How could you do it, Bill? How could you!"

The bitter disappointment was painfully evident in her eyes. Cos tried to make her understand. He told her about the gigs. He could get two hundred dollars a week. He'd tried to keep his mind on his studies, but studying the tapes of his comedy shows was more important. The jokes were running through his head. New bits. New routines.

"Your stuff becomes funny because you are delivering it. You're a talking cartoonist, painting images in the audience's head." Cos had told himself that, and now it seemed to be coming true.

As far as Anna Cosby could see, Bill had painted a fanciful image in his head—and had ruined his chances for a good career and a good job. He was so close to graduation, to being a college man! If he could just stick it out for another year and a half.

How long had it taken Bill to make it back when he'd dropped out of high school? Four years! How was he ever going to get a second chance and return to college?

Mrs. Cosby was inconsolable. Bill felt the burden of it. Nothing was funny at home. His brother Russell remembers the sense of gloom and disappointment that his mother felt, making it a tense time for everyone. Nothing was funny for Cosby when he went out to the nightclubs. Walking along the cold city streets, he said, "You could get depressed sometimes. Look at the people's faces and you see no happiness, no warmth."

He made the laughter happen in the clubs. The checks kept coming in. Some weeks he still came up short, but the momentum was building as the young comic made the club circuit throughout the Northeast.

He always dreamed about the time when he could definitively say that he'd made the right decision: big time and big bucks.

He got his paycheck one night on the road. He looked at the amount and immediately went back to the club owner, asking to have that week's earnings in cash. In five-dollar bills. Then he went back to his hotel room, grabbed that fistful of money, and flung it in the air, making a blizzard of bucks that came down in swirls of white and green. Four hundred dollars! That proved it! Bill Cosby: Comedian.

It was 1963, the new year, and he was beginning to move. In March he played the Shadows, a club in Georgetown, Washington, D.C., for five hundred dollars a week. Then it was back to the Gaslight for three months to work on new material.

The world of comedy was hot, and comedy albums were hotter than ever. And now, *clean, funny stories* were in. Forget about Dick Gregory. Look at Bob Newhart. Never on a nightclub stage in his life, an accountant who did some routines on local radio in Chicago, Newhart was signed to Warner Bros. Records. Literally flown off to a nightclub to record an album, Newhart's first few hours in front of a live audience ended up garnering "Album of the Year" honors, beating out everyone from Frank Sinatra to classical pianist Sviatoslav Richter. That kind of thing just wasn't supposed to happen with a mere comedian! And another unknown with no stand-up experience, Allan Sherman, had also produced a smash hit album for the label.

Roy Silver knew a guy in the Warner Bros. publishing division in New York. He said that Cosby was going to be big, and told him to get a contract ready. "As a favor," Silver recalls, a Warner vice president, Artie Mogull, began working on the deal.

Still, there were big questions about Cosby. Like, who exactly was he? Wasn't he going to be Warners' answer to Dick Gregory, who had done so well for Vee-Jay and Colpix? Now that Cosby had successfully removed the racial gags from his act—some of the big shots were expecting him to put them back in.

Cos had to set them straight, politely. "Rather than trying to bring the races together by talking about differences, why not bring them together by talking about all the similarities?"

"I had to be original if I wanted to fulfill my aspirations of becoming a big man in show business," he recalls now. But something was really wrong. People didn't always seem to get the message. He seemed to have to repeat himself. Again. And again.

Cosby fielded the questions politely, wittily, and tried to concentrate on the importance of getting press coverage. He had to shrug off the dumb questions that went with it.

Cosby stepped up his efforts to be more than a regional comedian, to be someone that Warners could sell all over the country. He had to zigzag all over the East Coast just trying to keep the momentum going and the money coming in. Down in Washington, D.C., a friend of his tried to fix him up with a date. He'd heard some nice things about pretty, nineteen-year-old Camille Hanks. But she had heard some pretty awful things about seedy stand-up comics. She refused to see him.

A psychology major at the University of Maryland, Camille enjoyed some of the middle-class lifestyle that was still just a dream for most blacks. The world of her childhood was far different from the environment that spawned Cos, the slick comical con artist from Philly.

Camille grew up in the suburb of Silver Springs. There was fresh air and plenty of room. While Cos and his gang had to tinker together go-carts from broken-up wood crates and stolen baby carriage wheels, Camille could go next door with her friends and ride horses, enjoying rural trails where the ground wasn't littered with broken glass and bottle caps. Cosby's dad cooked in a navy kitchen; Camille's father was a researcher working in the chemistry lab at Walter Reed Hospital.

"Growing up as I did," Camille says, "I believed in everything awful I'd ever heard about show-business people and I was afraid. But later someone brought Bill to my bowling class and he sat in the back, cutting up as usual. He didn't look at all like the ogre I'd expected, so we went out. The second week I knew him he asked me to marry him. Three months later I said yes."

A few moments following that, Camille's parents said no.

The engagement was off.

Cos kept trying to keep his relationship going with Camille, but he also had to leave for gigs all along the club circuit between New York and Maryland. Working at the Bitter End, in the Village, Cosby would finish up at two or three in the morning. Catching a quick nap, he'd start out for Camille's place at daybreak. Driving down in his used—very used—Dodge seemed to take forever. He'd spend the day with Camille, then drive back in time for the evening's show.

Sometimes when they'd go to the movies, Bill would zonk out, fast asleep.

Fortunately the more Camille's parents saw of the ardent young suitor, the more impressed they became. Eventually they came around, and the engagement was on again.

The summer of 1963 saw Bill's situation greatly improved in comparison to the previous summer's struggles at the Gaslight. He had perfected his "Noah" routine, told stories every New Yorker could identify with about subway nuts turning every car into a sideshow, and even did spoofs of commercials. As a dumb jock extolling the wonders of shaving cream, Cos, eyes wide in wonder, talked about how he could take a razor and remove "the little tiny hairs . . . comin' out of my face!"

Cosby was making a name for himself as a rising star, somebody to watch. The trouble was that most of America watched television, and Cosby wasn't getting that exposure. He was barely at the starting gate, earning a couple hundred bucks a week compared to the thousands offered cute clean comics like Bill Dana and Bob Newhart.

Bill was developing into an almost irresistible personality. So funny. So nice. But, when it came to auditioning for the "Tonight" show, the nice guy finished last. The affable smile he put on doing his act would turn into a poisonous frown as he left NBC in defeat.

That summer, Johnny Carson took a week off and hired guest host Allan Sherman. Roy Silver figured that this was going to be the perfect opportunity. Sherman had been an "overnight sensation" for Warner Bros. He had crossed two hot topics (comedy and folk music), adding a Jewish twist. A single, "Hello Muddah, Hello Faddah," earned him a Grammy. He understood what it was like to suffer and wait for a break.

Cosby was playing basketball down on the public court at Waverly and Sixth Avenue, and he barely looked up from the hoops when he got the news from his manager, Roy Silver.

"Allan Sherman's guest-hosting the 'Tonight' show. I got an audition."

"Screw 'em," Cos said, his shot rattling off the wooden backboard and sliding through the netless hoop. "They're all fucking assholes. They already turned me down three times and I'm not auditioning for them."

"This is different," his manager said. "This could be it! Give 'em another chance!"

"Yeah," Cos answered, thinking back to the humiliation and rejection, getting excited only to get kicked down. "Why should I put myself through that again?"

Cos shot a few more baskets. Then he stopped.

"All right," he said. "I'll take one more shot at them." When he told reporters that making it in show business took every ounce of guts and determination a guy had, he wasn't kidding.

Cosby raced uptown by cab. There wasn't much time now. He got to NBC at three, and taping was scheduled for five-thirty. Wariness and hostility were written all over Cosby's face as he stormed into the building. But he knew he had to cool it for the audition.

"Hi, Bill," Allan Sherman said. "I'm glad to see you. I've heard so much about you." Cosby nodded, still playing defense. "Why don't you do whatever you would do on the show tonight," Sherman said.

Cosby slowly worked himself into the karate bit, making all the gestures and moves in the awkward silence of the guest host's office. He began to get a rhythm going. Sherman wasn't exactly chuckling, but sometimes pros simply appreciate another comic's work without yucking it up.

"Okay, Bill," Sherman said when it was over. "I think that'll be real great. You'll do the show tonight."

Within hours, millions of people all over the country got their first look at Bill Cosby.

Cosby would never forget that night. Twenty years later, discussing it, ironically enough, with Johnny Carson (and no mention was made of who had been hosting the "Tonight" show that night), Cos set the scene:

"I came out—the guy put Lena Horne's makeup on me—I walked out and I was going to do my karate routine. And I hadn't really thought that it would be funny. But I guess the people were so conditioned to see a black person come out—they said okay, he's gonna talk about the back of the bus and the front of the restaurant and the side of the tree—and I walked out and I said I wanna talk about karate. And they went wooo hah hah—and I almost backed up and said, 'Well, what's so funny?' Then I went into the routine."

He did his impression of a guy who's just graduated from a karate school, proud of "the big slab of callus you got on your hand. It makes your hand look like a foot. Don't laugh. This is good. Keep your hand in your pocket for nine days, then when somebody attacks you, you take a swing at 'em and even if you miss, the smell'll kill 'em."

He showed how to break bricks with the proper histrionic karate shout. And then he told the folks that you could scare robbers without knowing karate—all you needed was the shout. With the crook cringing, you say, "Watch out or I'll shout again. Matter of fact, you give me *your* dough!"

He talked about a karate expert who knew the secrets of the sport: "He says, 'I'm thinking through this rock, I'm thinking two feet past it.' He raised his arm and it came down—unfortunately this rock was thinking, 'No you won't either,' and it shattered his whole elbow . . . now he picks on Jell-O . . . whipped cream . . . we still applaud for him but he's nothing. . . ."

Cosby was a hit. In August 1963 he went to Mr. Kelly's in Chicago for five hundred dollars a week and then in September turned up at the Hungry i making seven hundred fifty a week.

In January 1964, the stores had copies of *Bill Cosby Is a Very Funny Fellow . . . Right!,* a live album recorded on Bill's home comic turf, the Bitter End in Greenwich Village.

Allan Sherman produced the record with Roy Silver, and, just as stars as Harpo Marx and Steve Allen had done for Allan's first record, Allan filled the back cover with a heartfelt personal endorsement for Bill. Sherman, the top comedy seller of 1962 and 1963, lavished eye-popping praise on Bill Cosby.

Talking about the Noah routine, Sherman called it "a masterpiece, even though nobody has heard it yet. It's warm, and human, and honest, and deeply moving, and it's funny. It's going to be a classic . . . if Bill wanted to, he could make a living for the rest of his life just from the excitement and joy this one great bit will create. But Bill Cosby, if I am any judge of talent, will keep coming up with fresh, new material and will grow everyday in stature and importance on the American comedy scene. . . ."

He urged the millions of people who had made his albums gold to pick up on Bill Cosby. "I'm so proud and happy for the chance to introduce you to Bill Cosby," Sherman added. "It isn't every day that we come in contact with greatness."

In 1964, the record racks contained hit albums from many "overnight" sensations. There was the unlikely-looking Barbra Streisand, just another Greenwich Village hopeful a short time ago. And there was the unlikely-looking trio that people said resembled "two rabbis and a hooker," folkies Peter, Paul, and Mary. And suddenly hitting the charts were the most unlikely-looking people of all, the Beatles. Now it was time for something new in comedy. With the push from Allan Sherman, it was time to see a new name on the charts. Bill Cosby.

Warners, successful with the new breed of friendly, inoffensive comic stars starting with Bob Newhart and Allan Sherman, figured to continue with Cosby. They figured sales of his new album would be phenomenal. Sensational.

But they were mediocre. Barely ten thousand copies were sold. And that hardly seemed to suggest that Bill Cosby was a very funny fellow, right?

The important thing was that Cos at least had a record deal. That was a sign of respect, even though Warners only paid $2,500 to sign him up. Another important thing was that his nightclub earnings were getting higher all the time, some weeks topping $1,500. With the club work, and product now in the stores, there was cause to celebrate.

Best of all, Cosby started off the new year with a new bride. On January 25, 1964, he married Camille in Olney, Maryland. The Warner Bros. comedian and his wife had a whirlwind honeymoon.The newlyweds traveled all over the country. They went to San Francisco— because Bill was appearing at the Hungry i. They went to Los Angeles—because Bill was booked for the Crescendo. Then they went up to Lake Tahoe—where Bill played Harrah's and found himself a favorite of the club's owner, Mr. Harrah himself.

Cosby was part of the new, gentler wave of comedy. Just a few years earlier, stand-up had been dominated by hostile satirists who made their audiences squirm: Sahl, Bruce, Gregory, Berman, Nichols and May. But along with the Kennedy administration had come a youthful enthusiasm, a fresh sense of optimism, and the carefree sense of silliness typified by Allan Sherman's lighthearted parodies and such playful comedy teams as Allen & Rossi and the Smothers Brothers. And now there was Bill Cosby.

Or was there? Cos issued a new album, *I Started Out as a Child,* in the fall of 1964, and it sold only nine thousand copies. Warners, once high on Cosby, contemplated dropping him from the label.

The executives took another look at the sales figures. There was some cautious optimism: the first Cosby album was still holding on, selling a small but consistent amount. The second one was also doing steady business each month. Demographics suggested that Cosby was beginning to reach a totally new, untapped comedy record buyer: the teenager. Kids and teens hadn't bought Mort Sahl or Shelley Berman. But they liked the comics who spoke about things they could relate to. That included the Smothers Brothers with their "Mom Always Liked You Best" antics, and Cosby, whose second album had routines about playing street football, enjoying childhood luxuries like a first pair of sneakers, and the childhood misery of sharing the bed with a younger brother who wet the bed ("Hey—I'm tired of sleepin' on the cold spot!").

Kids loved Bill Cosby, the man who told them all about his childhood—and theirs. They didn't think of Cos as the Black Comedian. He was just the funniest storyteller they'd ever heard.

Unfortunately, some of the grown-ups weren't as smart.

They couldn't see what he was doing. They kept on asking him why he wasn't doing racial jokes. With Cosby onstage, so equal he didn't have to dignify the bigots by doing gags about being black, it seemed pretty obvious that Bill was on to something. But backstage, white reporters wanted to hear the Dick Gregory lines, and blacks were suspiciously asking what else Cos was doing for "the cause."

Cosby began to get the idea that no matter what he did, he wasn't going to be left alone. But he still kept to his image of the patient, laid-back comic, even if his answers starting coming out just a little bit slower, firmer, and with clenched-teeth enunciation.

"It would be easy to get on a stage and talk about 'the Problem,' " he would say. "Now, I have no crutch."

They didn't get it. "But Mr. Cosby, please elaborate."

"First," he began, "I'm tired of those old jokes about stereotyped Negroes. You know what I mean? I don't miss Amos 'n' Andy. Second, I'm tired of those people who say, 'You should be doing more to help your people.' I'm a comedian, that's all. Third, my humor comes from the way I look at things. I am a man. I see things the way other people do. . . . A white person listens to my act and he laughs and he thinks, 'Yeah, that's the way I see it, too.' Okay. He's white. I'm Negro. And we both see things the same way. That must mean that *we are alike. Right?* So I figure this way I'm doing as much for good race relations as the next guy."

Case closed? Of course not.

The lecture had to be repeated in interview after weary interview.

It might seem strange now, but in 1964 the idea of a black comedian coming out and doing "straight" material was radical. When Jack Paar booked Godfrey Cambridge, he had Cambridge's set filmed at an all-black college and prefaced the ten-minute clip as if the millions on TV were about to get an anthropology lesson.

While it was certainly laudable and liberal to give a black comedian a chance to tell racial humor, the idea of letting a black comedian do what every other comedian was allowed to do—well, that was too radical.

Cosby had to turn down TV work when it hinged on racial jokes. As he said at the time, "If somebody comes to me and says, 'I want to have you on the show because there's this thing I have about a white guy and . . . ' my answer is no. You need a show Negro. Now if you need a comedian, call."

Here and there, he got some TV work. The nightclub gigs were pretty steady. Cosby was now a better-known commodity. Not a big star by any means, Cosby was at least able to make a good wage if he kept to the road every week.

People were beginning to remember his name. Bill Crosby. Uh, Bing Cosby. That very funny new comedian Bob Crosby. Bill . . . Cosby?

(Cosby was an unusual name back in 1963, but it's actually quite an old one. Its roots are in the Old English Ceawas-by, which means "bold ruler's settlement." Now it's certainly doubtful that anyone, even Alex Haley, could trace Bill's relatives to England, but, interestingly enough, the emblem for the Cosby clan features the black leopard, three of them on a silver background.)

When the Cosby name was so firmly established he could afford some luxuries, Bill splurged. It wasn't simply the allure of knick-knacks. There was much more to it than that.

It wasn't the gleam of the gold, it was the gleam in his eye when he could walk into a fancy shop, stand up in front of some snide-looking clerk, plunk down a wad of bills and blow the guy's mind. Gold rings, gold cufflinks, gold tie bars. All those drippingly rich items advertised on the back of the *New Yorker*. Fancy clocks, decorator ice buckets, diamond stickpins. Cos picked them up like he was buying a handful of candy bars.

Cosby's passion, most of all, was cars. Now he was able to get something he could be proud to ride in. He picked up a Mercedes Benz 300SL.

One night in Los Angeles, Cos happened to meet an old friend from the Village, folk singer Theodore Bikel. When they went out to get their cars and find a place to eat, an interesting contrast was parked in front of them. There was Cosby's Mercedes, immaculate and shiny. And next to it, Bikel's old Corvette, with bumper stickers all over it saying things like We Shall Overcome.

Bikel looked at his friend's Mercedes, and asked, "What did the Nazis ever do for you?"

Cosby sold the car.

To replace it, he wasn't sure quite what to do. With all the irritations from handling "the Problem" and doing interviews about his "image," he felt guilty about wanting to get a Cadillac. Isn't that the stereotypical car that Negroes love to own? And how can you drive around in a Cadillac anyway if there are poor blacks somewhere without enough change to get a seat in the back of the bus?

It took a long talk with his wife, Camille, before Bill finally allowed himself the joy of sitting behind the wheel, tooling down the street in his new Cadillac Eldorado.

It took some more long talks with Camille before Bill reluctantly let reporters drive up and visit the Cosby house. He didn't want them in his California home, and he valued his privacy immensely. But he gave interviews because he felt it was important to show the world a young, successful black couple who had achieved "the Dream."

During the interviews, Cos would deflect questions about his childhood and marriage as much as possible. He wanted to let the warm, funny stories of growing up be accepted as fictionalized fact. As for the endless racial questions, he insisted he was just a comic, not a civil rights activist or political leader.

He didn't know that, within months, he would be just what he had long avoided becoming: the center of the rising civil rights movement in America, a reluctant leader who would become one of the key figures in an important moment of black-white confrontation.

Chapter Seven

Cos was doing his thing at the Crescendo, a late-night gig for the typical after-dark crowd. There were free spenders, the hipsters, the tipsy chicks hanging on the arms of dates hoping that liquor and laughs would equal love. He did the kind of bits they would respond to. Like the mildly risqué bit about Bobo, a zoo gorilla that didn't seem to know how to mate:

" . . . The guys from the Philadelphia Zoo sent up their best looking female gorilla. She was looking good, too. Long black stockings on. A girdle with hair on it. She was looking very shapely. And he did nothing. Of course she stormed out of there. One vet read him dirty stories. And that didn't work. Even the parts underlined. Another guy went in and showed him some gorilla stag movies . . . and he walked out in the middle of the stag movie. And the last method they tried was they took some darts . . . and they dipped them into this gland-secreting stuff they got from an old sailor . . . and they threw 'em and hit him in the back. The darts did nothing to him. He just pulled them out and threw 'em away. And they hit a hippo. And the hippo went wild. I mean, everything. Birds, trees, garbage cans. He was all over the place. As a matter of fact they have some of the weirdest looking animals out in that zoo now. They have a giraffe with a hippo's head, and the neck can't hold the head up. . . ."

Cos also brought out all of his polished best, like the bit about the karate expert fending off a mugger in a dark alley. He swings around to attack—only to see it's a midget holding the gun. Oops.

Backstage, Cos met an amiable, balding gent by the name of Carl Reiner. Reiner was impressed with the show. For Bill, who had studied and admired the Reiner and Brooks comedy albums, this was compliment enough. Cos, a stand-up comic for barely two years, was being praised by one of comedy's greatest writers. But Reiner had something else to say. His friend, producer Sheldon Leonard, was also impressed with Cosby, and had seen him do his karate bit on TV. Would Cos care to make an appointment to discuss doing some work with Sheldon?

Cos knew it could only be one thing—a guest spot on "The Dick Van Dyke Show," which was produced and directed by Leonard and Reiner.

Sheldon Leonard had a tough reputation. For years he'd played gangster parts in movies, and with his olive complexion, dapper short-cropped curly hair, murderously dark eyes and jutting lower lip, he possessed an intimidating presence. He matched it with a tough personality. He was uncompromising in his pursuit of quality. It was Leonard who chose the virtually unknown Van Dyke, defying network demands for a big star.

Before the riots that would underscore the restless demands for racial equality, Leonard was quietly turning around network concepts on race relations. An early Van Dyke episode had the lanky comic worrying if his newborn baby had been switched at the hospital. A "Mrs. Peters" was next-door to his wife, Mrs. Petrie. And so he demanded that Mrs. Peters and her husband come over and bring the baby. The gag finale was that Rob discovered his paranoia totally misplaced, not because the hospital kept good records after all, but because . . . Mr. and Mrs. Peters were black.

The idea knocked everyone out—everyone except CBS and the show's sponsor, Procter and Gamble. How could Sheldon Leonard even toy with racial humor? And what would the Southern affiliates say? Leonard stubbornly told CBS he was going to shoot the script anyway, doing it tastefully, using a handsome black couple, Greg Morris and Mimi Dillard. He made CBS a deal: if the live studio audience didn't laugh, if the sequence was offensive, he'd reshoot it with a different ending and different actors, at his own expense.

The gag ending got one of the longest laughs in sitcom history.

Going in the opposite direction, Leonard produced another show with guest star Godfrey Cambridge, a comic known for his broad racial satires. Only in this one, there wasn't a single line that had to do with Cambridge's color.

Cosby wondered what type of guest-role Sheldon Leonard had in mind. The answer was—none.

Leonard was thinking of Cosby to co-star in his new series, "I Spy," an action-adventure show. A show with an awesome $200,000 budget that would be filmed all over the world. A show that, on the basis of time and money alone, was a tremendous risk for NBC.

Cosby was astonished. He had his little karate bit—just about the only thing that suggested "secret agent." But he had no acting experience. A guest spot on a sitcom would've been enough of a "stretch." But—jumping into the co-lead on an action-adventure hour? An hour every week?

In 1964 spy shows were even bigger than sitcoms. "The Man from U.N.C.L.E." was a hit, and movie spies like James Coburn's Flint and Dean Martin's Helm were ready to compete with Sean Connery's James Bond. For the fall 1965 season, there would be Western spies ("The Wild Wild West") and comedy spies ("Get Smart") and, if Bill dared, "I Spy."

It was a daring offer that Sheldon Leonard was making to Bill. Not only daring for Cosby, but for a TV network at the time. Audiences had accepted an American and Russian working together, in the case of "U.N.C.L.E." 's Napoleon Solo and Ilya Kuryakin. But wait a minute. "I Spy" was was going to star Robert Culp and who? Bill Cosby? Culp and Cosby? White and black? A thaw in the nation's growing racial cold war?

This couldn't be possible, network insiders thought.

Cosby accepted the challenge.

This was big news all over the country. Newspapers actually headlined the event. The pressure stayed on. In January 1964, the pilot episode was in the can—but NBC was struggling to get it on the air. They were having trouble lining up sponsors. They were also having internal conflicts as some of their affiliates grumbled about carrying the show. With the possibility that not all NBC stations would carry it, and few sponsors would support it, insiders were already talking BOMB.

This was going to be the biggest, most expensive bomb in ten seasons, and a tremendous blow to any notion that the American public could accept blacks and whites together. And this was going to brand Negro comedian Bill Cosby as the risk that failed—and, the way show business was, probably drop him face forward into obscurity forever.

In a front-page story, *Variety* headlined, COSBY IN "SPY" PUTS NBC DIXIE AFFILS ON SPOT. They chronicled the tense waiting period involving "television's test case on integration," wondering what the fate would be of a show that "depicts a Negro and a white intermingling on an equal level."

The last time a black co-starred with whites on a TV series had been in the 1950s situation comedy "Beulah."

For Bill the waiting period was excruciating on every level possible. But the one he had to deal with, day to day, was trying to make it as an actor. Every day on the set of "I Spy" he had to try, try, and try again to become, overnight, a dramatic actor. All over the country people were likening Cosby to Jackie Robinson. Cos was the "big experiment." But imagine if Jackie Robinson had played football, not baseball, and had been expected to learn every baseball rule in the first season!

Cosby felt guilty. Maybe this part should've been played by an experienced black actor. Maybe somebody like Ivan Dixon, who was toiling away in bit parts on "Perry Mason" and lucky to get them. The cool, natural comedian was a very uptight actor. At the first reading, when Sheldon Leonard was inspecting the man he had chosen without a screen test, Cos was terrible. Cos knew it himself. He was wooden. He wasn't giving off the excitement and emotion he flashed on a nightclub stage. He was so busy trying to say his lines right that the meaning was wrong. He wasn't paying attention to what the other actors were saying, just tensely waiting for his cue to begin speaking.

Off the stage, he and Sheldon Leonard were giving interviews of optimism, whether they believed in what they were saying or not. Cos was under pressure to meet with the press, to endure days when he did nothing but talk, at half-hour intervals, to one glaring reporter after another, and always about the race question. "If [the show] does fail, I hope they won't say we'll never try this again with a Negro. I hope it's a case of Cosby did not come off, not a Negro did not come off.

"Leonard thought it was time that a Negro and a white could play together in a series that did not have any racial overtones," Cos would say, in as stiff a performance as he was giving in rehearsals. "The public," he said, "will accept my casting."

Sheldon Leonard sounded a little like Branch Rickey. Although he coolly refused to flag-wave for his cause, and tried as best he could to play down the hiring of a Negro, he let slip to a *TV Guide* writer a few words that indicated that, like Branch Rickey, he had made sure that if he was colorblind to talent, he wasn't foolish enough to wreck "the experiment" by hiring someone who didn't have the guts, soul, and stamina to stand up to the tension:

"I was sure he was the man I wanted. I make an intensive underground investigation before choosing a person for a long-range project of this sort. From every source I learned Bill Cosby was a tireless worker, a man striving to do his best. . . ." He added, "Cosby comes on as an engaging, warmhearted, intelligent man. If anyone takes exception to this man because of his color, it will have to be some nut."

Meanwhile, NBC, Leonard, and twenty-seven-year-old Bill Cosby had to wonder what kind of nuts were actually out there. Would any try to storm the studio? Or would there simply be a quiet, efficient boycott? When "The Nat 'King' Cole Show" went on the air in the fifties, it was killed in the ratings solely because Southern affiliates refused to carry it, dooming it to a small audience share.

Take a young comic with virtually no acting experience and stick him in a TV show seen by thirty million people. That alone has driven actors over the edge. Now take a man used to intimate nightclubs buzzing with live, appreciative people, and put him on a deathly quiet soundstage at seven in the morning. And instead of ad-libs and sure-fire jokes, give him scripted dialogue and long, dull stretches of time between every take for him to think, think, and think about it all.

And just for extra fun, make him black, the center of the TV season's greatest controversy.

"Ten years from now," Cos said, "nobody would probably notice that a TV star is Negro or white. At this point, we hope the story is all that matters."

But the story was the story. What made "I Spy" stand out from the start was the concept behind the show. Even in its embryonic treatments, the idea was to show a spy duo different from "The Man from U.N.C.L.E." 's Napoleon Solo and Ilya Kuryakin—guys who saved each other's lives but didn't share each other's lives.

"I Spy" was the story of Kelly Robinson (Robert Culp), a spy traveling the globe as a tennis player, and Alexander Scott (Cosby), spy and Rhodes scholar, undercover as Kelly's trainer-advisor. And it was the story of two men who were comrades, who enjoyed each other's company, who didn't care if one was "different" from the other.

On the set, the concept seemed to be working.

Bill Cosby and Robert Culp did enjoy each other's company.

Robert Culp didn't share Cosby's experience of ghetto childhood, but he did share many of Bill's ideals and interests. Professionally he had the same drive toward creativity and quality. Six years older than Cos, Culp had been a youthful loner, an outsider whose edge in school was athletics. He was a champ on the track field, a pole-vaulter with Olympic possibilities. Like Cos, Bobby was sidetracked in college and developed an interest in show business. He starred in a series, *Trackdown*, but got the reputation for being moody and difficult because he refused other shows, determined to hold out for better acting assignments. He also wanted to develop himself as a writer and director, things actors at the time were not supposed to do, or know how to do.

Sam Peckinpah, who directed a few "I Spy" episodes, assessed Culp as a man: "Bob is incensed by prejudice. He doesn't recognize it. He doesn't understand it. Yet he is not trying to carry any particular banner on the show."

Cos and Culp developed a style for the show. The idea was to show a hip, "beautiful" relationship. "My people would just like to enjoy an hour of TV where a Negro isn't a problem," Cosby said. "People can see I'm a Negro; we don't need to say anything else." Culp added, "We're two guys who don't know the difference between a colored and a white man. That's doing more than a hundred marches. We're showing what it could be like if there had been no hate."

As Culp and Cosby began to develop a working relationship, and their own style, Sheldon Leonard and the crew began to breathe a little easier.

On the set, Culp loosened Cos up, helping him when it would've been easy to upstage him and drive him from co-star status to sidekick.

"Bob gives me the help I need," Bill told writer Robert de Roos. "As an insecure entertainer coming in to work as an actor, I need all the acceptance I can get—not just hand-shaking, but real acceptance. Bobby gives me that."

Culp answered: "He is the fastest natural study I've ever seen. He is cramming ten years of education into a few months. No novice, no matter how talented, can come up with performances like Bill . . . to become another guy and have another guy's emotions with a bit of hero juice thrown in—that is painfully hard to learn."

It was stinging to have to be directed around the soundstage, to blow a scene because he was facing the wrong way, or not following the marks on the floor, or listening to the foreign language of technical terms shouted by the crew. The "natural" had to learn unnatural, staged choreography, and make it look natural again.

"They move you around from seven in the morning to seven at night as though you were an index card," he said. "I am still tumbling around the fringes of performances—playing with the outside edge. I've been trying to do the story lines without camping—to get a laugh as an actor, not as a comedian, and it's not easy. Everybody tells me I'm too self-critical. Well, we'll see."

Some around the set figured that maybe it wasn't just faith in himself, but perhaps some kind of religious comfort that was helping to pull him through. But Cos was never very religious. "I'm sort of a frightened atheist. If the sky were to open up tomorrow, I'd cop out. I'd probably try to con God. There are a few things I'd like to say to Him . . . but I don't think it can be done by prayer."

Anxiety was high not only at NBC, but at agencies like William Morris. Executives there screened an early episode of "I Spy," and they were aghast. How could sponsors be talked into advertising on this show? How could affiliates be persuaded to take it? Just look at what was going on!

There was a scene where Bill was on a bridge, making a contact with a pretty young girl. It was a long shot. All he really had to do was stay there for a moment, make the connection, and that was it. He kissed her cheek and walked off.

"You'll never get this on the air," one of the Morris men said. "Good God, he's kissed a white girl!"

Actually, Bill had done nothing more than kiss his wife, Camille. They'd needed an extra for the short scene, and they called the first lady they happened to see hanging around the set.

With each new episode, Cos began to deliver his lines with greater confidence, using a whole range of subtle facial gestures and physical stances. As he admitted with cautious optimism to those on the set, he had found his rhythm. By the seventh or eighth episode, the balance was struck between the character of tough, Rhodes scholar-CIA man Scott and cool, easygoing comedian Cos. The result was a sly spy, with a little dash of wry.

As more and more shows were completed and the date for the "I Spy" premiere crept closer, the affiliated stations around the country began to make their decisions. Since they were only affiliates, they were under no obligation to take every show the NBC network put on the air. They could grab something from CBS or ABC, produce their own show, or even fill the spot with reruns. CBS had not yet withdrawn the old "Amos 'n' Andy" show from syndication. Even that was possible.

Cos got the word at last. The returns were in: To the surprise of many in the business, the affiliates had overwhelmingly supported the show. They wanted to see Bill Cosby in action with Robert Culp. Only four stations declined the show—stations located in Savannah, Georgia; Albany, Georgia; Daytona Beach, Florida; and Birmingham, Alabama.

Chapter Eight

"At twenty-eight, Cosby has accomplished in one year what scores of Negro actors and comedians have tried to do all their lives," *Newsweek* wrote. "He has completely refurbished the television image of the Negro. He is not the stereotyped, white-toothed Negro boy with a sense of good rhythm. He is a human being, and a funnier, hipper human being than anyone around him."

When the first "I Spy" shows hit the air, the *New York Herald Tribune* assessed him as an actor: "Mr. Cosby may never get to play more than himself, but since he's an ingratiating fellow, he'll do fine. Gary Cooper went farther on less."

So that was a relief. And as for "I Spy"'s competition, the show was matching CBS's variety series starring Danny Kaye, and destroying the hastily rescripted "Amos Burke, Secret Agent," which had been "Burke's Law" (about Amos Burke, police detective) the year before.

Predicted to run dead last, "I Spy" was in the Top 20. And a man with virtually no acting experience except for his role in a fifth-grade production of *King Koko from Kookoo Island* ended the year winning an Emmy Award as best dramatic actor in a series. Yet there was no time when Cos could fully lift his head up and enjoy the triumph.

"I've been watching my step all the way," he sighed. "I never wanted to be judged as temperamental or nasty. If you're snotty then people would be sure to say, 'Those Negroes are all alike . . . I don't want them biting me!'

"The show is exhilarating in some ways and a burden in others. The character I play is a highly educated man and I'm nowhere near that. I was never a great student . . . and he is a Negro 'good guy' working equally with a white man for a patriotic cause—a premise which may not be accepted by every Negro watching."

And how could he pretend to support the CIA, and how could he do shows without inserting a few words on the growing civil rights movement, and why wasn't there a scene where Scotty is forbidden from coming into the same hotel as Kelly, and on and on and on.

And Cosby found himself defending, in interview after interview, against the innuendo that simply being Bill Cosby was not good enough. That his accomplishments toward equality were not good enough. That his milestone achievement in breaking into TV was not good enough.

"Bill Cosby carries as much weight on his shoulders as any Negro I know, and he wears it as well and as lightly as any man could. He may not be a front-runner in the cause—that's not his nature—but he's totally committed. He gives freely of his time and money. In Watts, he's worked hard for community theater. The cats on the street corner dig him, and he represents something very important to me."

Sammy Davis, Jr., said that. But then, many blacks and whites attacked him, too, for the very same reasons.

Those who wanted to could find a subtle message on how Cos felt by taking a look at the cartoon he clipped from a magazine and put on his dressing room wall. It showed a smiling prisoner in chains, up against a cobblestone wall, facing the hooded torturer who stood before him carrying a whip. "Well," the prisoner says to the torturer, "are we feeling any better today?"

Fortunately, Cos got to put the questions behind him and go out on location, shooting exteriors in exotic parts of the world. Sheldon Leonard reasoned that part of the allure of the international spy world was in the international locales. Instead of resorting to fakery, he insisted on bringing his actors to Hong Kong, Italy, and Spain to capture the distinct flavor of each country. It was in Hong Kong that Bill received news that his first child, Erika Ranee, was born, on April 8, 1965. It was also in Hong Kong that the Cosby cool was tested by a variety of natural and man-made problems.

On some days Hong Kong resembled a war zone, with storming ty-phoons whipping trees and debris through the air at a hundred miles per hour. The citizens fled the streets, even those used to the eye-popping winds that brought with them torrential downpours of sizzling rain.

Shooting sequences on the crowded streets of Hong Kong was often as chaotic as a typhoon. Cos and the crew would set up for a day's work, threatened by gray skies and mottled clouds above, with the teeming, curious citizenry swarming around on all sides. Simple scenes had to be done again and again as translators shouted instructions to the extras and snarled traffic was rerouted to flow more naturally. As it was, it was almost impossible for the roving cameras and walking actors to wend their way through the crowds without stepping over somebody or knocking into someone.

Sometimes a day's shooting captured the purple-blue waters of the bay, and the richness of the green and brown mountains, a tantalizing feast for lucky viewers at home who were just buying their first color TV sets, finally able to fully enjoy the NBC peacock. But just as often the out-takes would show tragicomic scenes of bewildered Orientals careening into the scenery and arguing with each other in voices of anger and woeful dismay.

Even though the camera crew took to hiding the cameras in boxes, and camouflaging them behind trees, there would be scenes of Cosby and Culp talking—obliterated by the huge, blinking face of an amazed Hong Kong citizen staring into the magic glass.

Cos and his manager had to keep a watchful eye on the script. In one lighthearted sequence, a curious Oriental child was supposed to be captivated by Cos, and then coyly rub his face. The child was supposed to say, "Oh. Brown no come off?" The only thing that came off was that scene in the script.

Gradually the scripts began to include more and more of the low-key Cosby humor. Cosby's tongue-in-cheek comedy was perfect for livening up the cloak-and-dagger drama. In one sequence, he and Culp are confronted and outnumbered by the bad guys:

"Let's rush 'em," Cosby whispers.

"I'll be right behind you," says Culp.

"That's no good. When we have to run away you'll be in front of me."

In another episode, Cosby is about to dive into the swimming pool (true to his spy nature, he's wearing sunglasses, in addition to the scuba mask up on his forehead). He's stopped by Culp, who has noticed that the pool is wired with electricity.

Shrugging off the narrow escape, Cos recalls another villain who used to like to shock people: "His name was Feeney. He was real trouble in school. He'd wire himself up, shake hands, and buzz ya. *Thipp!* He was the only guy the principal gave a diploma to with rubber gloves on."

Cosby's comedy and delivery were so infectious, Robert Culp began to pick up on it. After starting out as a "straight" hero, Bobby began using Cosby catch-phrases, offering a hip "Oh, isn't that wonderful" in the face of danger, or asking, "Is that a fact?" and "Does that shake your tree?" Culp ended up spouting some pretty Bill-ious lines, like: "If you don't get out of here very shortly, to enjoy the scenic wonders of this lovely land, the dwarfs are gonna come out and pull your beard down to your kneecaps!"

NBC was a little alarmed by all that, but it was certainly proof that a black guy and a white guy could communicate with each other. Offstage, Cos could say, "Bobby knows me better than anybody does. We're closer than brothers and we are equal in the show and out of it."

They were a matched pair when it came to causing trouble, too. In one scene they were supposed to rush up to a twenty-foot-high wall and pretend to climb it. Then the stunt men would take over, do the actual climbing, race over the rooftop, and then jump down into a convenient alleyway.

Well, the veteran track stars had other ideas. When they reached the wall, whispering suspiciously to each other, they not only took hold of the wall, but started climbing. The two athletes matched each other stride for slippery stride, making it up the wall with amazing ease. The awed crew watched as Bobby and Cos ran across the roof like real spies, skittered down slanted rooftops, and finally made their leap into the alley.

They'd done it! Only the crew had been so surprised, not a second of it was caught on film.

Sometimes Cos and Culp probably should've done the stunts themselves. There was the time two stunt men were ordered by producer Sheldon Leonard to hurry up and finish a scene that required a dive into the sea. Leonard found out they didn't know how to swim— "after they had followed my instructions and jumped into Hong Kong harbor. . . ."

Another scene couldn't be done until the crew found a fish—a large, beautiful sailfish was crucial to a particular harbor sequence. It took a long time for one of the fishermen to catch a suitable subject. But when shooting had to be rescheduled for the following day, the fish was carefully tied up and hooked to the side of the dock, kept fresh in the cool water. The next morning it was hauled up, nothing but a prickly skeleton. During the night it had been picked to pieces by scavenging harbor fish.

Writer Dick Hobson recalled the time Cosby ran up against Chinese superstition. "In Hong Kong the script called for him to be shot down, suddenly revive and shoot the pursuing 'heavy' dead. Unhappily Cosby had to fall with his face next to a pigsty. Which made him doubly anxious to do the scene in one take. But the Chinese heavy wouldn't die a convincing death. On the first take he died with one leg sticking up in the air; on the second he kept whirling around and wouldn't fall dead; on the third he 'died' in a sitting position. It took five takes for them to realize he thought cameras capture the soul. He was not about to simulate real death for fear it would come true." Meanwhile Cos had to keep dying with him, falling down and hoping that, for a change, his nemesis would also bite the dust and stay there.

Cosby's spirits were boosted by reports from stateside of the show's solid ratings. But the real lift came when Erika was, at four months, old enough to travel. She flew to Japan along with Camille and Bill's mom.

While the image of the "I Spy" duo was of two carefree spies enjoying the exotic locations and exotic women, and living the carefree bachelor life, the reality was far different for Cosby. And he loved that reality.

Wherever he went, he took his family, giving his mom a nonstop vacation, the chance to see the world in luxury and triumph. Meanwhile, the triumph included miles and miles of stockings in the hotel bathroom, tons and tons of suitcases for the ladies' clothes, and barely a grip or two for Cos. But it was all worth it. Even waking up extra early—when toddling Erika would come over, giggle, and slug him awake with a fist in the face.

"As a father," Camille said, "he's a very gentle man. He's just crazy about the baby and so patient. He loves to bathe her and feed her and dress her. He's just a very loving father. As a husband, he has the same qualities."

The globe-trotting spy adventures included stops in Spain, Venice, and Mexico. Back home, Cos capped another season with another Emmy Award.

In the summer of 1966, another baby was on the way. Cosby was getting in some nightclub work, but hoping that this time he'd be around to see his child be born.

It was on a Saturday evening that Camille went into the hospital. Cos wanted to stay, but he had a date to play. He called the airport and chartered a plane, delaying as long as he could.

He arrived barely in time for the show in Denver; a police escort with sirens blaring drove him to the concert. Cos did his full show, then zoomed back to the airport with another police escort.

He raced back to the hospital, arriving around 2:00 A.M. Sunday morning.

This child was certainly like her father: she waited until everybody was present, not showing herself until the wee hours of the morning.

Cos was thrilled to actually see the birth of Erinne Chalene Cosby. But pretty soon it was time to get back in harness for the new season of "I Spy."

It had happened on "The Man from U.N.C.L.E.," where the conventionally handsome Robert Vaughn was eclipsed by his lesser-known partner, blond, Beatles-haircut-wearing David McCallum. Now another somewhat blandly handsome performer, Robert Culp, was in the backseat while amiable, funny Cos won the awards. Cos was well aware of the situation. When he won his first Emmy he said in his acceptance speech, "I extend my hand to a man by the name of Robert Culp. He lost this because he helped me."

If anything, the show was supposed to be slanted toward Culp. Robert was supposed to be the main star, with cool, funny support from his partner, Bill.

After all, the show was called "I Spy," not "We Spy," and in the opening credits, only one silhouette—Culp's—was shown playing tennis, smashing overhand strokes, and then trading racket for gun and shooting up villains. But it was obvious that without Cosby, or some other very unique partner, the "I Spy" hour would be a long, slow one.

Culp could be as moody as Cos, fighting his own battles for professional respect. But the friendship between Cosby and Culp was strong enough to survive the very real, very tense time when the Emmys always went to Cosby and the reporters went to Culp to ask why.

Culp handled the questions tersely, abruptly, not wanting to get into a prolonged debate about the situation, not wanting to slip and lose his cool, blowing up his own disappointment while Cos was in the spotlight.

The spotlight on Cos was casting some glare, too. With every article on the success of "I Spy" came parenthetical questions. Yes, that Cosby is quite a fellow, but the show is spy fantasy and why doesn't it accurately mirror the average black man's experience in America? Yes, it's certainly wonderful that a black man is on TV, but can't he be a little more militant? For Cos, the whole thing was crazy.

One day he noticed the word "crazy" had been deleted from one of the "I Spy" scripts. The censors had taken it out. He discovered that it was a taboo word. You weren't allowed to use "crazy" in the dialogue because another adventure show had done that—and NBC had received too many complaints from crazy people.

One question that critics needled Cosby with was "how come Scotty never seems to get involved with women?" It seemed that any romance in the stories involved Culp's character only.

At first there was no love interest for Alexander Scott because it was felt that the image of the "sex-crazed Negro" needed to be remedied. Scott was going to be a hero, not the kind of smirking macho fantasy that James Bond was, with the sniggering sex jokes and obsession with bedding and forgetting his conquests. When the time was right, Scott did get a share of the ladies. And for the first time, young black actresses had more to do than play the part of personable maids or demure secretaries. Cos, who had deliberately wanted his character "sterile," was comfortable enough after a while to start requesting some romance in the scripts.

This still wasn't enough for some. Why, in the midst of the riots and the turmoil and the fight for equality, wasn't the Cosby character going to bed with *white* women?

In answer to a *London Times* article actually headlined WHY COSBY NEVER GETS A WHITE GIRL, he patiently told a writer, "Now don't get it wrong. It was my decision right from the start to play it that way. As long as I'm on the screen, whether television or films, I will never hold or kiss a white woman. Hey, our black women have just nothing to look forward to in films, nothing to identify with . . . tell me, how often do you see a black man falling in love and making love with a black woman? So as it is, I want to be seen only with our women—not Chinese or Filipino women, not yellow, green, pink, or white. Just our women, black ones."

With the concept of "black is beautiful" still pretty new as a slogan, Cos was determined to show the beauty of black women. "The black person has been taught for years that he's ugly and she's ugly. The time comes when you say, 'Heck, I'm not ugly, blackness is not ugliness.' "

Cos elaborated for *Playboy* magazine: "In cities like Washington, D.C., in fact, there are many Negroes who still feel a great deal of resentment if a dark Negro comes to date a light-skinned girl. The parents of that girl want to keep breeding lighter, so they can finally get rid of that badge and walk free. But most black people have finally discovered they've been deluding themselves."

Reporters continued to play up the racial question, sometimes goading Cosby, hoping to provoke an explosive controversy. Told that it was his duty to attend the nonviolent marches down South, Cos replied, "I don't want to go someplace where they're throwing rocks unless I have some rocks to throw back." He continued to resist the urge to throw a few punches at the reporters, preserving the dignity and image he had fought to bring to the character of Alexander Scott.

The year "I Spy" began, the Writers' Guild set up a "Negro Writers' Workshop." Now that "I Spy" was a hit, more opportunities came for black writers, technicians, and actors. One of the new spy shows, "Mission Impossible," featured Greg Morris in a non-stereotype role. He played the brainy electronics wizard, while white Peter Lupus was in the cast as the strongman.

The Culp and Cosby duo paved the way for shows that did choose to experiment with white and black themes. Only after a show like "I Spy" could there have been "The Outcasts," where Otis Young played a former slave and Don Murray a bigoted cowboy. They had lines that could never have been spoken by Alexander Scott and Kelly Robinson:

"With you or without you, I'm going down there tonight in the dark."

"Well, you do have a natural advantage in the dark, don't you, boy. Unless of course you smile."

"The Outcasts" were billed as "friendly enemies" but the *New York Times* reviewer said he missed the "Robert Culp-Bill Cosby camaraderie of 'I Spy' and saw that particular show as nothing special, except for "the novelty of seeing racial hostility made explicit in a television program." Cosby's approach seemed to be the one that worked—"The Outcasts" quickly vanished, while the more positive "I Spy" left a lasting impression and had an impressive three-season run.

It might've lasted longer but the spy craze had lost its steam, especially after dozens of secret agents had flooded the air: comedy agents (Red Buttons as "Henry Phyffe"), British agents ("The Avengers" and "Secret Agent"), spin-offs ("The Girl from U.N.C.L.E."), and spin-outs ("T.H.E. Cat" with Robert Loggia and "Code: Blue Light" with Robert Goulet). Even the show that had started it all, "The Man from U.N.C.L.E.," was limping to the end of its run. Shifted to Monday nights opposite "The Carol Burnett Show" and "The Big Valley," Cosby and Culp became invisible men. It was game, set, and match for Kelly and Scott.

Cos had mixed emotions. He was relieved that this ground-breaking grind was over. And he had to admit that, because of the exhausting schedule, some episodes of the show had emerged as little more than travelogues with some mystery thrown in. But at the same time, he felt that with another season he might've been able to add even more depth to the character of Alexander Scott, especially since his pal Culp had begun to assume more of the writing and directing duties.

Young fans could still play Kelly and Scott on the home board game of "I Spy," and everyone could take in the reruns. The show is still seen in syndication today. While the show seems dated, as any sixties spy show must, Bill's unique contribution is still clearly visible. He succeeded at presenting a positive image of equality where none had been before. As he told *Playboy,* he made Scott human because he made him like himself, "a guy who grew up in the ghetto, who went to school and took on middle-class values, who was trying to live like the white middle class. But he always knew he was black, with a real degree of black pride. . . ."

Cos had won three Emmy Awards in a row. Now what? He'd been talking about retirement, going back to school. Others thought he should star in his own show. And there was his stand-up comedy, netting him Grammy Awards every year.

"You mean," people asked Cos, "there's actually a decision to make between making a million bucks a year or going back to school?"

Cos wanted school. And he wanted to continue the momentum of his career. There was no compromise in Bill Cosby. So he vowed to defy them all and do both.

Chapter Nine

Nineteen sixty-seven had been a great year for Cos; the Internal Revenue Service told him so. They wanted their share: $833,000 in income tax.

He tried to outrace them in January 1968. With shooting virtually complete on "I Spy," he did a month of one-night stand-up gigs—twenty-five in all. The take was $750,000 for the month.

The tour reaffirmed in bold figures that, even if "I Spy" was fading away, Bill's popularity was as strong as ever. He was still the nation's hottest comic.

He had no shortage of material. Not only was he able to put together solid, twenty-minute routines about his brother Russell, he was now telling audiences about his new family, his daughters Erika and Erinne. Rather than talk about his childhood, he could talk about theirs. It was comedy through observation instead of filtered through memory, but the laughs came out just the same.

Bill wasn't doing a routine when he talked about his daughters to cooking columnist Johna Blinn. Johna wanted his personal recipe for Scrapple meatloaf, but Cos sidetracked her. "Did you ever watch a one-year-old eat?" he asked. "They never put the food in their mouths but stuff the string beans or peas into their ears or noses. Any cool cook knows that the mashed potatoes have to be just the right temperature before they can be mashed into the hair. . . .

"No kid that age drinks her milk; she just spills it down the front. And then there's always the dropping game, but you can beat that. You have only to fasten a rubber band on the cup handle and wrap it around the child's wrist. That way the kid digs the rubber band and has all the fun of dropping the cup."

Cosby's $215,000 California home was a happy one, with his wife, his two daughters, and his mom. The house had a game room, complete with pool table and card table. And if that wasn't exciting enough, you could always watch the fish tank: there, a pair of piranha showed how to make goldfish disappear.

The household expanded with the arrival of three dogs—Boogie, Sab, and Fat Albert—who somehow managed to keep away from the fish tank and the swimming pool. To keep his weight down, Cos favored a swimming-and-sauna regime, though he also liked participating in "Hollywood All-Stars" basketball games with friends like Bill Russell and Lew Alcindor, soon to be known as Kareem Abdul-Jabbar.

To get away from it all, Cosby enjoyed long drives. His favorite "toy" was his hot new Shelby, replacing in his affections the Mercedes, the Cadillac, and the Ferrari, and even the 1937 Rolls-Royce. Sometimes he would drive into the deserted flatlands and gun the motor, racing it almost up to its two-hundred-mile-per hour capabilities. He loved the car so much he began to talk about it in his act, eventually putting together a twenty-minute routine on sports-car driving, complete with rumbling, purring sound effects.

These days he could even insert a little timely racial humor. He imagined a sports car so dangerous that just stepping on the gas could propel someone down the block and into a tree. That car he'd give away—to George Wallace.

Cos was more and more interested in free-form comedy, meeting the audience face to face. "I feel that in-person contact with people is the most important thing in comedy. While I'm up on stage, I can actually put myself into the audience, and adjust my pace and timing to them. I can get into their heads through their ears and through their eyes. Only through this total communication can I really achieve what I'm trying to do."

He was also serious about keeping it a "family show." "It's a conscious effort on my part to stay away from anything that has to do with sex or what are known as four-letter words, unless it is to make a point. Not that I think it's bad; it's just that I'd rather work without using it."

He was staying away from traditional smoky nightclubs, preferring more family-oriented accommodations. "I like to see my people comfortable, not crammed into a small club and paying a hefty cover charge. I have nothing against the nightclub business, but places like Madison Square Garden and the Westbury Music Fair are better. Westbury even more so, because the parking is better and the people don't have to drive into the city. Plus, they're not drinking and there's no extra tab laid on them."

Sometimes Cos stayed out of nightclubs for other reasons. One day his agent asked him if he'd mind coming to his son's bar mitzvah. Cos agreed. But a short time later, the agent received a booking request from a nightclub: $25,000 for the weekend. The same weekend as the bar mitzvah. The agent was all set to accept the $25,000 date, but Cosby refused. The bar mitzvah was more important.

Something else was becoming important to Cos: his singing career. Although he insisted he was just an "amateur" having fun, he began to book himself into places like the Whiskey-a-Go Go for "music only" shows, starting in the summer of 1967. Nightclub audiences used to Bill Cosby, comedian, now saw "Silver Throat": Bill Cosby, R&B vocalist.

Was he for real? At first nobody could be sure. Now he was sporting a huge walrus mustache, and that certainly didn't look real. When fans picked up the *Silver Throat Sings* and *Hooray for the Salvation Army Band* albums, they heard some tracks that sounded a little funny—but who knew if that was intentional?

Many cuts were satirical, like Cosby's exaggerated shout-singing rave-up of "Sgt. Pepper's Lonely Hearts Club Band." But others were definitely sincere, like "Sunny," where Cosby's thin baritone attempted to solemnly croon some life into lines like "I want to thank you, girl, for the wonderful time I had."

The most successful cuts were the ones where he comically strained his voice and scuffed his way through R&B classics. For something like Sam & Dave's "Hold On! I'm Comin'," he knocked out the old lyrics and ad-libbed his own frantic words of encouragement: "You better hold on," he wails to his love. "Try and do something . . . run around the room a lot . . . I might be out of breath, but I'm coming!"

Those who considered Cosby's foray into vocalizing just egotistic, hard-headed indulgence had to eat their words when Cos punted one of his songs, "Little Ole Man," onto the Top 20 charts for a while.

Bill's comedy albums were the big sellers for Warners. Each new release met with instant success. The label's owner, Joe Smith, was surprised when he got a call asking him to bid for the rights to a Cosby album recorded at the Gaslight. The Gaslight? Why, Cos hadn't worked there in years. When he had, it was back when he was doing that Dick Gregory stuff about race and politics.

As it turned out, the owner of the Gaslight, Clarence Hood, was the owner of the tapes, which a long time ago were going to be released on the club's own Gaslight Records label and sold at the door. Cosby had felt the embryonic material was not suitable for release at the time. He felt just as strongly that this material wasn't professional enough for release now—and that his young fans wouldn't get their money's worth.

When Cosby and Smith found out the real reason why Hood was offering the tapes—because the Gaslight had fallen on hard times and Hood was in dire straits—they agreed to buy the material. They never put it out, of course. But they gave Hood a check for far more than Hood was asking—or that any label would've paid at auction. As far as Cos was concerned, Hood was an old friend in need.

By the time the novelty of Cosby's singing career had worn off late in 1968, he was already involved in plenty of other projects. He was hoping to fulfill his ambition of returning to school, and it seemed like the best bet was at the University of Massachusetts. He was even telling interviewers he was going to retire and become a schoolteacher. But he couldn't walk away from show business, especially since it seemed that no matter how much money he earned, taxes took out a huge bite, and bewildering investment options had to be taken into account to ensure that he would not be "embarrassed" by finding himself suddenly broke.

"When you talk about show business," he told an *Ebony* interviewer, "don't leave off the word 'business.' It's a serious, serious business. Most of us come from a low economic background where money is used to just pay bills. We are stunned when we realize that we can make a lot of money. We have no idea how the system works that is going to pay us so much money, so we leave off the most important part—protecting that money."

Now part of a growing corporation, Campbell/Silver/Cosby, he was working on investment deals that could net him a couple of hundred thousand dollars a year for life, even if he never worked again. Creatively, he had his $40,000-a-week stand-up gigs at Harrah's and other clubs, and had negotiated a sweet deal with NBC that would net him a new TV show, his own variety specials, and a few cartoon specials based on Cosby's childhood characters like Fat Albert and Weird Harold. Roy Silver was working on a movie deal with Warners, and Cosby formed a new record label, Tetragrammaton. (Silver was delighted to get away with that name, "the unspoken name of God—look it up!") Most of the deals were happening—although one, a proposed Fat Albert hamburger chain, never got off the back burner.

Tetragrammaton was a strange label that included in its list Deep Purple and Tom Smothers's friend, comic Murray Roman. The label also handled distribution for *Two Virgins,* the first John Lennon-Yoko Ono album (complete with a nude cover photo that Bill was not thrilled with). Since Cosby had been responsible for a healthy hunk of Warner Bros.' profits in the previous years, he was expected to get the label off the ground. His entry was a two-record set designed to show his "Vegas" style monologues. Instead of childhood riffs, it was an easygoing eighty minutes of Cos doing his laid-back audience-participation bits, joking about sports and gambling. He satirized gamblers who called out, "Oh God, help me" at the dice table ("Look, God has better things to do!") and shared gambling frustrations:

"I know one time I was down to my last two hundred dollars. I mean, not to my name, but I lost all I could sign for. And I said, 'I'm gonna win something. It can't get worse. . . .' Well, never tempt 'worse.' I went over to the roulette wheel and got two hundred dollars' worth of quarter chips. Covered the table. I mean, covered the table, red and black even up. I'm going to win something before I go to sleep. And the guy spun the ball and it fell on the floor."

He couldn't resist a little racial quip. Talking about poker chips, he said, "When we divvy up the chips, there's a way we're gonna do it: Whatever color the person, that's the color chips he's gonna get. No fair paintin' yourself."

When Cos began work on his first TV special, the network executives had a little racial quip of their own. "We don't know about this," they said. "We've got problems." Cosby was astonished. The network wanted to tuck the special out of the way, at ten P.M.

Cosby wanted it on early so the kids could watch. The network stalled on a date: then the one they chose was too late to qualify for Emmy nomination that year.

Cosby remembers what one exec told him: "One of them said, 'Don't forget, Bill, you're a problem. No matter how popular you are, no matter how many kids love you, you're a problem. All black men are.'"

Years before, Cos would have pretty much let things cool out. But in these times, after the stride forward with "I Spy," and when people were slowly beginning to exchange the term "Negro" for "Afro-American" or "black," Cosby went to the press with some of his complaints.

In an interview with the *New York Times,* he said, "The most difficult thing is for people to accept the American Negro as a full, total human being, without him being something different."

He confronted the female reporter: "You married? Okay, then. Say I work with your husband and one day he says to me, 'Hey, man, will you go pick up my wife for me? I got something to do.' So I pick you up, and I have to put a sign on the car saying 'This woman is not my girl friend. She is married to somebody else who is also white.'"

He talked about the double standard. People were bothering him about whether he was going to have blacks and whites on his special, and it didn't matter if he said "all blacks" or "all whites" or "checkerboard." Somebody was bound to find a reason to get mad at him.

He was growing restless. "When you belong to a minority group . . . you have to walk so that you don't upset the people who are in a position to give you the next step so you can eventually walk by yourself."

For the TV special, Cosby returned to Philadelphia. The idea was to shoot some background for his street-football monologue and use actual Philly locales.

Nothing much had changed. The brick walls of the tenements were scrawled up with graffiti, trashed up with chalk marks. Cos stood out on the sidewalk in front of the buildings, smoking his cigar, watching.

There was a strange contrast on the street this day. The shabby walk-ups were all around, but in the center of the street were thousands of dollars' worth of electrical equipment, cameras, and sound recorders. And while the people gathering to watch from the sidelines were dressed poorly, the guys operating the equipment were wearing

T-shirts made for the occasion, the words "The Bill Cosby Special" emblazoned across the back.

Surging forward were little kids, getting autographs from a man who was once one of them, who talked like one of them, and who was, deep inside, still one of them.

Cosby wanted some of the kids to get together and play some street football, like he remembered. But the kids who played with Cos when he was a kid didn't do it in front of TV cameras and people holding microphones and wielding lights.

The day wore on. The crew got the footage they needed. The restless crowd got a chance to praise their favorite son and envy him.

Cos made a splash in the old neighborhood, but response to the special was mixed. Cosby had done the unheard of: a special without guest stars. At a time when comics hardly had any respect at all, Cos had dared to do virtually an hour of stand-up. "Mr. Cosby is very funny when he is acting out his childhood games," the *New York Times* said, "but next time the producers should remember that there are very few performers who can carry an entire show by themselves."

Over at the *Daily News,* Kay Gardella praised Cosby: "His delivery and recollections had the same universal appeal that all our great humorists manage to impart when they dip into their treasured memories of the past and its hardships, with understanding instead of resentment and anger."

Cosby, still "the experiment" in the TV world after all those triumphs, now experimented with radio. Coca-Cola sponsored his five-minute daily show that gave a shot of comedy to Top 40 radio stations. Cos would appear as himself, or as characters like Brown Hornet and Captain Oh Wow, and impart unusual bits of wisdom, like "A ship without a sail has an engine in it somewhere" and "Hitch your wagon to a star and pay for it by the month."

As fast as Cosby was putting together new deals, others were unraveling. He was beginning to have conflicts with his high-pressure partners at Campbell/Silver/Cosby, and was worried about all the corporate risks. He was meeting some critical hatchets with his singing and fans who had already bought so many comedy albums didn't seem to need yet another—especially a double disc set.

As another hot summer threatened, with racial discontent stirring more violently than ever, Cosby journeyed to Harlem's Apollo Theater for the first time. He told the crowd, "In show business, you can be rich today and back in the projects tomorrow."

But most of the evening, which some saw as a test of how strong Cosby was without white middle-class support, turned out to be high hilarity and pure good times. Not only did the audience cheer and applaud him, even the stagehands got a special kick out of meeting their man, Alexander Scott, superspy. Some knew him as an actor, not a stand-up comic. Bill heard two of them talking when he walked in. "That's the cat," one whispered. "What's he going to do?" "I don't know, maybe shoot some cats!"

At a concert in Kansas just a few weeks later, on April 4, 1968, Cosby received the news that the Reverend Martin Luther King, Jr., had been shot.

It was hell night all over the country, a night of fear, anger, tension, and grief. Some places were burning, and some places were ready to explode. Some people were burning inside, whether it was a raging fire of pain or just a flickering candle of sorrow.

Cosby's own feeling of depression began to envelop him. He'd done his first show, not yet knowing more than the sketchy rumors. Now, facing the late show, he had heard the worst. King was dead.

He remembered what had happened when President Kennedy was assassinated, the unrelieved sense of loss and hopelessness, the bitterness and the tears. Death was on everyone's lips and there was no escape. The networks shut off all regular programming and staged a twenty-four-hour wake.

Maybe some people needed escape, Cosby thought. Maybe they needed laughter, and needed it bad. It could be a healing thing. Or it could almost be sacrilege.

Bill sat in the dressing room, weary from phone conversations with a tearful Harry Belafonte, confused and depressed, as tense as all of America, wondering what would happen next.

The crowds were filing in. Time for the show. Cosby got the word: five minutes to curtain. At last he left the dressing room and made the walk toward the backstage area. He could hear the buzz out front. Then he came out onstage and the spotlights hit him.

He began to do the show, shutting off the tragedy, rambling about the crowd, and gambling, and Kansas and stuff. It wasn't working; he couldn't concentrate.

Cosby faltered. He'd gone as far as he could in forty minutes, and stopped. He told his fans that he couldn't continue. The audience was stunned.

Slowly, they began to applaud. The applause reached a crescendo, swelling louder, until it seemed they couldn't applaud enough. The audience stood as one, standing and applauding.

And they let Cos go, audience and performer sharing a moment of understanding and pain, and wondering what the rest of the nation would do with their own sense of loss.

Back in the dressing room, the calls were coming in. He was going to meet with Belafonte in Memphis. A call came from Robert Culp. The two of them were going to go down together and be part of the Memphis march.

After Memphis, Cosby went to Atlanta for the funeral. Famous faces were there, but changed somehow by the moment—no longer looking like stars, just worn-out people. Along with Cosby, there were Stevie Wonder, Robert Kennedy, Ossie Davis and Ruby Dee. There was Dizzy Gillespie and Lena Horne, and all the people who had worked with Dr. King, marched with King, and were now marching for what was left of the dream.

Bill took it all in, the long ceremony marked with ripples of anger in the heartache, fury in the frustration. He stayed until the speeches began. When the politicians started to voice their profound sense of shock, and their heartfelt sympathies, he quietly slipped away.

Some time later, Cosby received a letter from Robert Kennedy about the King assassination. He had it framed and hung on his office wall, near the framed copy of the Emancipation Proclamation and a sculpture of Dr. King.

In June, Cosby appeared in an episode of the seven-part CBS series "Of Black America." In a fourth-grade classroom at the Old Tarrytown Road School in New York, Cosby and the teacher, Mrs. Lovely Billups, talked with the kids about black history.

"When I was growing up, we didn't get information about anybody but the usual people," Cosby recalled later. "Of course we learned how the Ku Klux Klan rode in and separated families. We lived in a ghetto, what must have been Philadelphia's first housing project—ninety-nine and nine-tenths percent black. I don't know whether any white person can imagine how that feels."

Cosby hoped to tell people more about black history and black leaders, and to "erase the stereotypes about what the black man is." And he remembered his vow to return to school, and to find ways of teaching the children.

"I think there's a lot to be said for fighting at the blackboard, with a piece of chalk as a weapon."

Chapter Ten

For his first solo TV series, NBC wanted Cosby to be a comical detective, but he wanted to play a schoolteacher.

"OK," they said, "how about playing a schoolteacher who moonlights at night as a detective?"

"How about I just play a schoolteacher?" Cos said.

NBC gave in. After all, Cosby had another option—he could continue his studies and really become a schoolteacher, just as he was saying he would do someday. They still wondered what kind of wild, zany sitcom plots his show would have.

His answer: none. No inane characters, no farce, and no booming laugh track. "The character I play will do certain things that will provoke anger," he told writer Kay Gardella. He will be "a human being: He makes mistakes, gets into trouble, and reflects quite frequently on the human condition. . . . What I'm really doing is a study of human behavior. My actions will be deplorable sometimes, but by being that way I'm saying to an audience, 'Are you really that pure?' My character will do all those things a person does when eyes aren't on him. He'll put his feet up on the desk, jump on the trampoline with his shoes on, and frequently act out of selfish motives."

One of the writers on the series was Ed Weinberger, who had been at Central High in Philly at the same time as Cosby. Preparing for the show, he noted, "People identify with Bill's humor because it's an honest admission of his vulnerability. He is happy to be vulnerable. It's a confession of his humanity."

With the premiere show scheduled for September of 1969, Cosby finished up some of his other projects, like a TV special called "As I See It," in which ten children got a chance to make their own eight-millimeter movies and show them, with Cos as host.

Executive producer for the NBC Children's Theatre project, George Heinemann, couldn't say enough about working with Cosby. "Boy, he's very much Mr. Casual. The kids love him, and obviously he loves the kids." Working with Cosby was child's play: "He invites us up to his house, and we sit around about three and one-half hours, have something to eat, chat about the good old days—his in Philly—and he listens to suggestions about how we think the show ought to go." And off it went.

Cosby had pretty much the same approach to his appearances on the "Tonight" show. He'd become a popular guest host starting back in January 1965. At that time, the *New York Herald Tribune* wrote, "Johnny Carson had best look to his squat-and-chat laurels," because Cosby's show, with Art Carney and Jason Robards, Jr., aboard, "was one of the better late shows in many a moon."

Cos no longer did set routines, preferring relaxed ad-libs. As he recalls, the change happened in the midst of a preplanned bit: "The audience started laughing at something . . . and I didn't know what was funny or why they were laughing, so I just started talking about something. And it turned out to be very, very funny. . . . Ever since then I've just been walking out and talking," mixing spontaneous observation with occasional lines from his nightclub act.

Things looked cool and calm when Cosby began guest-host duties one week in March 1968. Monday and Tuesday nights' shows went fine. Then on Wednesday night, March 19, Cos rambled through his monologue, including a few lines about visiting a Catholic church for the first time. His wife was Catholic, of course, and helped him understand the different rituals. But he couldn't quite figure out the wafers, those "individual pizzas."

Meanwhile, at the NBC switchboard, they couldn't understand why the room had gotten about one hundred watts brighter. The board was lit up with an overflow of four hundred calls.

For the first time, Cosby found himself swept up in coast-to coast controversy on a matter of taste. With those two words, "individual pizzas," the gentle, modern Mark Twain was branded as the worst kind of villain. How could the man prey on a defenseless minority group!

Eleanor Roberts, a columnist for the *Boston Herald Traveler*, was one of the many writers who felt that Cos had "done serious damage to his image. I don't buy this nonsense of the 'Tonight' show reaching a more liberal and sophisticated audience. That excuse is not open sesame to mock any religious faith." Pointing out that NBC had bleeped out a pair of curses (a hell and a damn, or perhaps it was two damns), Roberts charged "they took infinite care to delete two swear words . . . but they gave the green light to a blasphemy that won't soon be forgotten."

Papers all over the country picked up on the anti-Catholic attack from Bill Cosby. It was a sober, self-controlled young man who faced the cameras the following night and said, "I want to apologize for those offended by the routine. . . ."

Standing on the chalk mark and watching his step, he chose his words carefully. "I was merely giving an outsider's viewpoint toward religion in humorous terms," he said. "But I guess you can't do that on TV."

Ironically, when Bill's second annual comedy special was aired, barely two weeks later, it included a bit of biblical humor (his famous Noah routine, this time acted out with Cos in costume, complete with white beard). There was also a reference to his and Fat Albert's visit to church: "The coolest part was putting Scotch tape backwards on the fingernails and waiting for the collection plate to come around."

As with his first special, Cosby had no guest stars, carrying the entire show virtually alone. He did introduce someone sitting out in the audience—his mom. She called up to him, "Are you saving your money?"

The special received positive reviews, and Cosby was encouraged, hoping that fans of his simple, human style of comedy would respond to his new, low-key TV sitcom.

The first episode of the show was a slice-of-life study of Cos as Chet (only his mother called him Chester) Kincaid, enjoying his day off from teaching phys. ed. About the most exciting thing that happened was that a pair of cops pulled him over while he was jogging, thinking he might be a neighborhood prowler.

Variety was not pleased with the mild show, to put it mildly. With most premieres coming out running, "Cosby came out jogging. His preem episode was frail and contrived . . . short on humor and even shorter on story, and it was pointless besides. Presumably the intention is to key the scripts to the kind of fanciful anecdote that is the main stuff of Cosby's stand-up routines. The danger in that . . . is (1) that Cosby's tales may be better heard than seen and (2) that five minutes' worth of airy material may not stretch to a half hour."

It looked like Cosby's show was a prime candidate for quick cancellation. It just wasn't frantic, as most sitcoms of the era were.

At least nobody seemed to be bringing up the racial issue. Cos had jumped that hurdle with "I Spy," and the year before it had been Diahann Carroll's turn. As the first black to star in a sitcom, she took the same flack Cosby had for being an "unrealistic" role model, a cute, middle-class black who dared to act equal to and just like whites.

Diahann's show, "Julia," even included lines that naively suggested that some of the racial conflicts were over—or at least that the sight of a black face was no cause for alarm, as it had been when "I Spy" first came on the scene. In the opening episode, when "Julia" applies for a job, she tells the gruff-looking employer (Lloyd Nolan), "I'm colored. I'm a Negro." He hires her as a nurse anyway, answering, "Have you always been a Negro, or are you just trying to be fashionable?"

"Julia" was still on the air when Cosby's show turned up. Cosby could breathe a little easy. Maybe critics could attack him for being cute and mild, but now at least the question was about the comedy and not "the Problem." He had risen above it, with dignity, just as he'd planned.

Then a huge article by Faith Berry appeared in the *New York Times*: Bill Cosby was a cop-out, a disappointment to the black community. The *Times* criticized him for being "easy-going, likable, and at times too farcical to be true; he's everybody's friend, usually all the time."

Berry wanted to know why Cosby's sitcom didn't contain the racial strife of film dramas like *To Sir with Love* or *Blackboard Jungle.* She was furious that the comedy show had not covered "Afro-American history, community control of schools, teacher strikes, the black family, the black neighborhood, the busing of school children . . . soul culture."

How dare Bill Cosby show a middle-class black? And how about the family of Chet Kincaid? Why was it that Chet's brother works driving a garbage truck but "we've certainly seen nothing about the plight of any black garbage worker on this show." Berry allowed that the show was saying "blacks are human," but surely Cosby could do more than that!

It also seemed to gall the *New York Times* that this mild-mannered sitcom, which didn't seem to have any chance at all opposite "The Ed Sullivan Show" and "The FBI," was currently number one among the season's new shows. "It will probably remain a popular show, since many white viewers will continue to watch it because they find it refreshing. Blacks will do likewise, still hoping to identify with it."

In Hollywood, Cos quietly continued his work on the show. He kept the anger inside. "I help black people in my own way," he said. "It's just that I don't talk about it." He was tired of defending his philosophy to foolish white reporters and ax-grinding black ones. He didn't call attention to the fact that half the crew on "The Bill Cosby Show" was black, or that large numbers of blacks were getting their big acting breaks on the show, or that many episodes had all-black casts. This was years before the premieres of "Sanford and Son" and "The Jeffersons."

"The Bill Cosby Show" ended up number eleven for the season, just behind such superstars of American comedy as Red Skelton and Lucille Ball, and ahead of powerhouse programs hosted by Carol Burnett and Dean Martin. Not bad for a quiet, human little show about a person Faith Berry considered "a kind of half-man who, had he lived in the days of Nat Turner, might have sold Turner down the river."

Just as he had done in stand-up, Bill had a plan and stuck to it. The result in stand-up had been best-selling Grammy-winning comedy albums. Now, he had put together a year of wholesome, high-quality sitcom work and the public responded by making it a hit. Cosby's humor turned people around, and his own personal philosophy in comedy was vindicated.

The *New York Times* ran an article the exact opposite of the first. Another black writer, A. S. Doc Young, came to bury Berry, not to praise her:

"Bill Cosby, through sheer force of personality and great talent, has created a hit show, perhaps an improbable hit show. . . . Cosby looms tall among hero figures for black kids who need hero figures in the worst way. . . . Meanwhile, he relates in a constructive way to millions of adult viewers of all races. . . . Cosby would not be at his best as a professional civil rights leader, a Black Panther, or the head of a poverty program. But as Bill Cosby—comic, wit, humorist, and story-teller—he is making an important contribution to Afro-Americans, to Americans as a whole. His contribution is not to be taken lightly."

While he continued to overcome prejudice by simply proving his race-neutral equality, Cosby used a light touch on his show, one of the hardest things to pull off in comedy. When asked what was the most difficult style of comedy to write, veteran comedy writer Hal Kanter answered, "Subtlety. Innuendo." He said it was far easier to write zany humor or insult humor à la Redd Foxx, where you say "the most common, childish, aggressive statements and the audiences scream at them."

Instead, Cosby's writers aimed for realism and for character comedy. One show was simply a study of Chet's reactions to a neighbor's barking dog, who is keeping him awake nights. The neighbor is a comely young black girl—so Chet tries to be pleasant and friendly, even to the dog. But when he sees the panting animal, its tongue flapping in and out of its mouth, he grumbles, "You're making me tired, the way you breathe, you know that, don't ya?" As usual, any Cosby hostility translates into comic observation.

Chet tries everything to get to sleep, including wearing head phones and "sleep socks" over his ears, but the yapping dog never stops. The next morning, a numb smile on his face, his eyes glassy, Chet falls asleep with his eyes open during an important conference, snoring lightly.

A Dick Van Dyke would've done a rubber-band dance of exhaustion. Lucille Ball might've swooned into a dead sleep on top of everybody. Redd Foxx would've gone after the barking dog with a shotgun. But here, subtly and realistically, Chet just nods out, producing memorable chuckles. Viewers could turn to each other and say, "Yeah, that's exactly the way it is." No solution in real life to a barking dog all night—and the result is a groggy day the next morning.

Realism was so important to the show that even physical details were authentic: Perhaps for the first time on TV, a sitcom character went to bed not in neat starched pajamas buttoned up to the neck, but in a pair of undershorts.

Also, unlike most sitcoms, some episodes presented the star in an unflattering light.

When a halfback on the football team is so hyped on winning that he gets into fights when he loses, Chet lectures him: "The important thing is not winning. It's knowing what to do when you lose. Humility in victory; pride in defeat."

It's a nice speech, but Chet doesn't practice what he preaches. Competing in a handball tournament, he tries all kinds of sneaky tricks to win: cheap distractions ("Your sneakers don't look like they fit you"); pleas for sympathy ("My back's sore today"); and irritating ploys, like asking "Are you ready?" before every serve. And when he ultimately loses the tourney to a player who uses the same unsavory tactics, Chet becomes angry and sullen, argues with the referee, and storms off the court.

The student is shocked. "Mr. Kincaid acts just the way I do when I lose. It's kind of silly, Isn't it? Now I see how I look and, believe me, I'm gonna change."

The student changes, but Chet remains the same! After forcing himself to finally congratulate the new champ, Chet slinks away insulting him behind his back.

Cosby told his writers: "There are times when Chet will miss the point. He may be looking for something and it may be right in front of his nose. I do this deliberately, figuring that people will identify with Chet and become better teachers, better mothers, better fathers."

Chet wasn't always infallible with kids, either. In one episode (which featured an early TV appearance by Lou Gossett, Jr.), he tries to persuade some neighborhood kids to play basketball instead of hanging out on the sidewalk. When one kid tells Chet to get lost, he says, "Whatsa matter, nobody ever been nice to ya?"

The kid's heart is not warmed. "Here," the little boy says, walking away with his friends, "I'll leave the whole sidewalk to you in my will."

Of course, episodes showing the warmth of human nature and recognizable character comedy were more typical. Chet takes over his nephew's paper route, grandly proclaiming, "There's no labor a man can do that's undignified—if he does it right." He arrives at the newspaper truck at 5:00 A.M. only to be eyed suspiciously by the other paperboys and by the man handing out the papers.

"How do I know you're taking your nephew's place?" the man asks solemnly. "You got some identification?"

"Why," Chet pleads, "would I be here at six in the morning? What am I gonna do with forty newspapers?"

"Maybe," the man answers slowly, "you like to read."

At last Chet convinces the man, who says a line that kids have been hearing ever since parents and teachers were invented: "Tell ya what I'm gonna do. I'm gonna take a chance on ya. Don't let me down."

The rest of the episode involves Chet's misadventures delivering papers—to all the wrong houses—and trying to get them back again from crabby neighbors and vicious dogs.

Cosby's show was a great place for black technicians and crewmen, as well as many black actors and actresses, to find employment. Cosby's brother Russell was even around, studying to become a cameraman. But the show also offered young kids a chance to break into show business. The corridors of Richard Allen Holmes High (a reference, of course, to Cosby's home at the Richard Allen projects of Philadelphia) were filled with students—like Ed Begley, Jr., and a young Mark Hamill, who got to deliver the immortal line, "All right, you goons, you've had your fun. Cool it!"

Some episodes of the show were, as some critics claimed, a little preachy or slow-moving. One was nothing more than a history lesson (Chet teaching an Hispanic carpenter enough to become a citizen), coupled with a civics lesson (the carpenter stands up at the show's end to recite his version of the Bill of Rights—"People are people . . . they should be free and happy").

But more often the care and effort that went into these seemingly slim plots paid off. For example, one episode had Elsa Lanchester as an eccentric lady bent on preserving trees. "Save one tree and you will breathe easier," Chet says, giving her a slogan.

But despite all their efforts, the duo can't save one little tree that stands in the way of construction at a building site. Most of the episode had been involved with all the ways to try and save the tree, from protests to newspaper publicity to possible transplantation. But when it's destroyed, the episode poignantly stands still for a moment. Although the tree on this site has died, Chet and the lady find places along the highway to plant new trees. Chet tells a skeptical kid that, aside from shade and oxygen, it's important to have trees "as home base in hide-and-seek."

Buoyed by the ratings, Bill and the writers tried to experiment with new techniques in putting together a sitcom in keeping with his strong intent on educating, with valuable lessons that kids could put into practice themselves. Cosby, as Chet Kincaid, handled diverse problems: peer pressure from a baseball team when their star player, an Orthodox Jew, refuses to play on Saturday; teaching a girl how to drive a car without fear by using a lot of reverse psychology, etc.

Typical Cosby comic dialogue turned up in an episode about the cafeteria's poor menu. He tells the pretty black manager, "We all have to give up a little authority in the face of liberty. They want an end to the liver chow mein . . . and they want the tomato surprise not to be such a big surprise. They want an end to chipped beef on toast with creamed gravy and raisins."

"I think raisins help," she says.

"Dear, nothing helps chipped beef on toast."

There was room to experiment with all types of comedy, even the kind of funky black humor that would be the keystone of "Sanford and Son" a few years later. In one episode, Cosby used two of the greatest comedians of black vaudeville, Mantan Moreland and Moms Mabley. Cast as Uncle Dewey and Aunt Edna, they played a raucous, fighting couple.

"When a man starts to get old," Moms rasps, "get rid of him! He can't do nothin', won't do nothin', and don't want you to do nothin'!" Pointing at Mantan, she thunders, "There's a man that gets out of breath puttin' his pajamas on at night! That's a man who has to take naps so he can be rested when he goes to sleep!"

Moreland's gravelly comeback: "I wouldn't keep my eyes closed so much if my eyes had something to look at. I used to stay home from work just to avoid kissin' you good-bye."

Moms shouts, "He snores so loud it rattles my teeth!"

Mantan yells, "Then you should keep 'em in a glass farther from the bed!"

The episode showed that Cosby had respect for the old-time comedians and their ethnic character comedy, even if he wasn't willing to perform it himself. But as the kindly "Bill Cosby Show" slipped away after a second season, the comedian saw a troubling horizon. Mainstream sitcoms were getting nasty and the up-and-coming black comedians were selling a tough new attitude.

Into the turbulent late sixties and early seventies, there was a change from Negro to Afro-American to black. Along the way, the black community had convulsions over what was funny and why. Redd

Foxx and Sherman Hemsley would veer toward reverse racism, becoming black Archie Bunkers. Flip Wilson would do overtly ethnic characters like Geraldine, and Jimmie Walker would star in "Good Times." All would be accused, by various black factions, of damaging black pride, of not being black enough, of not being funny, or even of being too funny. And at the center of attention was still another black comic, Richard Pryor, the "crazy nigger" whose overt, stinging barbs about blacks and whites alarmed as many as he amused.

Would Bill Cosby try to navigate, as he had in the sixties, the bewildering, swirling waters of social change just to get a few laughs?

Cosby had some other plans. He had a home in Amherst, Massachusetts, and he was taking courses. There was the lure of retirement to the good life, of becoming a teacher, and of dumping all the controversy of his career. Voted Man of the Year in 1969 by the Harvard University Hasty Pudding Club (Paul Newman won in 1968, and Robert Redford would win in 1970), Cos could end his career on a high note.

And what about his kids? Ennis William arrived April 15, 1969, and there was a great temptation to stay home and watch him and the others grow. Even though he'd spent most of his past two years in California, Camille told him once, "You only see them six or seven months out of the year, and yet you know their personalities so well." But how much better could he know them if he was home more often? The children, Cosby said, "accept that they have a father who must travel for his work, but who comes home. That's the important thing. They know it's a job and I'll be back." Maybe it was time to come back for good.

Chapter Eleven

Cosby's dream home was a farm outside Amherst where he could raise his family and also work on his studies at the University of Massachusetts. More and more, he was drawn to the country life, and as his TV series faded, he told more and more people that his goal was to become a real teacher.

The 135-year-old clapboard farmhouse had cost $64,000 initially, but renovations siphoned off an additional $325,000 from the Cosby bank account. The sixteen-room house had five working stone fireplaces, making it especially cozy on those snowy New England nights. Cos had missed the snow during all those years living in the thirty-one-room California mansion he'd dubbed the "Cosby Hilton."

There weren't as many guests coming by as in the old days, but there was always room for old California friends like Clarence Williams III, or new ones, like pianist-composer Eubie Blake.

The country life, in both summer and winter, appealed to Bill. Fantasists might even say that it recalled the stories of Huckleberry Finn and Tom Sawyer that his mother read him as a boy, only instead of the Mississippi River, there was the nearby Connecticut River. In the summer, he could use the tennis court or commune with nature, going for walks on the 286-acre grounds with specially planted flower beds and fruit trees. In the winter, great fun could be had with old-fashioned sleigh rides, playing with the kids, or simply enjoying the serenity of a landscape gracefully covered in snow.

A quiet place, Cosby's estate was sufficiently off the beaten track to discourage tourists and fans. And it was far enough away from the local public schools—twenty-two miles—that Camille had to get up at six in the morning to drive the kids in each day.

Of the two small barns on the property, one was converted into an office for Cosby, and the other became a home for Cosby's mom. The place became more and more of a seductive, permanent home with each improvement and with the further acquisition of expensive period antiques.

The kids went to school, and so did Cos, in his own way. It was informal at first. The University of Massachusetts had a flexible program for their master's student. First of all, they admitted him even though he hadn't finished his four years at Temple, feeling he'd qualified on the basis of "life experience." (Temple would later gather up Cosby's massive volume of work and translate it into a bachelor of arts degree.) Second, because he was studying the link between television and education, he had to be free to work on projects in New York and Hollywood, like his Fat Albert cartoon specials, documentaries, and "The Electric Company."

"The Electric Company," aimed at bettering the reading skills of seven-to-ten-year-olds, was the perfect vehicle for Cosby's whimsical instructional talents. He could help teach kids how d could turn be into bed and, in song, demonstrate the value of the "Double E":

"Oh, you can flee to Tennessee for a three-day spree! Have yourself a time at a jamboree! Anywhere you go you find you can't get free from Double E!"

"The Electric Company" seems taken for granted now, along with "Sesame Street," but back in the early seventies it was an exciting breakthrough, something Bill was keen to become involved with even though he was sacrificing a lot of time and a lot of money. Skip Hinnant, one of the regulars on the show, recalls, "None of us were getting rich on the show and I know Cosby wasn't getting anything like his normal salary. He was intensely interested in the show as a new idea in reading. We had a research team working on the techniques for teaching, and for every dollar we spent in production they spent five in research, finding out what worked and what didn't."

Cos was magic on the set. Everyone called him either Cos or Bill, and right from the start, Skip recalls, "Bill was very open, very unpretentious. And he had the biggest collection of sneakers in the world! This was before running shoes became a fad. He'd come in with some leather sneaks or new tennis shoes and say, 'Look at these, Skip, look at these!' And I'd want to go out and buy a pair, or he'd bring me a pair. That's all he ever wore, jeans and sneakers.

"During the first year we didn't know what would work and what wouldn't, but he was laid-back and even-tempered even in the toughest times. It was eighteen-hour days, getting out of the studio at nine or ten at night.

"He was very cool about all that. I could imagine other stars saying, 'The hell with this, I'm goin' home, not for this kind of money am I gonna stay here till ten after coming in at seven in the morning.' But if he felt it had to be done, he worked as hard as the next."

Of course, Cos was not about to play "nice guy" all the time. He stood up for himself. "If he felt a sketch wasn't up to his standards, he'd say, 'I'm not going to spend a lot of time on this, just so you know up front. Let's get it done quick.' Or he'd say, 'This thing sucks, why don't we punch it up? Let's improvise.'" And Cos and the crew would cut loose and have some fun ad-libbing new lines. Though it was a monitored and carefully devised experiment, "The Electric Company" did provide ample opportunity for improvisation, and some of the best sketches were total ad-libs.

"He was a lot of fun on the set," Skip says. "He can be very casual and funny, but he has great dignity, too. You know you don't screw around with him, but at the same time you know you can."

To this day Bill enjoys the reputation of someone who loves to giggle, laugh, keep things loose—but keep enough respect and seriousness that when it's time to work, the fooling around ends.

There was plenty of Billfoolery on the "Electric Company" set. When Camille would come in for a visit, Bill loved to tease her in front of cast and crew. "He'd try to embarrass her to death," Skip Hinnant chuckles, "but Camille was cool. He'd flirt with somebody, and clown around, but Camille was still cool. A very, very even-tempered lady." Bill was literally a circus ringleader for silliness. Once when the entire cast was dressed up in clown makeup and costumes, Bill said, "Okay, everybody! Let's go out for dinner!" And suddenly a fancy nearby restaurant, Oscar's Salt of the Sea, was besieged by a bunch of crazy clowns, startling guests just by standing around with their happiest smiles on and their gaudiest, brightest outfits.

Harmless shocks for adults were only a part of Bill's impishness. One day some kids recognized him as he was leaving the studio. He smiled at them, began to jog, and then broke into a frantic dead run. The kids shrieked and raced after him, and for two blocks he led a ragtag, ever-growing group of giggling, laughing children on a merry chase. Finally Bill crashed into a trash can and went rolling over and over. The kids pounced on him, and there was a good-natured roughhouse right there on the street.

"He loves that kind of thing," Skip recalls with a smile. "It's real-life humor. It's funny and alive, and that's why I think everything he does works so well."

Cos kept up with the show for two full seasons, at the same time maintaining his own adult education studies. His new-found interest in education did clash with his old, long-standing frustration with schoolwork. Describing his studies at the University of Massachusetts, he said, "You look at things, and you say, 'Gee whiz, this is interesting, all these things. . . .' Then you find out, 'Gee whiz, this is going to take me eight hundred years before I'm finished with this!'"

The more involved Cos became in the academic community, the more inactive he was in mainstream entertainment projects. But as 1971 was drawing to a close, so was some of the comedian's enthusiasm for the sequestered life of academia. "I was starting to feel like I was accomplishing nothing. Nobody was pushing me. It's just that I seemed to lack something."

Cos went out on more club dates. He shared his traditional stories of childhood, but also included new material that seemed to reflect Chet Kincaid (a routine about playing handball and getting wiped out by a cool old man who just walked to the right spot, hit the ball the right way, and drove him nuts). He also did a bit about one of his most embarrassing moments, a visit with Ray Charles.

"Some people have their thoughts about what stars are like—like they never make a mistake. But have you ever been in a position where you were saying something and you knew that it was dumb? Totally without question just dumb? And as you got halfway through it your brain said *dumb, dumb, dumb* . . . but your mouth kept rattling it off?"

Bill came up to Ray's suite. "I go up, and I walk in. Now, the lights are out. It's pitch black in this apartment. And I said, 'Ray, where are you?' He said, 'I'm in the bathroom. Shaving.' So I said, 'Well, Ray, why are you shaving in the dark'—and I tried to stop it right there, but the rest of it came—'with the lights out?' Dumb! Dumb! Brainless human being!

"Ray was very nice about it. He said, 'I've been shaving in the dark all my life.' I tried to cover, 'Aw, I was just jokin', Ray . . . bet ya have a low electric bill, doncha . . . ?' "

As Cos made the rounds of the nightclubs, and as "I Spy" and "The Bill Cosby Show" turned up in reruns, Cosby still wanted to do something more, something different. Something he hadn't tried before.

How about movies? How about Bill Cosby becoming the next Warren Beatty?

Bill's film career could have started that way. Back in 1969, Cosby was scheduled to star in his first movie—*Heaven Can Wait.*

Bill's manager, Roy Silver, was crazy about the movie, which was originally made in 1941 as *Here Comes Mr. Jordan.* He even owned a sixteen-millimeter print of it. When the money started coming in, Roy bought the film rights with his own money—$250,000. He thought it would be great for Cosby. He'd play a black man who dies and comes back to earth in a rich white man's body. The viewer sees Cosby as he really is, but everybody else sees him—and treats him differently—because he appears to be an aristocrat.

Imagine *Heaven Can Wait* starring Bill Cosby—with a screenplay by Francis Ford Coppola. The script was ready, the project was paid for, but by the time Cosby was free to do the movie, he and Silver had split up. Now Cosby had to find a different film. He chose *Man and Boy.*

Cosby, presiding over Jemmin Incorporated along with Marvin Miller (who had produced Bill's TV show), found that the machinery that seemed to work pretty well for Silver/Campbell /Cosby was a bit gummy. Producer Miller told *Variety* about the problems in getting the project off the ground. "It's been intimated to me that this is not the kind of picture that people will buy today. It's a very old-fashioned picture, a family picture . . . a typical Disney-type picture, the story of a man's dignity and his love for his family."

Cosby's name, which meant three Emmy Awards and five Grammy Awards, didn't mean a thing in the land of the Oscars. Bill had no reputation in movies and was coming off only a mild success with his last television series. His last records for the Uni label were not the million-sellers the early Warners efforts were.

Miller discovered that movie executives weren't buying the concept of a black family's trials out West after the Civil War. One told him, "How can you make a film like this, when there were no black cowboys?" Besides, nobody in the movie was going to shed their blood or their clothes.

Cosby had determination, something the studios didn't understand. He had the courage of his convictions—something else the studios didn't understand. And he had money enough to start making the film himself. That was something the studios really didn't understand.

"Friends, with tears in their eyes, said, 'If you don't get a studio to put up the money, don't make the picture,' " Bill recalled. "There were just enough no's that I didn't like, the kind of reasons given that are why black actors don't act, black directors don't direct, and black writers don't write as far as the screen is concerned." Cosby told people he would go ahead.

His foremost supporter was Camille. She saw him brooding about the problem, spending hours on the phone, brightening with every glimmer of a promise, only to sink back when the answer was no. She told him to go ahead, even though he was risking the family's savings.

In Scottsdale, Arizona, Cosby and a forty-member crew set up shop. There was optimism, but also tension. They were starting a picture but weren't sure if it would ever be completed. They were racing against time, against money, hoping to find a backer before Cosby's bankroll gave out. Cos counseled his cast and crew that they were going to do the best job they could, as long as they could.

Visitors to the set couldn't believe it. Every step of the way Cosby seemed to be making success impossible. The script called for a villain, the perfect spot for a big name to help at the box office. Instead Cos rewrote the part for Douglas Turner Ward.

He explained at the time, "The original script had a white guy in the role, but we changed that. Bob Culp and I have done the black-white thing in "I Spy" as well as most movies have, I think, and I've had that. This confrontation between two black men is not only a fresh approach but real and a lot more dramatic. And why not have a good black actor playing a heavy?"

There would be no splashy black-white gimmick on this picture.

Cosby and the crew kept going, full tilt, treating the project like the quality motion picture they wanted it to be. No short cuts, no cheap shots. A porno movie can be made for under $75,000, even today. A quickie horror movie could be done for under $200,000. But here was Cosby, his film already costing $350,000.

Hardly a month into the project, they'd managed to put together some first-rate scenes. Marvin Miller took every scrap of film he could get his hands on, and kept trying to make a last-minute deal.

The ready cash was running out. Was this going to be another scene out of North Philly, with Cosby and his family being threatened with eviction because they couldn't pay?

Cosby began hearing from people who would back his movie. But they were offering some cons with the contracts. One man was going to give him the money—in return for being named Cosby's manager. Another promised to back the movie for a 70–30 split of the profits and, in fine print, a cut of his subsequent nightclub work and album sales.

Cosby had learned the business; he didn't fall for the con. He worked without salary, as did Marvin Miller, and he kept putting all his energies into the project. Sequestered in his office near the Scottsdale set, he heard a knock on the door. "Hey Bill," one of his young fans called. "come out and play!"

Cos paused, and answered, "I can't today, man. I gotta stay in and study."

While he was trying to find an answer to the financial problems, one of his co-stars, Leif Erickson, had to handle a problem of his own. Erickson had gotten word that his son had been killed in an accident.

Though numbed with grief, the actor remained on the set to finish his part in the *Man and Boy* project. Between takes, the shattered father was weeping, but when the cameras were on him he went through his lines without a mistake, to the awe of the entire crew.

"I can honestly say that this has been the most stimulating, the best thing I have ever been associated with," Cosby declared. "Only one-fifth of the picture has been put together and I am convinced that it is going to be a winner."

Finally somebody else was convinced. A white businessman had screened segments from *Man and Boy* and gave Marvin Miller the go-ahead. Cosby could now concentrate more on his acting than on his frenzied behind-the-scenes production work.

The basic story of *Man and Boy* chronicles the efforts of Caleb (Cosby) to set up a home for his wife (played by Clarence Williams III's real-life bride, Gloria Foster) and his son (George Spell). When the boy sneaks off to ride the family's horse, Caleb is worried. The horse is the family's life, the hardest-working and most valuable thing they have. While in the boy's care, the horse is stolen.

In the face of this cruel, discouraging blow, man and boy stay together as a unit, and begin the search for their horse, a long trek that tests their stamina, their dignity, and their love.

Caleb is forced to take menial jobs along the way, and he and his son must endure the hard work and the harsh insults of others, including a rowdy ranch hand (Yaphet Kotto), who delights in belittling the father in front of his child. Caleb must also handle the gunman who stole the horse (Douglas Turner Ward) and vigilantes who accuse him of horse theft himself.

Throughout *Man and Boy*, family life and the things that keep a family strong are underscored. The rugged problems faced by the pioneer family (including having to sleep three to a bed, and fight against those trying to take away their meager shelter) are meant to mirror problems faced by urban families. The family bonds are tested in every way possible. A test of love and devotion is shown in one sequence when Caleb meets up with a comely widow (Miriam Colon) who offers her board and bed, much to the son's confusion and disapproval.

Idyllic moments come, too, with the father and son living off the land, shooting birds for food, building a fire, taking care of each other against the elements.

The risky project was ultimately applauded for its honesty, and Cosby was praised for his dedication to his purpose. "The plight of the black man in the frontier West is a wonderfully provocative film theme," the *New York Times* wrote at the time. "It puts Mr. Cosby on first base in screen drama." The *San Francisco Chronicle* declared, "Cosby's role is believable and fresh with no cardboard heroes."

For a family picture, an unpopular item when only R-rated films seemed to draw people away from their TV sets, and when *Little House on the Prairie* was years away, *Man and Boy* did fairly well for a maverick production with no big studio push and limited distribution.

Bill had no time to brood over the box-office figures for *Man and Boy*. He was seriously involved with other noncomedy projects. The previous year he had narrated a documentary, *Give Us the Children*, about the problems faced by school systems in the inner cities. Now he was determined to go forward as a spokesman for a number of causes involving both children and inner-city life.

On June 18, 1971, Bill attended a dinner given to support the Congressional Black Caucus, honoring the election of such black members of Congress as Ronald Dellums, Charles Rangel, and Shirley Chisholm. Here was another side of Bill Cosby, one seldom seen by the public.

"Good evening," Cos opened. "I think all you niggers . . ."

The audience erupted into gales of surprised laughter. "I say good evening, niggers, because that's what a lot of you are gonna be when you leave this room. And I mean the white people sittin' there, too. Niggers come in all colors."

When the applause died down, he continued, "I'm going to support the caucus as long as I live. I'll support 'em because the black establishment for too long has been the entertainers. The black entertainers very seldom get to enjoy what white entertainers have . . . that is, to be able to go out on the Riviera with sunglasses and float around on a raft. . . . No, 'cause if you saw a picture of me on a raft with sunglasses on you'd say, 'Look at that nigger and we up here strugglin'!' You wouldn't even give me a chance to tell you I was floatin' on that raft for y'all!"

Cosby spoke about the need for black solidarity. Referring to the impassioned speech of the previous speaker, he said, "Ossie Davis just left here, poured his heart and soul into a beautiful speech so you could make the sign, give a half-hour handshake to each other and walk out and still be a nigger. . . . You don't need speakers to tell you every day who you are and where you have to go and who's cheating you. And you have to stop blaming people. Can't blame the Jew who owns the store—'We oughta go over there and take his store'—'cause there ain't but seven of you in this place can run a store!"

Over the laughter, Cosby told the audience to support black politicians and performers: "Ray Charles can't make the money he used to make 'cause Joe Cocker's doin' it. You can't blame white people. Who are you paying your money to support and see? When you leave here, it depends on just how long it takes you before you go back to being a nigger."

And, finally, he told the audience to educate their kids. "It's got to start with the young." He talked about the drug problem. "Kids taking dope today. They were taking it yesterday. Only reason why anybody knows about it now is that white kids are involved in it heavily."

Cosby's involvement in the anti-drug movement included a TV special on March 27, 1971, called "Bill Cosby Talks with Children about Drugs." "'The time spent acquiring a drug habit and kicking it is time you could have used to educate yourself," he said. "Every person I have ever known who developed a bad habit spent most of the rest of his life trying to kick it, staying with it, or never using it forever." On his *Bill Cosby Talks to Kids about Drugs* album, he sang songs about the effect of speed and downers, and underscored the theme, "Dope is for the dopies." At a time when there was virtually nothing out there, Cosby was ahead of his time in calling attention to the problem.

Kids listened because Cosby listened to them. "I listen," he said, "and I answer them just as seriously as possible. And if I don't know the answer, I'll tell them I don't know."

Aside from his antidrug work, Cos was chairman of the National Hemophilia Foundation, raised money for the American Cancer Society, VISTA, the American Heart Association, and others. The money he made from doing a toothpaste commercial went to the American Fund for Dental Education, an organization designed to help black students pursue careers in dentistry.

In the midst of all this, Cos was working on more TV specials, even one in which he played Aesop and told animated fables to a pair of children. He was also out on the road, doing stand-up gigs around the country. But something was wrong. Cosby seemed to sense it. Stand-up comedy was the cornerstone of his career, the very foundation. But it was cracking in two.

Chapter Twelve

As the 1970s began, Cosby had a dilemma. There were two Bill Cosbys in stand-up, and he had to make a choice between them. One was the old Cos, the childlike comic that kids loved, who talked about how horrible parents were. But lately there had emerged the Vegas comic, Cosby the parent, the adult talking about how horrible *kids* were.

The schizophrenic rip produced two very different albums in rapid succession: *When I Was a Kid* and *For Adults Only.*

At first, the question was simply which angle Cosby would choose to pursue.

It didn't look like "the old Cos" could make it anymore. The style that had produced so many best-seller records for Warner Bros. wasn't working. After seven years, audiences were getting itchy. *When I Was a Kid* was Cos in what had become his all-too-familiar role of storytelling nostalgist. Cosby always resented being labeled a "nostalgia" act: "It's larger than nostalgia. A lot of drama is going on up there. This is storytelling, one of the great lost arts of our time. It's not all, 'Oh yeah, I remember that.' Man, nobody's gonna laugh at that. You got to pay the people off. I try to take those moments and make them into situations."

But after so many years, he seemed to have run out of funny stories about the old neighborhood and his kid classmates. The album was "dedicated to all of the kids who were kids and are now big kids that

107

remember the fun they had when they were little kids because little kids have more fun than big kids because they forget pain a lot quicker than big kids."

It was a weak record, the first one with material that fell well below Cosby's standards. When he did a long, drawn-out routine on how he and his friends used to go to the theater and watch Buck Jones movies, it was a predictable, nostalgic ramble. In their adulation of Bill, critics often said that he could make anything funny, that his magical style was so effortless that anything retold in Cosby-ese would get laughs. This album proved that it simply wasn't so. Nobody could coast on personality alone.

As the dwindling sales proved, Cosby couldn't continue to rely on stories about kids. Especially at a time when the "cycle" in comedy had come back around to "cutting edge."

At the start of the sixties, Cosby had sailed in as part of the fresh new wave of comedians, the "wholesome" ones taking over from Sahl, Bruce, and Berman. But now, swinging into the seventies, cynical after Vietnam and Richard Nixon, audiences wanted to hear "the real word."

The ghost of Lenny Bruce emerged. A double-set, *The Real Lenny Bruce*, offered up his old routines. The Bruce revival, ignited by the stage and movie versions of *Lenny*, led audiences to flesh-and-blood satirists willing to pick up where Lenny left off: George Carlin and Richard Pryor.

If childhood humor was, for the moment, on the way out, what else could Cos do? He was able to make fifty thousand dollars a week entertaining the well-heeled Vegas crowd, and they seemed to favor his gambling bits, his sports routines, and encouraged anything that was on an adult topic and off elementary school and Fat Albert.

And so Cosby followed up the weak *When I Was a Kid* album with the exact opposite, *For Adults Only*, complete with a smirking cover shot of naughty Mr. Bill.

Bill had done mildly risqué humor once in a while—a bit on a silly gorilla too stupid to mate and an anecdote about him and Robert Culp in Spain, looking for Spanish fly, only to be asked by a cab driver: "You American? You have any . . . American Fly?"

Now he was ready to give the audience "the filth show." Besides, he was born, he said, in "Filthadelphia."

The album got a push from his nervous record company, with a full-page ad in the new, nasty humor mag, *National Lampoon*. Cosby's album was shown tied up in a brown paper wrapper and addressed to "George Whiteman" with the tag: "Amazing phonograph record brings renewed happiness to thousands of married couples . . . by one of the world's leading authorities on marriage and domestic affairs."

For his adult ringsiders in Vegas he talked about his hotel room: "They've got a mirror over my bed. I swear . . . I was uneasy going to sleep. When I sleep I toss and turn and when I woke up I thought I saw a naked skydiver coming at me. . . .

"But I don't know what it's there for. I really don't. You gonna shave in bed? What the hell you gonna watch? All I know is from the way I . . . ummmurrr, you get a broken neck tryin' to watch . . . and Camille's a virgin Catholic, I know she ain't peekin'!"

The crowd roared over Bill's verbal cartoon about the time his two young daughters, totally ignorant of the facts of life, sneaked into the bathroom and watched him stand in front of the toilet "doing God's work." They began to squeal, "Oooooh, Daddy, you got a Wallie Wallie!" And the next thing he knew, they were standing up, wetting the floor all over, trying to imitate him.

The Vegas crowd liked the new Cosby. But the loyal record buyers and old fans of the G-rated Bill were disturbed. They didn't want Cosby to tarnish his image. They didn't want a Pryor Cosby, they wanted the prior Cosby.

And suddenly, the man who had two directions to choose from, had none.

A restless Bill Cosby told writer Muriel Davidson, "I'm only thirty-four years old. My time is now. If it isn't now, it may be never. And I can't afford 'never.' I never could."

He tried to figure out where he should put his energies: film? Children's television? A new TV show?

Cosby tested all the options and embarked on a flurry of new activity. The activity became a frenzy, and it almost seemed to exhaust Bill—and suddenly exhaust the patience of columnists and writers. They started to turn on him and his one-man media blitz. What could they make of Bill's energetic efforts to explore all media all at once? Did he really think that he could be a TV star, movie star, and spokesman for wholesome family entertainment and values all at the same time? Suddenly the word for Cos wasn't cool or cute. It was Arrogant, with a capital A.

Chapter Thirteen

Nineteen seventy-two. Cosby had a bunch of record albums in the racks and *Man and Boy* in the theaters. He was also touring the country with his nightclub act; working on his master's degree from the University of Massachusetts; and appearing, with a painted face, in an educational TV special called "Prejudice," to talk about bigotry and ethnic slurs. He was making jazz albums. There was talk of a Saturday morning cartoon series based on his Fat Albert routines. And, when three CBS vice presidents, Fred Silverman, Perry Lafferty, and Irwin Segelstein, out-hustled ABC and visited Cosby's Amherst home, they came away with a contract for a new Bill Cosby show called . . . "The New Bill Cosby Show." And they were also prepared to star Cosby in his first made-for-TV movie.

At a press conference, a female reporter said, "But Bill, my readers think you're spreading yourself too thin."

Cosby stared at her for a moment and said, "Madam, I just don't care what your readers think, see?"

When he began to talk about all the projects he was into, the reporters turned off. When he let show some of the Cosby drive, and talked about his plans and ambitions, the reporters turned on him. This Bill Cosby was arrogant, self-centered, and even rude. What hostility!

Cosby simply was not going to listen to negative thinking or tol-

Cosby as an athlete
at Temple University.

"He was a real competitor!"
Cosby's coach told the author.
(Author's collection)

"What's a cubit?" That's the question Noah asked God in the first hit Cosby stand-up routine, ca. 1963. (Author's collection)

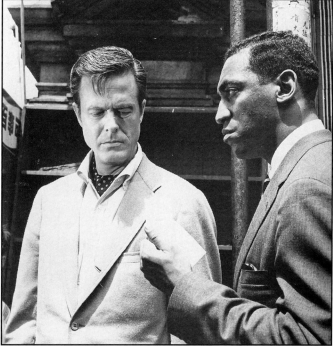

Cosby with Robert Culp on the groundbreaking "I Spy" TV show. To many, his becoming the first black to co-star in a prime-time drama series made him the "Jackie Robinson of television." (Author's collection)

An early sitcom success, "The Bill Cosby Show": Cosby as phys. ed. instructor Chet Kinkaid, with Joyce Bulifant. (Author's collection)

Bill's first theatrical release, and one of his best, the family Western *Man and Boy*, co-starring Gloria Foster. (Author's collection)

Cosby and the kids: Bill's been a favorite from his "Electric Company" days (seen here) to those famous Jell-O commercials. (Author's collection)

Hey, hey, hey!

Cos, seventies style, flanked by pictures of Fat Albert. (Author's collection)

Cosby for young and old: "Aesop's Fables," a 1974 CBS special. (Author's collection)

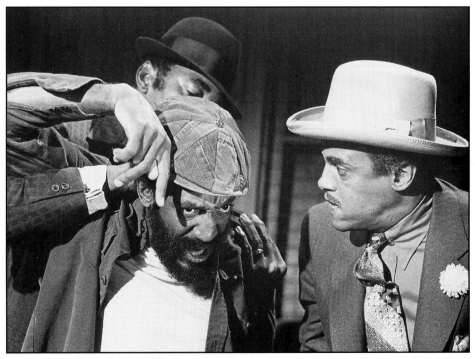

Behind the beard it's Bill Cosby, bringing quality to the burgeoning black film scene as he co-stars with Harry Belafonte (right) in *Uptown Saturday Night*. Copyright © by Warner Bros., Inc. (Author's collection)

In these two photos taken by the author on the set of "The Cosby Show," a skeptical Cos and a tired Malcolm Jamal-Warner wait out a technical delay by stage manager Gary Vinson . . .

. . . and then feign sleep.

Cosby takes some time out from taping a "Cosby Show" episode to chat with the studio audience. Photo by Ronald L. Smith. (Author's collection)

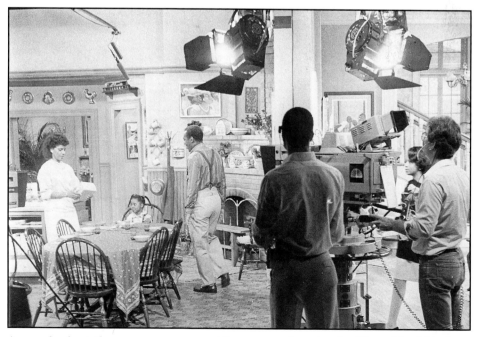

A rare look at the camera crew setting up a shot in the Huxtables' kitchen. Photo by Ronald L. Smith. (Author's collection)

The cast of "The Cosby Show," the undisputed hit series of the 1980s. (Author's collection)

Cosby and Phylicia Rashad reunite as a husband-and-wife team on his newest TV sitcom, "Cosby." (Courtesy Photofest)

erate it. He wasn't going to be told what he could or couldn't do. Too much was at stake. He had his own production company to keep afloat, he had to navigate a change in comedy style, he had to correct slumping record sales, he had to pursue his movie career, he had a family needing his attention and the demands of a dozen or more charity organizations. And he was going to teach a course in broadcasting at USC. Too big and just plain too busy to coddle the press, he alienated them severely with his talk of his goals, his philosophy, and his ambitions. But they were not going to interfere with his plans.

It didn't seem that anybody could. But an exception was Robert Culp, who visited Cosby with a script one day. Bobby, according to most observers, was having a rough time. Now he was hoping to get a break with a new movie, something called *Hickey and Boggs*. If Bill Cosby became Hickey, maybe the movie would get off the ground. Cosby was completing negotiations for his first TV movie, but stopped everything to help Bobby. Cos felt he owed him one.

As it turned out, there was still a certain amount of reluctance from the major studios. "I Spy" was a dinosaur, and many had forgotten about Culp and Cosby. Besides, Culp wanted to direct the movie himself, and Cosby was still unproven at the box office.

Fortunately, Fouad Said, a director of photography from the "I Spy" show, had made millions from the creation of the Cinemobile, a van that could transport sets from place to place. He was ready to support the duo. The script, rewritten slightly for Cosby, was provided by a promising newcomer, Walter Hill. Hill was ten years away from becoming the writer of Eddie Murphy's *48 Hrs.*

Behind the scenes, the men renewed their friendship, and Culp assessed the change in Bill. "When he came in to read for 'I Spy,' he was scared and angry. Angry because he realized what could be, what was, at stake. He has the fastest, sharpest, most flexible mind of any man, white or black, I know. Bill is a loner. The only way he has changed since our days together is those hangers-on. They're gone."

For the film, Cos and Culp rejected their super-spy stances and played a pair of luckless private eyes, relics from the bygone Raymond Chandler era. Culp explained that he was celebrating a pair of "classic super-losers in a losing profession, managing to pull it off one last time because of their devotion to each other."

They end up involved in a battle between mobsters, a Chicano street gang, and the police. The booty is $400,000 in stolen bank loot. Along the way they grumble about their domestic problems (both are divorced); find themselves the targets of a helicopter attack; and end up in gunfights all over Los Angeles, including Dodger Stadium.

In one scene, they take refuge behind a Rolls Royce Silver Cloud, which gets pumped full of bullets. Working on a very tight budget, they managed to get a used model and hoped to repair the damage and resell the car after it, and the scene, was shot. But, according to Culp, there was a perplexing mystery involving the car that even Hickey and Boggs couldn't solve: It was impounded by the Treasury Department.

"They tore it to pieces, ripping every bit of the upholstery off. They found what they were looking for—two pounds of heroin, about two million dollars' worth—hidden in the frame. . . . We were used by someone. Of course, it is possible that somebody made a terrible mistake. We may never know."

Reviewers who did manage to catch the modestly budgeted flick before it flickered out of neighborhood theaters didn't seem impressed one way or the other. The *New York Times* found the duo "a good deal less convincing" as private eyes than they had been as spies. "As anti-heroes, both Mr. Culp and Mr. Cosby are serious, sullen and extremely laconic. Terse passes at dialogue merely indicate their personal relationships and their concomitant, bloody, thankless mission. . . . Understatement is obviously the keynote here but *Hickey and Boggs* still owes us a fuller explanation despite all the chasing and carnage."

Now Cosby could devote himself to his CBS deal. Cos hadn't liked one aspect of it—having to live in Hollywood while doing the variety show. He had to agree, though, that it would be cheaper to do the show there, and was told that some of the money saved would be used to make the show better. Cos reluctantly went "bicoastal" again, with homes in Amherst and Pacific Palisades.

Robert Wood, CBS's president at the time, told reporters: "Bill Cosby has a total commitment to education. Fortunately for us, he realizes that television offers an ideal medium for narrowing the gap between education and entertainment."

Before the premiere of the variety show, or the new Fat Albert and the Cosby Kids cartoon series, there was the CBS movie. Filmed in Norwalk, Connecticut, and broadcast on February 25, 1972, Cosby's return to TV was in *To All My Friends on Shore.*

He played Blue, a family man with a mission. Driving a cab all day, he saves his tips in a secret hiding place, hoping for the day when he will have enough money to buy his dream house. He takes on extra jobs, works tirelessly for his cause, and sacrifices "today" for "tomorrow." He hardly has time for his wife, Serena (Gloria Foster), or son, Vandy (Dennis Hines). "I'm losing the man I love to a rotten old house," the woman complains.

Things change when Vandy becomes ill. He's diagnosed as having sickle-cell anemia, and it's fatal. For his dying son, Blue explains that there are yesterday people, today people, and tomorrow people. The past is for yesterday people. Blue has always been dreaming of tomorrow. But now all that matters is today.

What would make the boy's days happy? "I just want you," Vandy tells his dad. They begin to share the few todays that are left. It is on a boat ride together that Vandy is given the job of pilot. And it is there that Blue tells him, "Say goodbye to all your friends on shore."

The basic story was written by Cosby himself. The screenplay was by Allan Sloane, who received an Emmy for his work. Cos also wrote the musical score for the film, which was praised by the *New York Times* as "a warm, sympathetic, sentimental portrait . . . quietly appealing. Many of the family-life details are good. And the central performances are excellent."

Cos now began work on his variety show and on the cartoon show about Fat Albert. He brought with him a renewed sense of purpose and dedication. He had seen his career falter at the turn of the seventies as the "tough" comics and streetwise sitcoms took over. "People don't want Mr. Nice Guy," he fumed. "They want Archie Bunker. A lovable bigot." Cos was determined to do something about that, and bringing back the family-oriented TV variety show was part of that.

In the spring, Cosby received his master's degree, but vowed that he would continue onward, to his doctorate. And as the premiere date for his show, September 1972, approached, he gave his writers a taste of school discipline.

"If they write something very good," he said, "I shake their hand and tell them so. I grade their work the same as I would a school paper. Some get A's, some D-minuses."

Some people behind the scenes were not happy with Cosby's highly disciplined approach and his fierce determination to produce something worthy at all costs. In a way, it seemed incongruous. After all, why get so serious about this particular project? It was supposed to be one of those light, funny variety shows, with sketches and songs.

Hindsight shows that something else was out of place—the whole idea of doing a variety show in 1972. NBC's Flip Wilson, who had ironically inspired Cosby when the young Temple University student was first starting out, still had his variety show, which had inspired CBS to copycat with Cos. But Wilson's show wasn't as hot as it once was. Variety-type entertainment was dying. The old Hollywood Palace and Ed Sullivan-type programs were defunct. Just the year before, the host/dance routines/songs/comedy skits format had killed shows starring Glen Campbell, Johnny Cash, Don Knotts, Tom Jones, Jim Nabors, Tim Conway, Lawrence Welk, and Andy Williams. Tastes had changed. Especially musical tastes. Families couldn't agree on what kind of music to play at home—mainstream, country, jazz, rock, etc.—and the gulfs between each style seemed bigger than ever. As for comedy sketches, this was a deceptively tricky thing to put over. Only Carol Burnett, her show in its fifth season, seemed to be able to do it.

Cosby and CBS drove headlong into disaster. Scheduled at ten o'clock Monday nights, they were going to lose all the little kids who couldn't stay up to watch. Leading into the show at 9:00 P.M. was the wheezing "Here's Lucy" and the limping "Doris Day Show." The slim family audiences that did bother to sit through the sitcoms were dead snoring by 10:00 P.M., or so numbed by cuteness they needed to switch to ABC for some football violence with Howard Cosell.

With ABC football to the right of him, and "The NBC Monday Night Movie" to the left, Cosby charged ahead with his premiere show.

On the program, he was interrupted almost before he could begin by Foster Brooks, the "lovable lush" with the white beard parted in the middle. Brooks played a gaseously drunk CBS executive welcoming him to the network and at the same time humorously wrecking the show. Stumbling in from "my burnt mattress in the alley," the exec welcomed Bill to CBS, which stood for "Cocktails, Believability, and Sausage."

Sidney Poitier and Harry Belafonte were the guests. Keeping up with the times, one of their sketches with Cosby utilized racial humor. But a kinder, gentler racial humor than what was being offered on "All in the Family" and "Sanford and Son."

As a militant, Harry Belafonte tried to convert Cosby to his cause. "Come home, black brother!"

Bill looks at him. "To Philadelphia?"

In another scene, Foster Brooks goes over some CBS memos with Cos. "I hope you looked at your contract," he says, "because at the end of the year you have to marry Carol Burnett."

Sometimes there was more entertainment behind the cameras than in front of them. One day Flip Wilson came by during rehearsal. The "enemy" from NBC sneaked onto the stage at CBS's Studio 41, drew a toy pistol from his pocket, and suddenly made a grab for one of the script girls.

"I'm taking hostages!" Flip shouted. "I'm gonna hijack this studio to NBC!" Onlookers roared with laughter.

He got a mild smile out of Cosby, but Bill's amiable grin wasn't in evidence quite as much as it had once been. With his reputation on the line, some around him couldn't understand why he wasn't simply his TV image—silly and constantly smiling.

When he flew up to Vegas for a gig, audiences were astonished by Cosby's actions. Cos, the man who knew that you must never break in front of an audience and show anything but a nice guy in control, lost control.

A stagehand was sawing wood backstage, and the noise became more and more audible. Cosby's smiling, comic mask fell away as he stopped his act, put down the microphone, and suddenly stormed backstage through the swirling curtains.

A few minutes later the sound of sawing ceased. The confused audience waited. Finally Cosby pushed his way back through the curtains. Gone were the easy, laid-back ad-libs, or even the good-natured show of mock anger one might've expected.

He talked for a few more minutes, then said, "Good night." The audience just sat there in disbelief. The show was only halfway through, and suddenly it was over.

Insiders wondered how long it would take before the new variety show was over, too. There was word that Cosby wasn't getting along with his co-producer on "The New Bill Cosby Show," George Schlatter. Schlatter had a reputation for being a difficult, dominating personality. He'd guided "Rowan and Martin's Laugh-In" to the top, but left the show in a bitter war over its direction. The cast had always called him C. F. G., which stood for "Crazy Fucking George," and it was indeed both a compliment and a curse.

George and Cos could argue about almost anything. From the beginning, Schlatter was adamant about the set designer he planned to hire. Cosby felt a loyalty to the set designer he worked with on "The Electric Company," a man he knew to be quick and efficient. The two men tussled for quite a while before they stopped and realized they were both talking about the same guy—Bill Bohnert.

Bohnert noticed immediately that "they both had a different viewpoint on humor. Bill liked very long, sort of gentle stories building to a smile, and George wanted one-liners."

On some points, the two men did agree. Schlatter was more than willing to hire more blacks on Cosby's suggestion. "This was still very early on in television, when there were not very many blacks involved," notes Bohnert. "I do know that Bill was instrumental in getting a black cameraman and a black stage manager. These were big steps forward at the time."

Cosby's clothes and hairstyle reflected an updated image that was more overtly black than before. For 1972, Cos was sporting a kind of "Soul Train"/"Mod Squad" look, with bushy hair that might have been considered a conservative Afro. He wore long sideburns, a mustache, and a thumb-sized black liberation flag in his lapel.

Schlatter insisted the mustache had to go. "When you spend weeks growing a mustache," Cos reflected wistfully, "you almost fall in love with it. I had a good, big, thick mustache. Everything you drink with it, you drink twice. But Schlatter felt it covered too much of my face. I took the sideburns off as well. He said something like, 'Gee whiz, I think it would be groovy if people could see your face.' "

They didn't see it for long.

If there was any consolation for the demise of Bill's variety show, it was that he wasn't alone. Julie Andrews, the movie superstar lured at last to do her own variety show, suffered the same ignominious fate.

The happiest thing about the ill-fated series was that it gave Cos the chance to meet with some of his Hollywood friends and even put them on the show. Of the comedians, Cos had a special fondness for Groucho Marx, and it was mutual. Groucho was always raving about Bill to his friends: "Have you ever seen Cosby in a nightclub? He's fantastic. He doesn't tell any jokes. He does impressions of people. Like how a mother will talk to her child, and how a father will talk to the same child. Things like that. . . . He's brilliant, this man."

Writer Charlotte Chandler taped some of the informal get-togethers between Cos and Groucho in 1972-73, and they appear in her book on Groucho, *Hello I Must Be Going.* They showed the mutual respect and love of fun the two shared, singing old songs with wacko titles—from an a cappella version of "The Darktown Strutters' Ball" to "You May Look Like a Hawaiian, but You're Just Another Nigger to Me."

When Groucho received an honorary Academy Award, Bill was at the party with him, along with another admirer, Jack Nicholson. Later, after appraising the Oscar, the only major award Cos hasn't won, Cos said, "Now, you take this gold streaker . . . he looks like one of my people as opposed to one of yours. Got some nice buns. And a great profile. I could see a woman at home getting quite horny over that, and going out in search of it."

Groucho was fun. So was Cos. But nice fun wasn't where prime-time TV was going. Referring to the short-lived "Jimmy Stewart Show," Cosby noted, "Jimmy Stewart went down the drain the same as I did playing Mr. Nice Guy."

It looked like Cos was out of touch, too mild in an era when Flip Wilson was jiving it up as Geraldine and Richard Pryor was hurling racial epithets at both whites and blacks. But the children were still there. Cosby's other TV project proved to be a rewarding success on all levels.

The idea of a cartoon show based on the Cosby Kids had been in the works for a long time, but at last "Fat Albert and the Cosby Kids" got a Saturday-morning spot. With that program, Cosby was fighting a battle against mindless junk TV, violent superheroes and inanities like "Scooby Doo," "Motormouse," and "The Brady Kids" cartoon show.

"The way I see the show," Cosby told journalist Cecil Smith, "it will be so casual in its teaching, the children will never know they're being taught. It will have Fat Albert and old Weird Harold and those other characters I made up, but they will get themselves involved in things like mathematical equations and what geometry is all about and why."

If the show was educational for kids, it was, in a way, an education for Cosby, too. Dr. Dwight Allen at the University of Massachusetts had arranged to make the show part of Cosby's studies. He'd be earning college credit, turning in the scripts almost as though they were term papers, working with the professors on evaluating the techniques Cosby was using for combining education and entertainment.

Once more the critics were skeptical—until they saw the finished product. *TV Guide* proclaimed it "perhaps the best cartoon program on television, and the most thoughtfully presented. . . . Cosby presents the cartoon material (in live action introductions) acting as a parent or adult friend. He makes the transition for the child from the real to the fantasy world, much in the same way a parent or grandparent says, 'Now I'm going to tell you a story.' He reappears during the show to explain the actions, define words, and point out a moral."

"This is Bill Cosby comin' at you with music and fun. And if you're not careful, you might learn somethin' before it's done." With simple introductions like that, Cos became a Saturday morning pal.

Like most cartoons made for TV, the animation wasn't much and the shows tended to be "amusing" rather than "funny," but the series maintained its standards through more than ninety half-hour episodes.

The cartoon cast included a youthful version of Cosby, his squeaky-voiced brother Russell, and three of the oddest kids ever seen. There was Fat Albert, of course, a sort of benign Muhammad Ali type, who spoke softly and in rhyme most of the time (after falling down and creating a giant hole, he says, "Hey, hey, hey, made my own subway"). There was Dumb Donald, whose strange, loose stocking cap fell halfway down his face with just his eyes showing through. And there was Mush Mouth, who talked with sputtery extra b's. "Are you kidding?" would come out "Ah be-you be-kibbeding?" About the only name he could possibly have pronounced right would've been B'nai B'rith.

Some episodes were overtly "message" oriented. In one, Fat Albert and the gang play hooky to go skateboarding and play in the junkyard. Then they meet two bums and learn that the "easy life" means bum food, sleazy surroundings, and no friends. After all, if you can't read or write, how can you even get a letter from your pal?

Suitably chastened, Fat Albert comes to school the next day two hours early. "Ever hear of drop-outs?" he asks. "Hey, hey, hey, we're drop-ins."

After the cartoon, Cos offers a few more words on the subject. "School may not be the greatest," he admits, "but the worst thing in the world is not going to school when there is school."

Then Albert and the gang sing a song about the coolness of school. To those who play hooky they sing, "You think you're the smart guy, just 'cause you stayed away/ If you're so smart, well, think real hard: Tell me, what did you learn today?"

The show was a learning experience for Bill's own children. Young Ennis was a faithful "Fat Albert" watcher for years. When he was eight, the little boy received a treat. He was brought into the recording studio to watch a "Fat Albert" soundtrack being recorded. He stared wide-eyed at the imposing array of tape recorders and mikes, and the technicians doing their jobs.

When Cos came to the microphone and started to read from his script, the little boy was awestruck.

"Dad," Ennis whispered in surprise, "*you're* Fat Albert?"

Many episodes of the show were drawn from Bill's monologues, such as the classic one about him and his brother having their tonsils taken out. In cartoon format, a black doctor with a Transylvanian accent frightens the boys. They tell their parents, "We can't go. Tell the doctor we can't go. We're too sick to go to the hospital!"

When they're forced to go, the boys gather their gang around to hear "our last will and tenement" and dolefully hand out all their "good junk," like decoder rings and kazoos, knowing they are about to die. The hospital stay has moments of comic misery, too. "My neck itches," Russell whines. "Why don't you scratch it?" asks Bill. Russell responds, "It itches on the inside!"

That particular show offered a lesson of a different kind. It showed to what lengths Cosby and his crew would go in order to be absolutely truthful and instructional. Someone asked if it was such good advice to tell the viewing kiddies that a tonsillectomy doesn't hurt. And what about ice cream? In Cosby's monologues and in the script, he had said, "The best part is you can eat all the ice cream you want." Well, was that true? And was that such a good idea considering the calories involved?

The show's producers actually contacted the assistant dean at UCLA, Gordon L. Berry, and put the question to him. He in turn put the question before a panel of teachers and professors for approval. The panel could not reach a decision because one of their members, a professor in the UCLA psychiatry department, was out of town, and his viewpoint was vital. Production waited while a pediatrician was consulted. The pediatrician pointed out that not every child can eat ice cream anyway, because some kids are allergic to it. The question was tossed back to Dr. Berry, with the suggestion that a few more doctors and nutritionists be brought in. This was in addition to Dr. Berry's CBS- and Cosby-approved panel of anthropologists, psychiatrists, sociologists, and specialists in children's education.

In the end, the simple joke about ice cream was left in, as well as the sight gags of Fat Albert and the gang crashing into the hospital corridor in search of the room where Russell and Bill were having their ice cream feast. Cosby turned up at the end of the show to admit, "Having their tonsils out did hurt . . . but they'll be over it soon." The gang sings: "Don't be scared of a hospital . . . you'll get good care at a hospital . . . you'll be repaired at a hospital."

The "Fat Albert" series covered a lot of different subjects. As if to vindicate once more Bill Cosby's profound point of view on racial equality, a study conducted by CBS confirmed that Cosby's approach— treating blacks and whites as people first and stereotypes dead last— was paying unexpected dividends.

Polling a sample of black and white kids, CBS found that only twenty-nine percent even mentioned that Fat Albert and his gang were black. When asked to describe the show, and how the characters were like or different from themselves, less than a third even thought to answer that there was a racial difference. This was remarkable, especially since the show did have an all-black cast, had some realistic lower-income locales, and even injected a few childish racial jokes now and then (Fat Albert, seeing that Weird Harold keeps his spare change in his shoe, says, "Hey, hey, hey, you're a real sole brother.")

Cos devoted much of his time to the "Fat Albert" show and to his studies at his Amherst home. He still played stand-up gigs, even in his hometown, though Philadelphia was hardly as lucrative as Atlantic City or Las Vegas.

He loved going back to Philly to meet with friends from high school and Temple, and sometimes he'd even go back to the old neighborhood to surprise the new crew of kids there. Once he and a group of fans got into a stickball game on a sidestreet. There wasn't much room to stretch out. The buildings on either side were foul territory and a ball bouncing off the far wall in back would carom back so quickly that nobody could get more than a double out of it.

So Bill got up at bat, studying the situation carefully. The street stickball **veteran took** an uppercut swing and popped the ball straight up, about six stories in the air. Cos took off like mad, loped around the "bases" (touched the wall, stomped on the sewer lid, then around to the Buick) and home. Home run before the ball came down.

That's how you play the game, kids.

Meanwhile, Cosby tried to break in with the real big boys. Cos bought into the Golden State Warriors basketball team. "It's more a sentimental gesture for me," he said. "The team originated in Philadelphia and that's where I'm from. I just bought a percentage of the team for old times' sake. It's not really any big deal."

As for his own career, Cosby cast a bitter look at the new television scene. Of "All in the Family" and its comical bigot Archie Bunker, he said, "Some watch the show and love Archie because they think he's right. . . . Names like kike, nigger, and the rest of them never seem to die." Through the years he maintained a smoldering dislike for the show. On a 1985 Phil Donahue broadcast, he reiterated: "My opinion is that the man never apologized for anything. He had a wife who said, you shouldn't say that, and a son-in-law who said, you shouldn't say that, and a daughter who said, you shouldn't say that. But the man himself became a hero to too many Americans for his shortsightedness, his tunnel vision. And I'm really a believer that that show never taught or tried to teach anybody anything."

At the time of his variety series Cosby issued a new album, *Inside the Mind of Bill Cosby,* but it wasn't a big seller. Reluctantly he had to admit that "the market is saturated with Bill Cosby" albums, and they weren't moving.

Cosby had released one jazz instrumental album on Uni. For Sussex, he released one more, with exactly the same title as the first, which may have been an act more of stubbornness than prudence. After all, the title *Bill Cosby Presents Badfoot Brown and the Bunions Bradford Funeral Marching Band* was a tongue twister.

The album notes showed Bill's irritation with critics and seemed to underline that he was rehearsing for retirement. After disclaiming the record as something "fun" and not to be taken "seriously," he wrote: "I wish the critics reviewing this album to know thusly. It is no big thing, until I notify you of such. . . . No matter how small the fans of the Bunions Bradford album, if they can purchase enough, the next album shall follow. If they don't, the Bunions Band is playing its own funeral march."

The main problem with Cosby's instrumental albums, aside from testy album notes, were the actual notes. Cos liked jamming, the joy of rambling on for ten or fifteen minutes. But hearing it isn't the same as participating in it. And at a time when some in the audience were getting impatient with an ad-libbed Cosby ramble on stage, fewer wanted to hear him ramble and riff as a musician. (Not even a "musician," since technically he was the composer/arranger and left the actual playing to studio musicians.)

Cosby's reputation as a strong seller of records was eroding fast. His TV shows were having progressively smaller runs. As for making more movies, he was leery of all the "blaxploitation" films now on the market. "Give them some sex, some guns, and some cocaine to capture the black audience," he said, describing the movie moguls' thinking. "It is a proven formula, man. Maybe they will throw you a *Sounder,* but in the end it is easier to throw some dude $500,000 and tell him to give with the sex, tits, and coke."

When he did agree to an infrequent interview, he complained about past interviews. He remembered how Earl Wilson sat around his hotel room ordering floppy deli sandwiches and asking incoherent questions with his mouth full. He remembered others who were drunk. He remembered being used to liven up other people's articles and make them look good with his jokes. And he recalled Rex Reed misquoting him, sticking in soul phrases he'd never uttered. Cos figured that Rex must've confused him with Godfrey Cambridge. It was Godfrey who punctuated his speech with "hey, baby" this and "hey, baby" that.

More and more, Cosby felt that the direction to go in was education and children's programming. His Fat Albert cartoons won him the Children's Theater Association Seal of Excellence. If Cosby had definitely lost ground in prime-time television and in record sales, maybe retirement was the answer. It was something for Cos to think about as he spent time at his Amherst retreat with his wife and children.

Chapter Fourteen

"I thought kids were the simplest little creatures in the world, once upon a time. That was before I had any of my own. But me, I'm someone who likes to do things in the overkill method. I had a kid—my wife helped, of course—and then another and another . . . and well, you get the picture, don't you?"

It seemed there were so many Cosby kids there weren't enough days for them to arrive on. Bill and Camille's fourth child, Ensa Camille, arrived on April 8, 1973, the same birthday as their daughter Erika.

A month later, Cos had a gift for other parents—a prime-time cartoon special, "Weird Harold." In it, Cos and his pals, including the Weird One, put together go-carts and have one of the wildest, most violent races in the history of childhood. After the carnage, the kids end up before a judge, handcuffed by cops. But all ends well: The kids are allowed to race again, under adult supervision. The story was based on monologues from Cosby's *Wonderfulness* album, recorded nearly a decade earlier.

Actually, Cos had found quite a different sport to occupy his attention during this slack period in his career. He was developing into an excellent tennis player and had begun making the rounds at celebrity tournaments across the country.

He took the short trip down from his Amherst home to compete in the Robert F. Kennedy Memorial Tournament in New York, in August 1973. At the benefit for minority children, Cos demonstrated both his tennis form and his comic form.

With the crowd watching, Cosby defended himself against the awesome serving power of Stan Smith. He braced himself defiantly. But just as Stan tossed the ball up, Cos comically fell apart, the racket flying out of his hands, his legs flapping back and forth in shuddery terror, his face a mask of eye-popping fright.

Smith dropped the ball and doubled over, wandering away from the court in laughter as the crowd roared.

Later on, Cosby was back again, in a weird mixed-doubles match. He was paired with Alan King, and the sight of the two cigar-chomping comics wearing equally oversized tennis hats was bizarre enough. But playing opposite them was the most mixed male-female doubles opposition anybody could face: Bobby Riggs in drag. Wearing a bonnet and an old-fashioned red-checked dress with puffy lace sleeves, Riggs baffled Cos and King completely, and even when Riggs threw a bunch of chairs all over his side of the court, making it an obstacle course, the two comics couldn't solve his lobs and spins.

But Cosby got the last laugh. In the midst of play, Riggs lost control of his dress, and the top slipped down. Cos immediately ordered the game forfeited on account of this braless breach of tennis-court etiquette.

When it wasn't a charity game for comedy, Cos was a good player who could give most any semi-pro a tough time. "This is probably the first sport I've entered where I really feel like trying to achieve my full potential," Cosby enthused.

In those days, he had plenty of time to practice his game. Cos still went out on the road for his stand-up engagements, but was more interested in watching his three daughters and son grow up.

Television audiences didn't see Cosby trying to compete with the new trend—the racial comedy riots of "All in the Family," "Sanford and Son," or "The Jeffersons." Instead he appeared between those shows, in his commercials for a variety of products.

Even in this, he was a trailblazer, although some have trouble finding redeeming value in commercial interruptions. Before Cosby, it was rare to see a black man in an ad. The few blacks who did appear usually pitched some product with an ethnic slant, like Southern fried chicken. But Cosby would become the spokesman for products and companies that symbolized America: Coke, Ford cars, Texas Instruments calculators, Jell-O. It proved that Cosby was very special indeed, one of the very few stars who could be appreciated—if not loved—by all of America. Big corporations and big advertising agencies don't take risks that could offend potential buyers. Cos proved to be the perfect choice.

Meanwhile Cosby continued to work on his studies at the University of Massachusetts and involve himself in educational projects. He visited inmates at the Pennsylvania State Prison and made a film for kids of the ghetto, called *A Date at Craterford*.

In it, Cos talked about the road to prison—beginning with street gangs and petty crimes. He interviewed many inmates, including one who was in jail for a senseless murder committed during a gang fight.

Now, the inmate reflected, "One of the things that I've always felt I needed in my life were people who understood me, so I feel that maybe a lot of the problems the young children or the young adolescents are encountering can be possibly overcome, or some solutions can be found if they can just sit down and talk with somebody."

Cosby's face was sober. He pondered, "You had to kill someone and be laid away almost for life before you found you're an intelligent human being."

Some wondered when Cosby would do another movie for theatrical release. "I don't do blaxploitation pictures," Cos said. "I prefer doing things I can feel good about."

Out on the Coast, several actors were trying to feel better about Hollywood's product. Paul Newman, Barbra Streisand, Steve McQueen, Dustin Hoffman, and Sidney Poitier banded together to form First Artists, a company that would give the stars the same creative control over their projects that Charles Chaplin, D. W. Griffith, Mary Pickford, and Douglas Fairbanks had when they started United Artists fifty-four years earlier.

Poitier was hoping to begin filming a series of family pictures featuring blacks. In the past few years, it seemed that every black in a movie was either a superdetective or superpimp. Cosby was eager to join in the project, and with Harry Belafonte joining as well, Poitier had a film with blockbuster possibilities, the first black "superstar" movie.

With these big stars, Poitier received financing, and more than 1,300 blacks won jobs on the project, behind the cameras as well as in front of them. Filming for the movie, *Uptown Saturday Night,* went without a hitch.

As time for the premiere approached, everything was looking good. It seemed that nothing could stop the movie from becoming a triumph. Just to add icing to the cake, Cosby went into the studio to cut some promotional radio commercials for the film.

Cos had so much confidence in his ad-libbing, he didn't want to over-rehearse. That could kill his easy brand of humor and make the commercial sound phony. The Muhammad Ali of comedians, Cos sometimes treads the fine line between confidence and cockiness. He often uses just enough of his skills to thrill audiences with a performance that could, if he weren't a consummate showman, meander into coasting. Somehow, after giving away a few rounds with ringside chatter and audience jokes, he always comes back with knockout punchlines.

This was his knockout commercial:

"Hi, this is Bill Cosby. Remember the good old days when you used to go uptown to Harlem and have a good time before it became very dangerous? Well, you can still go uptown without getting your head beat in by going downtown to see *Uptown Saturday Night.*

"This way the people are all on the screen and won't jump off and clean your head out. Bill Cosby, Sidney Poitier, Harry Belafonte, starring in *Uptown Saturday Night.* This is PG, Parental Guidance. I thank you."

After the ad had aired on July 3 on a few New York radio stations, it was the subject of a newspaper review.

BILL COSBY INSULTS HARLEMITES, roared the *New York Amsterdam News,* the city's powerful black paper.

Some black leaders demanded to know how white radio stations WINS, WABC, and WCBS-FM could dare run such an ad. Then they learned that black stations like WBLS-FM and WWRL had run it, too.

Seizing on the Bill Cosby slur, the manager of the Apollo Theater fired some bullets to go with the bombshell controversy. "Why should blacks have to go downtown to see a movie about themselves?" demanded Bobby Schiffman. He had been furious long before July 3. On June 16, when the movie had its sneak premiere for the press in mid-Manhattan, he distributed ten thousand cards reading, "Wonder why uptowners can't see it uptown now? Because Jim Crow lives;

125th Street is still the back of the bus, moviewise that is." Even though the press party was held in Harlem, at Vincent's Pub on 125th Street, Schiffman was still angry.

Once again strides forward toward pride and dignity were met with resentful sniping and conflict. And there was Bill Cosby, stuck ankle-deep in the mire of his admirable ad-lib ability.

If both black and white radio stations were guilty, then there was no scapegoat. If every film company's policy was to give first-run films to expensive downtown movie houses before uptown and neighborhood theaters, then there was no scapegoat. The press soon ignored the radio stations and Warner Bros. and went after Bill Cosby.

Along the way, they grabbed Melville Tucker, the film's producer, and demanded to know if he was *with* Cosby and *against* them. "Being perfectly objective," Tucker said, "I can see where some people in Harlem might feel some resistance to [Cosby's] statement."

Cos was in Europe at the time. When the storm raced over the Atlantic, he took no shelter. He didn't ad-lib his answer, he sent a carefully worded telegram instead:

"I wrote the 'blurb' with the intent that it be humorous. Like lots of things humorous, sometimes a person has a lapse of taste. I retract it. I take back everything said and am sorry for any harm done. I apologize to the Harlem community and to black communities in all other cities. Had I listened to it after having done it, I'm certain I would have wiped it out myself."

For a decade Cosby had been working hard to present the right image, and he had worked hard on the project, proud to join with Poitier and Belafonte to produce an important film that was for blacks without being "blaxploitation." The sting of the mistake was hard to take—and the anger that met his joke—the fury of being turned against for a quip gave him a feeling of bitterness, even betrayal. Cosby had always known how easily audiences could turn.

The next time Bill picked up the papers, he was expecting more bad news. In the *Los Angeles Times*, he read that *Uptown Saturday Night* was "one of the year's most enjoyable movies, the old-fashioned kind that leaves you feeling good all over." The *New York Times* called the performances "marvelously funny . . . Mr. Cosby is particularly good. . . . [The film is] so full of good humor . . . such high spirits that it reduces movie criticism to the status of a most nonessential craft."

There really was nothing to criticize. It was a nice film and that's what it was intended to be—a likable film, a film to get people together, a family film with some positive black images. Its goals far outweighed any complaints over the actual amount of laughs, or Poitier's ability to direct comedy.

In fact, the film is more an action-adventure epic with some humor thrown in. It follows a factory worker (Poitier) and his good-time pal (Cosby in a porcupinish mustache-and-beard set) in a mix-up with gangsters.

At first, there's some unintentional comedy as the very straight Mr. Poitier attempts to spout earthy dialogue. "You know something?" he tells his wife. "After twenty years, two kids, and four jobs—you still got the biggest butt I ever saw." A viewer would have to conclude from the view supplied that he hasn't seen many.

Cosby also has some exaggerated lines that sound strange coming from a man not usually given to talking in ghetto dialect. Coaxing Poitier to come with him and visit Madame Zenobia's after-hours parlor, he smiles broadly and says, "They be some fiiine mamas comin' in that place!"

The better lines have the trademark Cosby deadpan. At the dice table, Cos is all fey smiles, checking out the foxes and the galloping dominoes. The hostess roars, "If you can't stand the heat, stay out of the kitchen. Harry Truman, 1952." Cosby answers, "I remember. I was in the kitchen when he said it."

The fun and games end when gangsters break in and rob the joint. It's a menacing moment, and for Poitier and Cosby it means the loss of their winnings—and the lottery ticket in Sidney's wallet that turns out to be worth $50,000.

The two men hit the street trying to track down the gangsters. Under Poitier's leisurely direction, the men take time out to visit church. Flip Wilson has a tiny, jokeless sermon to give on loose lips: "The looser the lips are, the faster the ships sink. And some of the lips in this congregation could sink aircraft carriers." Richard Pryor has a cameo, too, doing his frightened, trapped-mouse act. He plays a faint-hearted private eye with eye trouble. "See my right eye? See how bloodshot it is? That's from sleepin' with one eye open." Then he whines that the "supernigger" detectives in the movies get the drop on whites and crooked cops, and romance women, and "I ain't had a woman in months!"

Cosby actually gets to drop the comedy completely in one unusual scene. He enters a bar and lectures, "I am off the corner! I get mean when you mess with my green!" Not only does he pick a fight with a very tough-looking patron, he even punches him out. When Poitier attempts a similar feat, complete with insults ("You're so ugly it's against the law in twenty states to marry you!"), he nearly gets his head handed to him.

Eventually they meet up with Harry Belafonte, who parodies Marlon Brando's godfather with puffed cheeks and a raspier-than-usual voice. Flanked by his gang, he informs the duo, "We gonna beat the black off both of ya." And if he doesn't, rival gangster Calvin Lockhart will.

Caught between the warring gangs, Poitier and Cosby get involved in high-speed chases and some tense moments of kidnap and near execution before the movie ends with tears of joy mixed with the laughter.

For Cosby, the film marked his first full-fledged movie success, even if he did it in hirsute camouflage. The film may have added to his image among more militant blacks, who could appreciate his "new look" and the dialogue that was closer to the street.

The presence of Pryor and Cosby together, early on, showed the difference in their performing styles. Pryor was funny with his woeful, frightened expressions, his knitted brows. He was the perfect victim. Cosby had more dignity and sympathy. The scenes where he and Poitier were frightened (Poitier did quite a bit of eye-popping) didn't work. Cosby simply doesn't have fright comedy in his repertoire. Impersonating a child, in a comedy monologue, yes. But while playing an adult? Definitely not.

In stand-up and in comedy records, Pryor was the exact opposite of his screen image. He was relentless, sharp, and scathing. In 1974, with Cosby no longer signed to a record label at all, the Grammy went to *That Nigger's Crazy*, by Richard Pryor. In fact, Pryor would end up with three Grammys in a row.

Out along the concert route, Bill was still strong with the Vegas crowd, but his appearances elsewhere sometimes proved disappointing. At the 3,200-seat Nanuet Theater-Go-Round in New Jersey, Cosby barely drew twenty-five-percent attendance. He took it pretty well, demonstrating that the relaxed, rested Bill Cosby of 1974 was far different from the harried workaholic of only a few years earlier, the one who had lectured columnists and, in one notorious performance, walked off in mid-show because of a backstage noise.

Looking out at the sparse audience he quipped, "I had some opening remarks like 'I'm glad to be here,' but that was before I saw the crowd! Is there a flu epidemic? Is this a Jewish holiday or something? Are the stores open late? Give me some sort of an out!"

Now, at the movies, Cosby was suddenly a better draw. Sidney Poitier recalled, "The success of *Uptown Saturday Night* told me that black people wanted to laugh at themselves and have fun. They were weary of being represented on the local movie screen by pimps, hustlers, prostitutes, private detectives, violence, macho men, and dirty words. They wanted to have good, clean, family-type fun."

Family fun and sports fun seemed to be the answer for Cosby. Into 1975, Cos kept up his vow not to bother with records, and to avoid TV. With the arrival of another daughter, Evin Harrah, he had a full house: Erika, Erinne, Ennis, Ensa and Evin. The E's, he always said, referred to "excellence."

Cosby was setting the example, pursuing physical and mental excellence. He was working on his doctoral dissertation, entitled "An Integration of the Visual Media Via Fat Albert and the Cosby Kids into the Elementary School Curriculum as a Teaching Aid and Vehicle to Achieve Increased Learning." He wanted "to show my children that, although their father does one thing, it's possible to do many things."

Cos also published a book, *Bill Cosby's Personal Guide to Tennis Power, or Don't Lower the Lob, Raise the Net.* It's filled with pointers on improving tennis skills, and also some stern warnings: "If you and the ball happen to arrive at the same place at the same time . . . body spasms will not help you execute the stroke!"

The same competitive spirit Cosby brought to Temple University could now be seen on the tennis court. In one memorable pro-celebrity charity match, tennis trainer Alexander Scott faced his old friend, tennis pro Kelly Robinson. It was an I Spy Cosby-Culp reunion that brought the crowds to their feet.

In the mixed-doubles event, Cosby was teamed with Fred Stolle, and Robert Culp was joined by Arthur Ashe. Cos dazzled the crowd by winning several heated exchanges with Ashe, and charmed them with a little clowning in between matches.

Cos later teamed up with Elliott Gould, Dean Martin, Jr., and others to play basketball in an exhibition to help Sugar Ray Robinson's Youth Foundation. But their opposition was members of the Los Angeles Rams football team, and they were blown away by a thirty-point margin.

At home, Bill was still getting blown away by the simple things in life. Like teaching kids how to keep their ice cream on the cone. Cos surprised some visitors to his house by insisting on picking up a fallen scoop of ice cream, rinsing it off, and putting it back on a daughter's cone. He asked them, "Have you bought ice cream lately? Do you know the price of ice cream?" The Cosby kids learned not to waste food, and even to watch out for sloppy eating where the ice cream dribbles down the sides of the mouth: "Each dribble's worth maybe three cents!"

Cosby made his lone major television appearance of 1975 in November, starring in a Monday-night special, "Cos: The Bill Cosby Comedy Hour." It was a relaxed, coasting kind of special, closer in concept to the failed variety show of 1972 than to the Emmy Award-winning monologues he did on earlier one-shot shows. The guests were mainstream performers that had no flair for Cosbyan comedy: Tony Randall and Karen Valentine. And the supporting music was supplied by country star Loretta Lynn. Despite some help from such veteran writers as Alen Robin and Art Buchwald, *Variety* spoke for most critics in reporting that "this was a disappointing use of an extremely ingratiating performer. . . . The scissors-and-paste production was flat."

It just seemed to confirm that movies were the way to go. Agreeing with him was tennis partner and friend Sidney Poitier.

Chapter Fifteen

With the success of *Uptown Saturday Night,* Poitier and Cosby said, *Let's Do It Again,* and that film was even more of a triumph than the first. When it arrived in 1976, TV shows like "Sanford and Son," "Good Times," and "The Jeffersons" had covered most phases of the "new black comedy" style. With nothing more to prove, Poitier and Cosby could strike a relaxed balance between overtly ethnic, funky material and general jests, without having to answer to either black or white extremists.

"Sidney's looser," Harry Belafonte said, dropping by the set one day. A $2.6 million budget contributed to Poitier's confidence. For the first film Cosby basically had worked for a percentage of the gross and $75,000 up front. In order to appease Poitier and stay with the movie throughout its long shooting schedule, Cosby even suspended nightclub gigs that could have been worth, in his estimate, $500,000.

The superstar cast assembled for *Let's Do It Again* included the distinguished actor who had paid many dues in his long stage career, Ossie Davis, and two hot TV personalities, Jimmie Walker and John Amos. Again, Cos plays a feisty kind of guy, picking a fight with somebody far heavier and taller.

"Watch your lips or they may get you into something your behind can't get you out of!" he shouts. But when push leads to fight, he decides to forgive the man. After all, it happens to be George Foreman, in a cameo role.

Poitier wisely stayed the straight man, leaving Cosby more room and time to play around. In a very Cosbyan scene, Cos lets a little girl sit on his lap, only to find she's wet his leg. "She's all finished now," he announces, giving the moppet back to her mother. When he eyes a hot-looking lady in the parking lot, he smiles at her—forgetting that his pants are wet and that he looks like some kind of perverted bum.

Cosby and Poitier belong to a mystic lodge that wants to build a day-care center. So he and Sidney concoct a scheme: Take the lodge's money, gamble it in New Orleans, and earn enough to make the dream come true.

The guys bring their wives to New Orleans with them, mixing business with pleasure. In the pursuit of pleasure, Cosby speaks the most R-rated dialogue of his film career. At dinner in a fancy restaurant, his wife (Denise Nicholas) kisses him on the cheek, thanking him for the vacation.

"Is that all I'm gonna get?" he asks.

"That's all you're gonna get in public."

"I'm gonna lay a blockbuster on you tonight," he teases.

"Yeah? Well, I have a block for you to bust, baby, so you better bring a whole lotta hammer!"

"Have hammer . . . will travel," Cos enunciates coolly, "and go deep . . . into . . . your crevice!"

This shocks Poitier's wife. How can they act so blue (or, perhaps, too funkily black) in public? But in *Let's Do It Again* the relaxed attitude lets people be what they are. When the woman wonders aloud "what people would say" if they heard such coarseness, Denise answers, "They would say I was having a horny conversation with a man . . . and he was pickin' up on my thighs! Are you gonna sit there and say Clyde ain't been hittin' your switch regular?"

"We don't let the whole world know about it," the woman huffs.

"No," Poitier agrees, "we whisper a lot!"

Cos and Poitier find a scrawny fighter (Jimmie Walker) from Possum's Paw, Alabama, and hypnotize him into thinking he can defeat the champ. When the scam works, they must stay one step ahead of the furious bookies—and try to keep Walker on his weirdly concocted winning streak.

It was a pleasing film on all counts. Con man Cos proved here that he could easily have assumed some of the slick, lovable, comic hero roles given to actors like George Segal or Burt Reynolds. The movie broke box-office records when it opened at the Criterion Theater, achieving a three-day gross of $64,000.

Even the New York premiere, with money going to Harlem's YMCA and YWCA, reflected the relaxed attitudes of the times. Once Steve Allen made a joke to a black audience, "It's so nice to see blacks, Negroes, and Afro-Americans all living together in harmony." Here, John Amos showed up in a dashiki and cap. Poitier and Cosby wore their business suits. And Jimmie Walker turned up in flashy threads with a blonde on his arm. Three very different points of view, but all seemingly acceptable that night.

Praise for Cos was lavish. The *Christian Science Monitor* wrote, "Cosby shows flashes of pure genius." The *Village Voice* loved "the free-wheeling jiving, put-down artistry" he showed. His success in the two hip Poitier films proved he could be a big star in movies.

It led to his first "mainstream" film (discounting the quickly made and quickly forgotten *Hickey and Boggs*). Cosby shared star billing with the female superstar of the era, Raquel Welch. The movie was a hard, hip, "M*A*S*H"-style comedy, *Mother, Jugs and Speed.*

The two Poitier films had been funky, cool black comedies. Here Cosby was cast in a ferocious, hip "black comedy" of semi-sick humor. Cos plays Mother Tucker, an ambulance driver and medic who works for a sleazy company run by scuzzy, sloppy Allen Garfield.

"Times are tough," Garfield lectures his crew, "the country's goin' to hell. You take inflation, welfare, recession . . . there's nothin' we can do about that. But thanks to mugging, malnutrition, assassination, and disease, we got a chance to make a buck!"

The grimly humorous ambulance calls include: a lady wrestler thrown out of the ring and doused with soda by jeering fans, a giant black woman who has fallen off a chair while changing a light bulb, and an overdosed hippie stretched out in his underpants.

The patients' problems are treated with cruel humor. The wrestler is propositioned by ambulance driver Larry Hagman, who turns out to have necrophiliac proclivities toward any dead or unconscious woman. The black woman is strapped to a gurney and ultimately hurtled out a window, down a fire escape, and into the path of an oncoming truck.

The overdosed kid is nearly taken away by the cops until Cosby rushes in with a paper, calling, "That's our stiff! Read 'em and weep!"

In a devilish moment, Cos drives along mumbling, "Oh! Why did the Lord tempt me this way?" A bunch of nuns are daintily crossing the street, single file. He jams on the siren and rides right into them as they break into a panic-stricken run for cover. Cos chuckles in amusement as he flies by.

Raquel Welch initially plays a thankless "Hotlips Hoolihan" role. Everybody calls her "Jugs," even Cosby. Eventually she's allowed to go out on calls. Cos makes Raquel handle the problem of a loathsome fatty who's caught himself in his pants zipper. As she grimaces, trying to free him, Cos grins and says, "She has the dedication of a jungle missionary." Then it's off on more cases, some with peculiar in-jokes ("Mrs. Natasha Gurdin got her hand caught in a garbage disposal," one call goes, referring to Natalie Wood's real name).

Cos, dubbing himself the "Brown Hornet," has fun with his job— most of the time. One case involves a strung-out junkie who pleads with one of Cosby's partners, "I need drugs. Morphine, Demerol, whatever you got." It's Toni Basil, about seven years away from rock stardom. Just to prove she's frustrated, she takes out a rifle and blows the medic away.

Back at the office, grisly Larry Hagman has a pool going, betting on how many corpses come in each day. He's bet on eight for today. With Cosby's dead partner, it would be nine. "He doesn't count," Hagman protests; he's not really a paying customer. Cosby smiles, comes forward, and suddenly attacks Hagman, pummeling him to pieces, sending him crashing to the floor.

Cosby is unquestionably the star of the movie, handling the comic high points, and having all the no-nonsense authority to take charge during dramatic shoot-outs and punch-outs. His performance once again proved he could enjoy a full movie career, playing everything from tough private eyes to the kind of seriocomic romantic roles Elliott Gould, the star of the movie *M*A*S*H,* seemed to be getting in those days.

But the movie's jumble of sadistic comedy, violence, and pathos put critics off-balance. The *Los Angeles Times* praised Cosby's "strong, coherent performance" in a film that they felt should be awarded "a tarnished cup for shrill sludgery." *Time* praised Cosby's "affectless cool." But just to show that ethnic digs would forever pop up even in totally nonracial films like this, Andrew Sarris of the *Village Voice* limply labeled Raquel Welch "pure plastic" but then attacked Cosby for doing "a Stepin Fetchit imitation."

The film had some success as a cult item, enough so that, when "M*A*S*H" ended up a tremendous TV hit, *Mother, Juggs and Speed* also became a TV show. In 1978 a pilot episode was screened by *Variety*. Although an extra *g* was added to Jugs to appease feminists, nothing of value was added. "The cool, relaxed presence of Bill Cosby was missed, and, worst of all, the actress playing Raquel Welch's part didn't fill it to its full potential: "Her breasts are exiguous compared to the ones flaunted by the robust Raquel."

For Cosby, 1976 was not just the year of his renewed movie career. He also made headlines for achieving one of his most coveted goals in private life. It would give him lasting pride—and give detractors fuel for some of the nastiest sniping of his career.

Chapter Sixteen

It was a picture-perfect May afternoon in the country. Camille wore a softly shirred pastel dress that touched the ground and a wide-brimmed picture hat, neatly tied with a bow around her conservative neckline. She was the very model of elegance, recalling the Gay Nineties in demure sweetness. Her mother-in-law was in "Sunday best," too. But the hero of the hour was Bill Cosby, in mortarboard cap and gown.

With a smile and a handshake, Bill stood before University of Massachusetts Chancellor Randolph Bromery and accepted his degree, doctor of education. From now on: Dr. William H. Cosby, Jr.

"Mom just went crazy today," said Bill with pride. "She used to say 'Education's a must.' If she was dead, she would have gotten up to come here today. Her tears mean so much."

The man with the degree was also a man with a renewed purpose. In just three months, in fall 1976, he was going to show off his commitment to education in entertainment with "Cos," a new variety series. Who better than Dr. Cosby to teach kids and make them laugh at the same time?

But was this the right time?

The warning signs were up and the lines were drawn. The time between 8:00 P.M. and 9:00 P.M. had been ruled "Family Hour" in an attempt to curb the networks' tendencies toward shows with violent heroes and violently jiggling heroines. For this first hour of prime-time, G-rated entertainment only!

What happened was disaster. Shows stuck in the 8:00-to-9:00 P.M. time slot were wishy-washy failures that quickly dripped down the drain. Without .38-caliber guns and 38-D bras, "family" shows came and went: "Swiss Family Robinson," "The Captain and Tenille," "The Tony Orlando and Dawn Rainbow Hour," "Holmes and Yo Yo," "The San Pedro Beach Bums," "Young Dan'l Boone." High morals? Yes. And low ratings.

With such a high mortality rate, who would dare try to entertain without sex or violence? What star would risk professional disaster for a cause?

Dr. Bill Cosby.

The educator and father of five would champion a family show that didn't take on racism, abortion, vasectomy, crime, or other Norman Lear-y topics.

The doctor theorized, "The Family Hour has to do with something very, very technical. It has to do with using the tube to address itself to educational values, to teaching, to subjects that have to do with morals." If that didn't sound entertaining, the doctor assured critics that his show would not "be turned into a university instead of a variety. This hour will be funny without preaching and teaching."

Just to make it even more of a challenge, ABC put Cosby up against the only praiseworthy family show on TV, "The Wonderful World of Disney," and the blockbuster "60 Minutes." Cosby's steely determination never wavered. He vowed to be "more inventive" in finding ways to reach the family audience.

Kay Gardella was, for over a decade, the kindest, most supportive columnist in Cosby's corner, a woman who plugged virtually every Cosby special, TV show, and movie. But even she cautiously questioned his heroic charge into TV's wasteland: "Of late Cosby . . . gives the impression he's carrying the burden of responsibility for all the young people of the world on his shoulders. It's a good thing somebody does, I know, but it tends to inject a little of the preacher into the comedian. Dangerous inflation of opinion can result, and must be guarded against."

Cosby's admirable vision was tunnel vision, and it led him down a long, bottomless shaft. His one chance was that folks would be in the mood for something funny. Disney and "60 Minutes" weren't funny. But neither was he.

The simple TV show "Cos" produced a simple reaction from critics: diabetic shock. They cringed when he did an Art Linkletter bit, interviewing little moppets for forced humor. They fumed at wholesomely boring guest stars like Cindy Williams and Bruce Jenner, and snored through the music of Chicago, a band most any age group could tolerate, but few really could get excited over. There was a roving cast of "bright young players" and some animation, and, in the middle of it, Bill Cosby and his monologues.

Variety called the show "an uneven mixture of clever and silly material . . . deliberately tailored for tots' brief attention spans." There wasn't enough of pure Bill Cosby. *TV Guide's* critic had less tolerance: "Cosby comes on the way he does in those commercials in which he persuades little children to eat their canned peas. sixty seconds of Cosby being cutesy-poo in a commercial is one thing: sixty minutes of the same every Sunday night is another."

TV Guide also took time to trash Cosby's newly won doctorate: "With Cosby's new Ph.D. in education . . . perhaps he feels he has a professional obligation to be boring. . . . Bring back "Lassie." At least that show admitted that it was a dog."

Surely Bill could could count on somebody to say a kind word. Like, how about the Black Writers' Caucus?

When Bill began "I Spy," there was no such thing. Now, a decade after Bill's breakthrough, the group finally singled out Bill Cosby—because Bill Cosby was being unfair to blacks.

"We don't feel anyone owes anyone anything," chairman Jim Tisdale told the newspapers, "but we felt it would be only fair or rational that a show with a black principal would be represented with blacks in all creative, craft, and technical areas." Sure, Cos may have done a couple of good things and broken a lot of ground for the race, but only two of the twelve writers on this show were black.

The Black Writers' Caucus vowed to set up pickets outside the studio and show Bill Cosby a thing or two.

"I'm really on my countdown to retirement," Cosby said in the midst of all this. "My first series, 'I Spy,' ran three years. 'The Bill Cosby Show' lasted two years. My first variety hour lasted one year. And this show? If I'm lucky, it will run thirteen weeks."

Try a lucky seven weeks. Trick or treat: On Halloween, Cos became one of the season's earliest casualties. He'd given them sweet treats—but it looked like viewers wanted nasty tricks.

Frustrated by the show's demise, Cos turned up at a party at the Playboy mansion in Los Angeles to relax. One of the guests was Tommy Smothers. Tommy and Bill, both purveyors of childlike comedy, were not buddies. During the late sixties, when Tommy had turned into an activist-comic with a penchant for political satire, he couldn't understand why Bill remained so neutral. Sometimes when they crossed paths, Tommy would chide Cos about getting into the game a bit more.

The Playboy mansion was neutral ground, and everyone was having a good time. Tommy walked over to Cos, smiled, blinked up at Bill with his one blue eye and one green one, and began talking.

The next moment, Cosby said "You've been asking for it."

And there was Tommy sprawled on the floor from a sudden right-hand lead from Cosby.

The crowd was hushed. Tommy was an athlete in his own right, a gymnast capable of some picture-perfect push-ups and handstands, but he was no match for a sudden whack from Cosby.

There were no other punches thrown that night, but in a town as small as Hollywood, there was worry that the two men would meet again, and soon.

Tommy was asked what would happen the next time he happened to run into Cos. He answered, "I guess I'll have to hit him again—with my face."

A close business associate of both Bill and Tommy, who noted that both men could be moody at times, recalls, "They never really liked each other. Tommy can be really strange . . . Tommy is very physical. And Bill can be very physical. I can easily see the two of them punching the shit out of each other."

Most fans who heard about the incident were shocked. Even intimates were surprised. Most people who have seen Bill angry say that his rage takes the form of "smoldering," and that the look in his eyes and the grim-set jaw is enough to send people walking briskly in the opposite direction.

Fortunately the Cosby-Smothers confrontation was restricted to that one punch. Probably somebody clued Cosby in to what was pretty much a misunderstanding. Tommy had gone over to congratulate Cosby on the new show—unaware that it had been canceled that very day.

"Cos" may no longer have been a target for critics, but Cosby was.

He had always seemed "too good to be true," and now was the perfect time to attack him for his "goody-goody" outlook. With the violent success of Richard Pryor, there was some backlash against Cos for remaining a mainstream "Tom" performer à la Sammy Davis.

Cosby wasn't helping the cause. Like a parent, he lectured columnists who didn't understand his vision. And his conservative viewpoints seemed out of touch with the times. Guys like Pryor were putting on the toughest of street-jive dialects, while Cosby took a dim view of Black English: "We're lighting a fire that has no use, a fire that doesn't warm anybody, where you're going to make up your own language, your own mathematics and sciences. That's just an easy way out. We need black people in space and science programs and in many other areas. While these hoodlum packs are out roaming the streets and saying, 'What it is, is what it is' and 'Right on' and giving handshakes and challenging each other over a piece of cement that the city owns, there are some very bright ones . . . who could contribute something to society."

On another passionate subject of the times, interracial sex, Cosby was on record as a moderate. "Many white chicks feel they'll get soul if they ball a black man they don't even care about," he'd told *Playboy*, "and the black goes to the white because of the white's status in this society; the black person is supposed to gain from making love to a white. And the white is giving up status. . . . If a white chick is with a black guy, she's saying, 'Look at me, look at what I'm giving up, look how I'm going against society. Man, am I brave.'

"Now, I'm not talking about love, just balling. . . . I've been with white cats who've looked at black chicks I wouldn't be seen with anywhere and heard them say, 'Man, she is fantastic-looking. . . . I'm talking about whites who have a desire to make love to a black . . . [to] dig that African or extra blackness that says this person is 100 percent black."

Typical of the prickly heat he was getting lately was this from the *Village Voice*: "Cosby has become unfunny in recent years, a monotonous young fogey capitalizing wherever he can on his splendiferous teacher thing . . . clubby-kissing the ruling-class hand of Johnny Carson, making spokesman commercials for such established heels as White Owl cigars and Pan American airlines. He has evolved into a kind of self-parodying sap."

For months critics had been giving Cosby a piece of their minds. Now, for peace of mind, he spent the Christmas season at home in Amherst. Camille told *Essence* magazine, "It's like what you read about in books. There's snow, sleigh rides, tobogganing and sledding. We roast chestnuts and marshmallows in our fireplace."

Their formal Christmas dinner, for twenty people, featured homemade bread, two different main courses (meat and fish), and three types of desserts. Eubie Blake played the piano and told stories.

At that beautiful time of year, Cosby had the satisfaction not only of time with his family, but of remembering, by contrast with those dire years in the Philly projects, how much he'd been blessed. It was unfortunate that, to judge by the failure of "Cos," some of the old-fashioned sentiment, love, and humor he knew was gone from many American TV screens. And not even missed.

Chapter Seventeen

Nineteen seventy-six was a big year for Richard Pryor, not Bill Cosby. While Cosby's TV series crashed, Pryor was at the top of his game with the scorching album "Bicentennial Nigger." A reporter came up to Pryor and began to compliment him, saying that he appreciated the tough satire, such a change from the "cute" comedy of Bill Cosby.

Pryor snapped, "Bill Cosby's one of the funniest men in the world, and I don't like being compared in those terms. Saying Bill Cosby is cute, that is offensive to me. Bill Cosby is not cute, he is one of the funniest men in the world."

He once admitted, "Bill Cosby paved the way for Richard Pryor." Indeed, Pryor had been borrowing Cosby's style ever since he saw Bill work in Greenwich Village nightclubs. His first TV exposure, on "The Merv Griffin Show" in 1965, wasn't long after Cosby's TV arrival.

Pryor was now the comedian that most talk shows wanted to book. He was controversial, sharp, and unpredictable. In the talk show world, the rumble was that Cosby was merely unpredictable. "Tonight" show talent coordinator Craig Tennis reported that Cos was mercurial in temperament, veering from cordiality to rudeness for no apparent reason. Of course anxiety on the "Tonight" show was always high when a guy like Cosby was around, because he disliked pre-show conferences to map out questions and topics, preferring to wing it—

which always had an element of uncertainty. Tennis recalled having "both very good and bad experiences . . . Bill changes from moment to moment—you never know where you stand with him. I've seen him come on the 'Tonight' show completely unprepared and yet work himself into a monologue that is warm, original, and killingly funny. At other times he's been cold and aloof, maddeningly playing the superstar, and even talking down to the audience."

It was through the "Tonight" show appearances that most fans saw the gradual change in Cosby's monologue style over the years: He changed from an impish, childlike performer to a more adult figure, coming out in a vested suit, walking his special stately walk, and enunciating through the cigar flaunted between his teeth. It had been a struggle for Cosby to be accepted as he grew older and became "the parent," talking about kids rather than being the kid himself, or the older brother rapping about all the younger Russells of the world.

Now that both the "parent" and "child" routines weren't working that well, Cosby had to, at least temporarily, look elsewhere for a humorous subject. He found it in an unlikely place: R&B music. Spurred by the success he was enjoying from the Poitier films, Cos shifted into comedy funk on records, signing with Capitol and releasing an album called *Bill Cosby Is Not Himself These Days, Rat Own, Rat Own, Rat Own.* He certainly wasn't himself, except in one way—he was, as usual, taking a bold step and doing it largely on instinct.

What really made Cos think he could succeed with an R&B comedy record anyway? He hadn't made any record in three years, hadn't really had a successful comedy record in five years, and had had no success with a musical album in more than a decade. And he was aiming at a very slim target. Back in '76, rock and soul fans weren't known for having any sense of humor when it came to lampoons of their idols.

His first single made the charts: "Yes, Yes, Yes," a parody of Barry White's school of butterfat balladeering. With a female chorus cooing "yes yes yes" over and over, the deep, intimate vocal oozes, "I wowna ask ya a question, darlin' . . . last night baby . . . did you go through my pockets?"

The song turns out to be a ballad about the miseries of married life, and a chick who wrecks the car, cheats, and drives her man nuts. On the album Cos lampooned gooey R&B love songs with such observations as "My love is so deep for you, you can't find it" and "I picked a brick up and waited for you . . . wanting to smack you dead upside the head . . . yes, I've been in love . . . and you can have it!"

The other tune making the charts was "I Luv Myself Better Than I Luv Myself," a James Brown rave-up with Cos crying, "Good God! Feeling Good! Good God! Yow!" before trying to quack and bark out his soulful joy.

Cos remembers that tune well: "Through the song, in the humor, I kept saying "Good God. Good God." People bought the album—and then some of them sent the album back to me with a note: "You have crushed my faith in you by using the Lord's name in vain."

Fortunately there were enough other people holding onto the record to give Capitol some faith in their newly signed comedian. Bill followed up the musical parodies with his first new album of monologues in years: *My Father Confused Me, What Must I Do?* It was a beautiful comeback album blending contemporary humor and stories about parents and children. He lampooned pot smokers unable to handle simple reality, even seeing a hamburger grilled and eaten. Wild-eyed and frantic, Cos cries, "The dude took a piece of round meat! And threw it on the grill! Then he turned it over! It had black stripes on it! I said far out! And the dude ate it! I can't deal with it!"

He drew a bizarre picture of his runny-nosed daughter whose shimmering face made her look like "The Glazed Donut Monster." Given a rest for several years, his childhood routines sounded fresh and more vibrant than ever. In one he talked about his mother's clichés of violence, like "I will knock your brains out." That one really frightened young Cos:

"That's horrible, man. She's gonna hit you in the head and your brains are gonna fall out on the floor! I always wonder what would've happened if I went to the store, got some calves' brains, and when she hit me threw 'em on the floor . . . pow! Knowin' my mother she'd say, 'Pick those brains up and put them back in your head and don't let your brains fall out of your head again! Or I will knock you into the middle of next week!'

"Please do, 'cause I'm having a rough time this week."

Cosby proved to be closer to his old, amiable image—even when pressed by pushy reporters. One time he was appearing in a celebrity tennis tournament and refused to grant individual interviews to the press. A reporter—from the notoriously trendy *Interview* yet—who used the byline Tinkerbelle, disregarded the ban and came up to Cos anyway. Cos actually invited the reporter's company, and answered some very precocious questions.

Tinkerbelle asked if Cos went "to Temple . . . the college, I mean, not the synagogue." Cos answered, "Both. It's fifty-five percent Jewish." Tinkerbelle quizzed him on another vital matter: "You get propositioned much, Bill? You must. How do you deal with it?" Cos answered, "I just tell the guy to go to hell."

Cos enjoyed himself on the tennis court—and he would soon be named by *Tennis* magazine as the top male celebrity star in the country. He was also having fun at home with his five kids. He had fun the day he dropped by the Sotheby Parke-Bernet gallery in New York and bid on a painting of a black child and his Sunday school teacher done by Thomas Hart Benton. He got it. He only had to pay $105,000.

He had commitments to various causes that cared about him as much as he cared about them. He was a member or active on the advisory boards of the Mary Homes College, Ebony Showcase Theater, the Black Film Foundation, Workshop for Careers in the Arts, the Communications Council of Howard University, the Smithsonian Institution, Institute for Creative and Production Studies in Radio and Television, the American Sickle Cell Foundation, and the Studio Watts Workshop. Among others.

The warm reaction to Cosby's new comedy album seemed like a thaw in the cold, hip world that stand-up comedy had become. It was something of an irony that Richard Pryor, hoping to increase his success with his own TV series, was rebuffed for being *too* rude and satiric. Cosby, who saw his Fall 1976 series get the quick ax on October 31, watched as Richard's Fall 1977 show was killed by October 20th. This didn't mean Cos was ready to try again.

"I've got nothing to offer in a series," he said. "I don't know how to get lucky with them when you've got fifteen writers sitting around throwing paper airplanes and handing you stuff to rewrite and try to make good. That's why I was glad to see Pryor pull out because they eat you alive."

Soon enough, Richard Pryor and Bill Cosby would be joining forces in an attempt to warm up Richard's image and give Cos a little more of the hip edge. But that was still a year away, with both men having other commitments to deal with.

"I've done so much people can't box me in," Cos said. He kept juggling the club dates, records, talk shows, and TV commercials. He was even in the news again when, after he had received his master's and Ph.D., Temple University belatedly, officially, gave him his bachelor's degree. Also, he had a new film coming out with Sidney Poitier, *A Piece of the Action*.

"What the picture touches on," Poitier told reporters at the time, "is the question of young people who are underprivileged, unemployable, or unemployed in major cities." The story also dealt with the punishment of crime, because "our system is punitive rather than rehabilitative. . . . I believe our system of justice helps create criminals."

In the story, Poitier and cat burglar Cos have Robin Hoodish intentions of taking money from those who are taking from the poor. They end up rehabilitating themselves and thirty kids, with the help of a retired policeman played by James Earl Jones. They naturally have to battle corruption and bad guys along the way—with Cos in a derring-do highlight leaping from a twelve-floor office building to safety.

Cos found "something very new and different" in his expanded romantic role opposite Denise Nicholas, who had played his wife in *Let's Do It Again*. Here she and Bill had a chance to flesh out the relationship. She played the coordinator at a community center who has no idea his occupation is slightly larcenous until they get to know each other much better. "It's a nice clean relationship," Bill said. "They discover each other and like what they've found."

Shooting was low-key, and, when the crew went on location to Chicago, they would sometimes find Cos passing the time with neighborhood winos, joking and rapping. The film was more warmly emotional than the first two, and *Newsweek* applauded: "It touches the funny bone and the heart and leaves you feeling good. This is by all means superstars Poitier and Cosby's best effort."

When the returns came in, though, the film had failed to generate quite the response at the box office that the two previous Poitier-Cosby movies had. Cos was disappointed. He liked the film because it had less "foolishness" and more of a story.

Poitier also was crushed by the public's lukewarm reception: "*A Piece of the Action* was my own original idea. I then had to work for many months with the scriptwriter. And then I had to make the picture, direct it, and act in it, and once it was finished I had to edit it, oversee the scoring and all the manifold details attendant on getting a picture out. . . . I have to rest my bones, restore my juices. You will not see another movie of mine until two years from now."

Cos put out a few more records for Capitol, both music and comedy. They broke little new ground, though in keeping with the style of the seventies, Cos was covering territory he couldn't have covered in earlier childhood remembrances. Like wet dreams:

"First time it happened, I got scared. I didn't know what it was. I said uh-oh, I ate too much cornbread last night. . . . I rolled up the sheets and went down to the laundromat, five in the morning, did my own sheets. Nine twelve-year-olds down there doin' their sheets, too, man. After that I'd get out of school, three-thirty, four o'clock I was back in bed again: Come on, whatever it was! Yes indeed, three glasses of water and a picture of Dorothy Dandridge and I was on my way."

There was talk of Cos starring in another black superstar film, *The Wiz*, playing the Tin Man. Other commitments prevailed, but it might've been cute if Cos had played the wizard, and the original songs were kept. Then Dorothy and her friends could sing "We're off to see the wizard, the wonderful Wizard of Oz. We hear he is a whiz of a wiz, if ever a wiz there was. . . . Be Cos, be Cos, be Cos, be Cos, be Cos . . ."

The new year brought Cosby into "mainstream" movie-making once again. He joined Jane Fonda, Maggie Smith Michael Caine, and Walter Matthau in *California Suite*. Even though he was technically in a "blacks only" segment of the movie, with Richard Pryor, this was a film that was geared for mainstream tastes.

Screenwriter Neil Simon's idea was to present four stories about guests at a Beverly Hills hotel. The subject was relationships in crisis situations, in situations of need, love, and support. Two of the episodes were heavy; Matthau's segment, and the one for Cosby and Pryor were going to be slapstick-filled comic relief. The trouble was that neither the director, the writer, nor the stars were especially noted for slapstick.

Matthau bristled at director Herbert Ross. "Herbie wanted me to pull out all the stops, to be outrageous," he fumed. "I said that I liked myself better when I speak very quietly." His segment was an artistic embarrassment, an overdone slapstick farce in which he made inane faces, wrung his hands, and popped his eyes over the dilemma of keeping his wife from finding the hooker who'd stayed in his apartment overnight.

Bill and Richard didn't voice any opposition to their director. They welcomed the challenge of doing some slapstick in the silent-movie tradition. It would certainly be a challenging change of pace for Bill, who had settled down into a slower-moving, cigar-chomping parent/philosopher mode in stand-up.

Bill and Richard play doctors who, while on vacation with their wives, are hapless victims of a broken-down car, bad plumbing, and other hotel nightmares. All could've been clichéd but funny sequences —except that this modern comedy broke a key rule of old-time slapstick: violence must look harmless.

The climax of the segment begins on the tennis court, where the doctors and their wives get hit with balls and smack each other with tennis rackets. Unlike the old slapstick, where a Buster Keaton instantly bounces up after a fall, or a smack to Curly Howard's skull is accompanied by a weird sound effect, these bits were played straight. When one of the ladies trips over some balls and falls flat on her face, it's not funny. It looks like she could be hurt.

Back at the hotel room, hobbled by injuries, Pryor's wife smacks her head on the bathroom mirror—painfully. She knocks over a ninety-dollar bottle of perfume.

"Of all the stupid-ass things to do," grumbles Cosby.

"Hold on," Pryor shouts. "She did not do it on purpose."

"You mean it was a planned accident?"

The men start bickering, and it escalates rapidly. Pryor becomes a wild man, threatening to bash Bill in the head with a tennis racket at the count of five. Cosby, in perfect control, barks, "Never threaten a man who spent two years working the drunk ward. Back off!" And when Pryor shivers, unable to find the courage to count the final five, Cosby goads him into it.

Pryor's puny attack is met by powerful Cosby arms. He hurls Pryor down, the tennis racket smacking into the TV set, blowing it out Pryor charges again, only to be bounced off the far wall.

The madman rushes forward yet again and catches Cos around the legs. "Don't bite me," Cos warns sternly. "You could give me a blood disease!" In his frustration, he gathers little Richard up like a pile of laundry, and, exasperated beyond control, grabs the man's head, pulls it forward, and bites him on the nose.

When next observed, the two couples, all in bandages and casts, are trudging haplessly through the hotel lobby, the perfect vacation over. And so was the enthusiasm for the team of Pryor and Cosby. Most critics dismissed the film as simply unamusing.

The influential critic from the *New Yorker,* Pauline Kael, also declared that the film was . . . anti-black.

She pointed out that white actors had played Cosby and Pryor's roles in the original stage version: "When the roles are played by black actors, the skit seems to be saying that the men may be doctors but they're still uncontrollable, dumb blacks."

Attacking the film's art direction (the hotel had white wallpaper and pastel-colored furnishings), she insisted that the men's blackness was deliberately distorted: "The recessive whitened decor turns them into tar babies."

As for the slapstick, the ineptness of the accident-prone duo proved that blacks "don't know how to handle cars. . . . When they stumble around a flooded room, crash into each other, step on broken glass, or, even worse, when Cosby bites Pryor's nose, it all has horrifying racist overtones." She decried the offensive film that showed "blacks who act like clowning savages."

Talk about giving offense. When Dr. William H. Cosby, Jr., read the piece, his blood pressure could've been charted on the Richter scale. Taking out a full-page ad in *Variety,* he wrote: "Are we to be denied a right to romp through hotels, bite noses, and, in general, beat up one another in the way Abbott & Costello, Laurel & Hardy, Martin & Lewis, Buster Keaton, and Charlie Chaplin did—and more recently as those actors in the movie *Animal House*? I heard no cries of racism in those reviews. If my work is not funny—it's not funny. But this industry does not need projected racism from critics."

The controversy stewed for days. The film's producer, Ray Stark, accused Kael of irresponsibility. Others simply dismissed the review as typical of a lady whose views seemed to veer drastically between scintillating and senile. Of the protests, Liz Smith said, "Kael probably won't care. She is used to being attacked."

Cosby was used to being attacked, too. But, to quote Bob Dylan's song about Lenny Bruce, Cos fought his war "on a battlefield where every victory hurt." Every step of the way, Cosby's triumphs as a comedian, as an actor, as a trailblazer for civil rights, as one of black America's most positive images—every step of the way Cosby heard criticism ranging from outrageous blasts to inane sniping, and much of it confusedly racist.

But whenever one avenue was blocked off, Cosby found another. His versatility enabled him to strike new fire in stand-up, on TV, in movies, on records—even as a singer. The moment he was stuck, he simply unstuck himself and changed direction—but he always moved forward.

Now he shifted gears in his movie career, returning to children's entertainment. He turned up next in Disney's *The Devil and Max Devlin*.

"That Walt Disney was the slickest guy who ever operated in this town," Cos once said. "Do you realize that for every three people who see a Disney picture, there are probably two who didn't really want to come to the theater? That's right. Parents go because that's something their kid can see. And, man, when you got one or two out of every three people going to the theater when they don't even want to be there, you got something going for you."

What a natural idea: Bill Cosby matched with Walt Disney. It was an idea whose time had come—too late. At the time Cosby arrived, the Disney Studios were losing prestige—and sometimes money—with their rigidly G-rated, mild live-action films.

If Cosby thought he could turn things around, so did his fans. Ads for *The Devil and Max Devlin* promised only slightly less excitement than *The Devil in Miss Jones*. With wickedly smiling Cosby and lovable clod Elliott Gould, the one-minute TV teasers promised a feast of devilish pranks. Sitting through the whole film turned out to be purgatory.

Gould plays a creepy landlord who evicts people on any pretext. Tripped by a blind old lady and sent sprawling into the gutter, he's run over by a truck full of Hare Krishnas. A colorful beginning, but the beginning of the end.

"Welcome to hell," an unsmiling Cosby intones. He's not the devil after all, but "Barney Satan," evidently one of the devil's soul brothers. Gould is justly awed by the sight of exploding fireballs and gaunt, corpse-white zombies. Cos lays out the plot: Gould will be restored to life if he can bring in three "fresh, unsullied, innocent" souls. The souls of three kiddies.

The plot is paced like a taffy pull. Gould tediously goes about his work, introducing himself to his adorable targets: Julie Budd, Sonny Shroyer, and too-cute, pudding bowl-coiffured Adam Rich.

Gould doesn't know if he can con all three kids. "Oh, God," he mutters. Cosby says, "I wish you wouldn't say that." And that's as witty as the script ever gets.

Though Gould and Cosby shared the billing, Gould had about seventy percent of the screen time. Cos was left to pop up now and then to see how Gould was doing, and he had no time to say anything more than "What about those contracts? . . . Your time is almost up."

In one brief, amusing moment Cos teases Gould by popping up unexpectedly, pursing his lips in the famous Cosby smirk, and giving him the eye. Cosby could easily have played a lovable devil throughout. In another, even briefer moment, with Cosby losing patience, he delivers his lines with Sheldon Leonard-like menace and a baleful stare. This, too, could have been chillingly effective if it had been carried on throughout the film.

Instead the movie went from fun to funereal within the first five minutes, and Cosby was blandly wasted—until the end. Then the film took a shocking turn for Cosby-watchers. It was obvious from the beginning that Gould would double-cross the devil. When he does, Cosby's hellish temper comes out. No longer is he wearing a business suit. Suddenly he blazes onto the screen as a hairy, red-legged satyr with woolly crimson goathair on his head and a bare chest. He warns Gould, "Eternal damnation is yours! You'll know the unmitigating pain and horror of limbs torn from their sockets. You'll feel pain you never imagined in life, yours forever! Flesh you'll smell burn! Rotting forever!"

It was a tantalizing peek at a raging Cosby viewers have never seen before or since—and it slips by in less than a minute.

Now that he had followed *California Suite* with another turkey, it looked like the only way Bill could get satisfaction in a film was if he wrote it, directed it, and starred in it himself. As for trying television again, Cos reflected, "I just haven't been able to put together the kind of show where the public will say, 'Hey, let's watch!' It's as simple as that." And in stand-up comedy, the leading attraction was still fiery Richard Pryor. Tastes were definitely turned toward the hothead and away from Cool Cos.

He was now forty-four, and it looked like the best of Bill Cosby's career, like the best of an aging sports star's career, was well behind him.

Chapter Eighteen

"We comedians have a staying power of maybe twenty years," Cosby said, nearing his twentieth year in show business. "Unless we come up with something new, we can run out of welcome."

It seemed that the welcome mat was down for Cosby only on admirer Johnny Carson's "Tonight" show and out on the road. Like others who couldn't get a TV series, or had movie careers and seen them peter out, Bill became one of those people called "celebrities," who, to the average TV viewer, don't seem to do much except sit around being a star. Bill joined comics like Don Rickles, Buddy Hackett, and Shecky Greene in the ritual Carson interviews promoting club dates.

Now middle-aged, Cosby appeared to be coasting. He described slowing down in an article for *Ebony*. He wrote that he was having trouble keeping weight off, wasn't able to keep his body as finely tuned as he used to. As for such basics as food and sex, Bill felt these areas were also not going to get any better.

"When you reach middle age, you find that everything you eat turns to gas . . . your stomach changes, too, as to what it can and will accept." And in the bedroom, "you come home late . . . you get into bed and touch and start to make your move. She says, 'No,' and you roll back over the other way and say to yourself, 'Thank you so much,' because you were not all that serious in the first place. All you wanted to do was go on record. The first thing you say at breakfast the next morning is, 'You know, I made my move last night, and you weren't ready.' "

Cos complained that, aside from the body, the memory was going too. He'd walk into a room and forget what he'd come in for. And he'd get mad at himself for forgetting. "There are, of course, some advantages that occur in middle age," he wrote. "But now that I'm forty and my mind has started to play tricks on me, I can't remember what they are."

On the "Tonight" show, audiences saw him wearing glasses more often. One time he admitted that he would probably have a long life, even if it included needing thicker glasses. He mentioned that his grandfather lived to be ninety-eight years old.

"But they were taking pieces away from him," Cosby added. "They cut his legs off. He had diabetes. And my Aunt Clara went in and she said, 'Oh, Daddy, you've lost your legs!' And he said, 'Be quiet. You didn't say anything when they took all my teeth.' And that was important to him. Your teeth go, then your legs, and they were just chipping away at him, so he said, 'I think I better leave.' "

Carson asked, "Does aging bother you?"

"No," Cos answered evenly, "it doesn't bother me at all. I'm just happy to be here no matter what the punishment."

The punishment appeared to be parenthood, the main theme of many of his monologues. More than ever, Cos was reaching out to all those fans from the sixties who were now parents themselves—and coming back to Cos to hear all about what they'd let themselves in for. That included kids whose favorite words were *I dunno* and *mine* and having to talk like a tobacco auctioneer to get them to "Stop it stop it stopitstopitstopit."

"Some people are disappointed because I still do a family show," Cos said, "but if something pulls and holds a family together, and makes them laugh at themselves . . . that's a part of life I want to give."

Cosby's interest in children's programming was still high. Cos was involved with Bob "Captain Kangaroo" Keeshan and the *Weekly Reader* in producing "Picture Pages," a series of five-minute video shows helping preschoolers learn to read.

Cosby's high profile on TV was mostly for all those commercials he did with kids. Sure, kids loved Cos, but he clued folks in on those Jell-O ads: "The kids really respond to me . . . well, you know how they do that? They get about five hundred kids in a room before I even get into the building, and they show them me in "Electric Company" tapes, and they watch the five hundred for the five kids who are most turned on . . . and they grab them and give them to me for the ad. The rest is easy."

Cosby had become another Mr. Whipple or Josephine the Plumber, a famous funny character in commercials. But even here, Cos had to worry a little. After being named *Advertising Age*'s "Star Presenter of 1978," Cos was dropped by one of his major clients, Ford Motors, in 1979. While he was doing Ford commercials, their sales had gone up from 2.3 million to 2.6 million, but a new ad agency had come in and someone had said, "We'll let the products be the stars." There was a hint that Cos had overextended himself.

In the summer of 1981, Cos made an appearance at the Kool Jazz Festival, where he was invited to put together an informal "dream concert" of some of his favorites. Bill assembled Arnett Cobb on sax, Jimmy Smith on keyboards, Mickey Roker on drums, and B. B. King for guitar and vocals.

"This is a happening," he said happily. "It's for people who love jazz and love to laugh and love to have a good time." He saw a definite link between comedy, his way, and playing jazz. "With B. B. King you know the song, you want him to sing it, but each time he is constantly challenged to hit it right," and yet make it come out fresh and different. Cos would write out material on a yellow legal pad, but always improvised from there, never doing the same bits the same way.

Guest-hosting the "Tonight" show, Cos continued to give air time to favorite jazz performers like Dizzy Gillespie and Sonny Rollins, but was disappointed that there wasn't much new comedy talent, anyone with "a good five minutes." He'd visit East and West Coast comedy shops, but the clientele were mostly vacant-eyed yuppies and the only way comics could reach them was through inane shock comedy.

The new rage in stand-up was young Eddie Murphy, who turned out to be a cross between the outrageous Richard Pryor and cool, likable Cos. Murphy actually did both of them on stage. He started out doing "a salute to Richard Pryor" with bits copped from records. Once he became famous, doing a variety of characters, he perfected a Cosby impression complete with vested suit, wire-rimmed glasses, cigar, and self-satisfied smile.

Murphy recalls his first contact with the real thing: "Bill Cosby called me up and said, 'You can't get onstage and say fuck you.' That was the most bizarre thing that's happened in my career. Bill Cosby calling me up and reprimanding me for being too dirty. Wow."

But Eddie had great respect for Bill. He followed a little of the Cosby lifestyle: no smoking, drinking, or drugs. "You never hear any garbage about Cosby," Murphy said. "He has a happy home life."

Meanwhile Murphy and Pryor continued to dominate in comedy. The middle-aged Cos didn't seem to mind. Like the singer of "Ain't Misbehavin'" he was happy on his particular shelf. Cosby's audience wasn't the misbehaving Murphy and Pryor crowd. Bill realized "the young swingers would probably be the most difficult for me as an audience, because my act is not designed to cover lovemaking or sex; it's designed for the philosophy of people who are thinking of having a family, or already have one."

Cos was content to be himself, remembering from his brief "adults only" period in 1972 that changing his style would be futile. "Let's say that what Bill Cosby does, he is known for. And the people who like him, like him for that."

In the family arenas where he began to play, the concert halls and suburban theaters, Cosby became a family institution in stand-up, another George Burns or Jack Benny. He could take ten or twenty minutes for a leisurely warm-up, and the audience would wait with respect and devotion. Cos developed a friendship with the crowd that went against the traditional "kill the audience" hysteria of many frantic and hostile comics:

"I used to want to destroy people with laughter. I wanted to make their stomachs hurt. But that isn't fair. It really hurts and it makes people tired. So now I pace myself. I don't want people concentrating on their pain rather than their laughter."

A review at the time, from the *Daily Iowan,* described his heartland strength: "There were times when the jokes became obvious, when everyone knew what was coming. But the way he said things, the tone of voice, made predictable lines belly-splitters. . . . His delivery was timed with deadly accuracy." Simple lines were "delivered so marvelously" that the audiences were roaring with laughter. On paper it has almost no impact, but when Cosby, after a long lecture from his dad on how hard money is to come by, gets to the punchline, the audience howls. All he says is: "I did not ask you, 'Have you suffered, old man?' I asked you . . . for some money!"

"Bill Cosby is nothing less than the most gifted monologist of our time," Steve Allen wrote. "One of the reasons . . . is that he is, richly and purposely and openly, the most childish," reaching "the child that each of us was, the child that still lives within us."

He does it with a limitless array of voices, faces, cadences, movements, not to mention his own inimitable delivery, where the words come out like they're being coaxed, shoved forward with a little bit of wobbly wonder and good-natured surprise.

Yet for all the adulation, Cosby has never rested on audience acceptance. He's aware of the nature of each different crowd: "You have to work differently in different places, but you still have to be Bill Cosby. Take Lake Tahoe. That's a family crowd . . . I can do a loose show and they'll stay with me. Vegas is something else . . . the people are intimidated. They've paid to have a good time . . . the prices are so high. . . . I do a tighter show. I don't digress as much. It's like driving a car. Sometimes you make all the lights, sometimes you go bumper-to-bumper, but you still get there."

But in the eighties, Vegas wasn't the attraction it once was. By attrition, there were fewer fans for old-fashioned acts like Wayne Newton or Engelbert Humperdinck; more people were going to rock concerts or simply staying home. The co-owner of the Aladdin Hotel, John Jenkins, sulked, "which of these lousy monkeys is worth $300,000 a week?"

Cosby, playing the Vegas Hilton at the time, was furious. But he answered "the terrible slur" with his brand of honesty, dignity, and self-respect. "I'm proud of my drawing record. It's up there with the best of them. I would never ask for more than I'm worth, but it's not fair to get less." With cool logic, he pointed out that it was Vegas club owners who ballooned star salaries in bidding wars, and it was their problem in failing to understand the public's point of view on entertainment value.

Often Cosby declined concert dates in favor of appearing at schools. As he told a writer from *Essence*, "In many of the lower economic areas, people constantly say that the children have no positive images. So they ask entertainers to come out and give speeches." He found that the kids were not interested in hearing Cosby lecture on staying in school or staying off drugs. They wanted to know how many cars he had and how big his house was. Bill would tell the kids that they had their own positive images to look for: "Look at your mother . . . see how she has to get up and do your clothing, do your food, give you money so that you can have something for lunch. Then she goes out and works and comes home to fix your dinner. What kind of image is that?" He felt it was important for kids to understand their parents a little more, be more aware of what it takes to raise a child.

At the Cosby home, he maintained a firm, loving hand. Sometimes the technique was a threat, sometimes just a logical discussion. As his monologues describe, sometimes nothing worked. But often, all that was needed was a little more communication and attention between parent and child.

Being on the road was tough. When Cos took his kids with him, sometimes even Bill the Model Parent couldn't control them at all times. Like the time his son caused a commotion at a hotel:

"Ennis—I don't know what got into him—but he was bored and he went out on the roof of the hotel, and he just wanted to see what would happen to Coca-Cola bottles . . . that were full . . . and the security guards came up and Coca-Cola was all over the place and they said, 'There's a little boy up there throwing bombs at the people.' And I didn't know it was my child. After that I had to keep him with me, and talk to him."

All the Cosby kids turned out well. Erika Cosby, at age eighteen, turned out exceptionally well. She posed for fashion photos in the June 1983 issue of *Harper's Bazaar*. "Even though there was so little time," she reflected, "we feel very close to our dad. There's a special bond among us. You know, fathers just have a way of putting everything together."

Late in the year, Cosby teamed up with Sammy Davis, Jr., to create a blockbuster show that he figured even the slightly diminished Vegas crowd couldn't ignore. And he was right. The team of Sammy and Cos was hot stuff in the hot town. As Sammy recalled, "the rapport was positive between us, no upmanship, no 'how many laughs is he getting. . . .' "

Sammy was drinking heavily at the time, unable to figure out why he was feeling so sluggish. One night Cosby had enough.

"What the fuck is wrong with you?" he asked Sammy.

"Age, babe," the little singer replied.

"You're drinking all the time now," Cosby warned. "Whatever you're doing . . . don't end like this."

The serious, concerned look on Cosby's face touched Sammy. He would eventually get a check-up and discover that liver damage was behind the sluggishness, pain, and bloating that was giving him so much trouble off-stage.

On stage, the duo decided to continue their triumph and take the show to Broadway—the only facet of show business Cosby had not tried before. Sammy insisted that Broadway would be a fantastic experience.

Talking about *Sammy and Cos,* Broadway's two-man show, Cosby told Johnny Carson, "We went to Broadway and bombed. We had about seventeen people sitting there, man."

"How do you explain that?" Carson asked.

"Well, it was Sammy's fault," Cos deadpanned. "he wasn't drawin' at all. My people were there."

"Maybe," Carson began apologetically, "they just weren't used to seeing two performers on a legitimate stage."

"Maybe," Cos answered, "they just weren't interested!"

Actually fans were interested, but they wanted to pay five bucks, not fifty. And they were getting what they wanted, thanks to a new phenomenon called the "live in-concert" movie. Richard Pryor had been incredibly successful filming his stage act so everybody could see it, and cheaply. In the same way that rock videos brought the music industry out of the doldrums, these performance movies jump-started demand for stand-up comics.

Up until Pryor, stand-up stars were confined to seven minutes on a variety show. TV specials or movies of a solo show were rarely done— and rarely successful. Now movie producers began to see dollar signs. And the new cable TV market started to sign up Eddie Murphy, Buddy Hackett, George Burns, and Robin Williams for solo shows. The ratings were high, videocassette versions sold well, and suddenly stand-up stars were earning big bucks. Robin Williams, for example, received $25,000 for his first special in 1978. In 1983, his price went to $750,000.

If all these comics could do it, like Richard Pryor and Eddie Murphy, why not the original . . . Bill Cosby himself?

With the national release of his performance film, *Bill Cosby Himself*, Cos emerged from what the public considered "semi-retirement." In a loose show that Cos also directed, the comedian covered some familiar territory, offering his brilliant "Dentist" routine, and some other material from his *My Father Confused Me* album—from a hysterical dissection of parental threats to his father's whimsical way of letting out gas: "Come here and pull my finger."

Cos was up to date with some satire on cocaine: "I asked a guy, 'What is it about cocaine that makes it so wonderful?'"

"'Well, it intensifies your personality.'"

"I said, 'Yes, but what if you're an asshole?'"

Cosby's brilliance at pantomime was evident in his routine about drunks walking, and happy babies wriggling, and the bizarre squinting and staring doctors do while they view a woman in the stirrups about to give birth. His genius with sound was highlighted in his dentist bit: He imitated the unique cadence of a dribbly patient with Novocained lips, the sound of drills, and the various gurgles and gasps of an open-mouthed victim of modern dentistry.

Most of the show was about becoming a parent. It started when Cosby saw his first child: "They washed it off and it wasn't getting any better. . . . I said to the doctor, 'Can you put this back? It's not done yet.'"

Then came a discussion of parenthood, including a report on a nighttime three-child brawl over flipping towels and sudsing faces in the shower. "Parents are not interested in justice," he concluded. "They want quiet." Quiet from kids' screaming and crying and acting "brain-damaged" and answering every question with "I don't know."

The movie was generally greeted with enthusiasm. "I know it's hard to keep pushing yourself into different areas," Cos admitted, "but you have to if you want to be around in a few years. In this business, if you stand still, you disappear."

Cos, who seemed on the verge of disappearance, who hadn't had a TV show of his own in eight years, was now about to try television again. He was about to make one of the most explosive comebacks in TV history. And this time, he surprised everybody—even himself.

Chapter Nineteen

Cosby was home watching TV. He rarely tuned in. He tried to get his kids to refrain, too, and to read more instead. "I decided to stay up and watch what was on cable. That night I saw three movies about rape. They all seemed designed to do the same thing—show women having their clothes torn off.... The next night I watched again. This time I heard people cursing for no reason other than to get a laugh.... Next I began to monitor the networks and the independent stations: women degraded, cops-and-robbers shows with the guns getting bigger and bigger."

He took it all in and said, "I'm tired of shows that consist of a car crash, a gunman, and a hooker talking to a black pimp." But had the public tired of it, too?

Over the past dozen years, Cosby had only appeared on TV in two shows; both were "family-oriented" and both were disasters. Even so, he decided to try a comeback. "We have about six television sets in our house, and it's less expensive for me to do a television series than it is for me to throw them all out."

He told writer Bill Davidson that he approached the networks offering "a detective show . . . I would solve crimes with my wits, as Columbo once did, and my girlfriend would be a strong woman with her own career." There would be "no guns, no violence, no car chases." The networks said, "No way."

But when Cos turned up on the "Tonight" show and performed some of his routines on family life, NBC's executive Brandon Tartikoff was intrigued.

Tartikoff's pet project was "Family Ties." He saw that there was a new generation out there: baby-boomers who were settling down, finding themselves in the unlikely position of raising a family—just as they'd seen on their favorite TV shows growing up, "The Donna Reed Show" and "Father Knows Best." Only now, those shows were gone.

Cosby's discussions about a new TV series centered on a situation comedy. He'd be out there doing humor about human beings—a family's love and understanding. Basically the tone of the show would not be that different from Cosby's first situation comedy, with its emphasis on low-key slice-of-life vignettes.

As teacher Chet Kincaid, he handled students' problems and his own imperfections and foibles. As obstetrician-gynecologist Heathcliff Huxtable, he would handle his five kids' problems, and share the chores with his wife, a practicing lawyer. But he'd be laid-back; as he put it, "a man in search of a perfect nap." And he'd have his hands full, being "not as in control as I pretend."

As the NBC execs watched Cosby's "Tonight" show appearances, they saw all the possibilities for entire sitcom shows that were glimmering in the observations Bill was making. Like: "One of the things you learn when you become a parent is the horrible thought and the reality that your children will be your children for the rest of your life! That's why there's death."

They could visualize his anecdotes fleshed out in loving detail. Like the time Cos described an incident at home with his eight-year-old daughter Evin: "I just finished eating and my stomach was swollen from the food that went in it. And she patted me on the stomach and said, 'Dad, you have a big stomach.' I tried to give her wisdom and so I said, 'Dad's stomach is full of food, that's why it looks this way.'

"She said, 'Yes, and you have a big nose because you don't pick it.' "

Cos had a glazed smile on his face as he added, "I don't like her anymore . . . but she's too cute to throw out."

As the idea developed, both NBC and ABC expressed interest. Cosby still had a tremendous "likability quotient," one of the latest network tools for gauging a star's popularity. Aside from his long résumé in show business, and his recent success with the solo movie,

Cos was still the popular pitchman on TV commercials—and for commercial TV, this was a big, big selling point. But the networks were still worried about a show based on "warm, gentle humor." Was Don Quixote Cosby again galloping toward a "quality/family" vision that was just a mirage? Would the millions who were supposed to be watching just disappear?

ABC backed off. NBC held on, but only wanted six episodes. Cos decided that in that case, he'd film his show in New York. "If I'm canceled," he said, "I'd like to be a little closer to home."

NBC wasn't even sure of Cosby's name: Heathcliff Huxtable. Heathcliff was okay, kind of funny. But Huxtable was uppity. They asked him to change the name to Brown.

Cosby discovered that some things never changed. His "game face" came on. He took a hard line. He wanted total control and would accept nothing less. He wanted at least thirteen weeks to get his show going, not six.

NBC was amused, but, just to make sure, they insisted Cosby do a short pilot show. Knowing the network mind, Cos decided to film a vignette of Dr. Huxtable talking to his daughters about sex. This got NBC's attention and slowly the concessions came. NBC even found a studio in Brooklyn for Cos.

Before long, the studio set was redone in Cosby's image. By now Cos had a permanent Big Apple residence as well as the Amherst and California homes, and was about to buy a house outside Philadelphia, too. Dr. Huxtable's home would be a replica of Cosby's townhouse. Duplicates of Cosby's Oriental rugs, antiques, Queen Anne chairs, and the rest were made, and the walls held paintings by a favorite artist of Bill's, Varnette Honeywood.

The Brooklyn studio itself had a down-to-earth feel to it. Located about an hour away from midtown Manhattan, the square brick building was smack in the middle of a quiet, suburban part of the borough. There were a few prewar apartment buildings nearby, but most of the streets were flat with rows of humble two-story houses, some peeled and worn and in the throes of neglect, others sporting fresh paint, new gates and fences, and other signs of urban renewal. Down the street from the studio on Avenue M and Fourteenth were a humble fruit stand, a hot bagel place, and a cluttered newsstand—nothing fancier for "The Cosby Show" staff, nor for the cast of "Another World," who also used the obscure Brooklyn facility.

Behind the scenes, Cosby got involved in endless story conferences, total rewrites, and dissections of each script for motivation and realism. Cosby's eldest daughter Erika was away at Princeton; the character corresponding to her, Sondra, would be away at college, too, for the first episodes. Each script was treated to an almost psychiatric appraisal. There was even a real psychiatrist on hand as an adviser, Harvard University's Dr. Alvin Poussaint.

The show had to be faithful to Cosby's attitudes toward life and comedy. He cautioned his racially mixed writing staff to stay away from sitcom cliché. "If this was 1964," he said, "my wife could do the cooking and I could be the guy on the sofa who just says, 'Let your mother handle this.' But today a lot of things have changed and I want the show to reflect those changes. A family where the father cooks, too, and pitches in with the kids, and where everyone has responsibilities."

Guiding the show along, Cosby once again seemed to shoulder most of the burdens. "I feel a great responsibility," he admitted, "to make it as good and as real as I can." Cosby's standards were so tough that three writers quit after the first six episodes. The hectic rewriting and clashing over focus and nuance caused head writer Earl Pomerantz to quit, too. "Bill challenges you to do your best," he said, "but I must say that I was awfully tired." Cosby's humor always came from richly defined characters and situations, not from one-liners and cheap sight gags. It was hard to turn out half hours with as much polish and charm as Cosby's ten-minute monologues.

"I said to the writers I don't want sitcom jokes. I don't want jokes about behinds or breasts or pimples or characters saying 'Oh my God' every other line. What we want to deal with is human behavior." Save the wisecracks for "Webster" and "Dif'rent Strokes," "Benson" and "Gimme a Break." Save the leering for John Ritter and the unbelievable corn for "Night Court."

When Cosby planned his family show about upper-middle-class blacks he met with more criticism than praise, more derisive pessimism than encouragement. While he worked on deadline, keeping a close watch on the show's characters, comedy, and quality, he had to do publicity—which meant meeting with doubting reporters.

As he was trying to keep an upbeat perspective and a focus on his goals, he was asked: Bill, why do a family show? Aren't you out of touch? How many whites will be on the show? Will you show the real black American family? What about social problems? What about white versus black? Isn't it a fairy tale to portray blacks as doctors and lawyers? How come you don't talk like George Jefferson or Fred Sanford—isn't that real black dialect? And why aren't you having the family live in the ghetto?

"All we're trying to show all America is that in a lot of ways behavior is the same all over," Cos would say, again and again. It was like twenty years before when he said, "Let's talk about the similarities, not the differences." But people weren't listening.

All they did was complain. And each reporter had a definite point of view about how blacks were in real life, and how they should be portrayed on TV, and Cosby was supposed to agree with every single one.

"Why do they want to deny me the pleasure of being an American and just enjoying life?" Bill asked. "Why must I make all the black social statements?"

Why not do a show his way, "a class way . . . something to be proud of . . . to show that we have the same kinds of wants and needs as other American families."

Looking at sitcoms in the 1980s, the cycle between so-called "blacks in whiteface" and "funky soul families" had spun way off course. New shows had smart blacks—who played maids and butlers to doltish whites. A bizarre fad had black children acting extraterrestrially superior to the white families that adopted them. The only holdover from the previous decade was "The Jeffersons," with its gleeful reverse racism and "honky this" and "honky that." And now Cosby was already getting heat for simply showing his conception of a normal, upper-middle-class black family. Not a fake family based on fairy tale—his family.

And nobody believed him. Twenty years and he was still fighting negativity, still defending his style of comedy. Two decades and too many questions. Cosby'd had enough.

At a press conference he told reporters that he would answer only to himself. As for the upper-middle-class black family bit: "My wife plays a lawyer," he enunciated, "and I'm a doctor. For those of you who have a problem with that . . . that's your problem."

Uh-oh. Boy, Bill's a little touchy, isn't he?

No, not touchy. Bill Cosby is arrogant!

"The Cosby Show" had barely been on the air for a month when a damaging cover story on Bill appeared in *TV Guide*. Its title was a sarcastic warning: WITNESS THE HUMORS OF BILL COSBY. Writer Kathleen Fury said her interview with Cos "was unpleasant. He made no attempt to be amiable and was by turns combative, defensive, challenging, threatening and hostile . . . one of the most arrogant celebrities I've ever met."

Was this just a case of the wrong writer interviewing the wrong star at the wrong time? Was it a misreading of a star's protective ego or a comedian's innate anger? Was it the pressure of Cosby's responsibility for his show?

If it was, Ms. Fury reasoned, then Cosby wasn't as intelligent as his Ph.D. claimed—he should've been smart enough to answer her questions politely. He'd refused to talk about his father when she asked him why she hadn't heard much about him lately. (One reason was that he was now deceased.) She said Cosby intimidated her by grousing about an old *TV Guide* article that mentioned how many cars he owned. She called him "clamlike" for his concern about privacy.

She pointed out that in public he was rude, too. When she was on the street with him, he was mobbed by cheering, devoted fans. She noted that after signing autographs over and over, "for some reason known only to him, he stopped."

Looking for other signs of Cosby arrogance, she complained: "While educated people talked Zero Population Growth, he and his wife had five children."

The piece caused an immediate stir, and the woman's quotes were gladly repeated by disgruntled newspapers that had failed to secure private interviews with busy Cosby. *Us* magazine couldn't get to Bill, so they quoted *TV Guide*. *Newsweek* admitted they, too, were turned down, so they also quoted *TV Guide*'s arrogance line.

In *Jet*, Cosby was quoted on the problem: "That makes me sound like a real bad guy, doesn't it? But I turned down requests because the magazines said they wouldn't put me on their covers. Is that arrogant? I see so many magazine covers featuring blood and violence and sex. I didn't think it was an unreasonable request, since our show deals with important family relationships."

Thirty million people seemed to think that, whatever his moods at times, Cosby was still a very funny fellow. Even as *TV Guide* hit the stands, Cosby's show hit number one, one of the biggest upsets in TV history.

Who could have predicted it? Not Cos.

On the "Tonight" show with guest host Joan Rivers, Cos said he was surprised by his success. He'd only hoped to post enough numbers to keep the show going. After all, the deck had been so stacked against him. Not only were sitcoms on the decline and smutty prime-time soap operas favored over family fare, Cos faced tough competition from "Magnum, P.I.," a powerhouse detective show with great appeal. Kids and fans of violence loved it; men identified with Tom Selleck and women loved the guy. But now Magnum was shot and Cos was king. In one eleven-week stretch, Cosby was number one nine times. Once in a while "Dynasty" or "Dallas" would nudge him out, but even blockbusters had a tough time. The Super Bowl beat him, but he beat the Academy Awards.

"Yeah, it feels good," he told Rivers. "It's like seeing a fat pitch comin' down the middle and you have a big bat!"

Johnny Carson joked about his success. "It's number one in the ratings," he said during one night's monologue. "Now I hear they're trying to get Prince and Tina Turner for a remake of 'Ozzie and Harriet.' "

The critics now began to side with Cosby. *People* called the show "revolutionary" while decrying "The Jeffersons" as "an obnoxious parody of white upward mobility." *Newsday* also compared the two, saying, "The Jeffersons are rich. But they are absurdly nouveau riche. The Dr. Cosby family . . . are upper middle. And they belong there. This is a real breakthrough." The *New York Times* enthused: "Mr. Cosby, here at his very best, can take the ordinary and make it seem delightfully fresh."

Plaudits like that helped water down the occasional whine, like the one from the *Village Voice*. Though the paper championed gay causes constantly, they snickered that Dr. Huxtable, black gynecologist, was "going to awaken the well-buried racism of genteel America," because heterosexual America couldn't help but cringe at "the notion of black fingers messing with their womanhood's collective Down There."

With less of an ax to grind, *Mad Magazine* simply went after the show because . . . they went after every hit show. "The Cosby Show" became "The Clodsby Show," and Cliff Huxtable "Quippin Yockstable." Cos took a ribbing for his endless "Tonight" show appearances (he was shown reading a medical text on "Terminal Carsonoma"). Lampooning Cosby's ubiquitous TV commercials, *Mad* suggested that Dr. Yockstable's most pressing emergency call was not from a patient, but somebody from Coca-Cola. The show itself was lampooned for its cute-ness. There was a caricature of Cosby with little Keshia Knight Pul-liam. "Isn't that the most adorable living doll . . . Look at those incred-ibly cute facial expressions." Gag line: they were referring to Cosby, not Keshia.

But even *Mad* magazine had to throw in ethnic insults and take some cheap shots. The doctor's son is punched and develops "a white eye." Later he's made to say, "If we're black how come we're so well off? How come we act white . . . and think white?"

When he appeared live on yhe Phil Donahue show, Bill had been joking with the audience, taking time to explain his point of view on his production of a family show filled with gentle humor. It seemed that he was among friends and fans, not nitpicking TV critics and social commentators. Then members of the audience began to ask about blacks versus whites.

What about breaking the cycle of "all-white television"? What about "black girls running and hugging on white guys" and rock videos where black men are with white girls? Cosby's face clouded with anger. "I would like to right now stop with this program," he said. "I am not an authority on blackness. I didn't come on this program to discuss blackness. I came on this show to discuss human beings and let's get into that. . . . I don't want to spend the time when a black per-son shows up on a show talking about blackness and what you all have to do in order to make America better. When Bob Newhart comes on here let's have him talk about it. When whatever person comes on let's have them talk about it. Right now, why don't you see if I can be a h-u-m-a-n b-e-i-n-g."

The audience applauded.

Still, with all the negative remarks in the press, and the cries of "arrogance," some viewers had to wonder: "Is the Bill Cosby I see on 'The Cosby Show' the real Bill Cosby?"

"The character he's playing," Robert Culp told *Newsweek*, "is very close to the real Bill Cosby. He's taken off all the veils."

Okay, that's from a Cosby friend. How about someone who was once in business with Bill, and close to him, but no more? Ex-manager Roy Silver puts it this way: "Bill Cosby was and is intrinsically funny. If you sat in a car with him and drove from New York to Philadelphia, he'd have you in hysterics. In many ways he's really remarkable. He never drinks. He never did drugs. Married to the same wife, has five kids, well-spoken, articulate, sincere—my God—charismatic. What else could you want?"

Ernie Casale, Bill's athletic director at Temple, also expressed surprise when asked about the "arrogance" rap. Is the Cos we see on TV the real Cosby? "Oh, yes," he says, "that's Cosby. Once you get to know him, his actions are the same, you can tell. The things he says, the way he moves. People are seeing him. That's Cosby.

"I've never seen Bill as an arrogant person. I've seen him go out of his way to be nice to people all the time. I can't believe that. God, he'll do anything to please people when he's around us."

In an interview with *Rave* magazine, Bill described himself simply: "I like sports. I like to read. I'm not a loudmouth. I'm not instantly witty. But I'm pretty much what you see and have seen and heard. I don't have two dozen layers to me."

Bill visited Temple regularly, and Casale insisted that, even in private situations, without the spotlight, Cos was down to earth. He recalled that when he and Bill were at an airport in Houston, "a crowd gathered, and Bill and I sat there, and he just practically put on a show for these people. He didn't say, 'Let's get out of here' or anything like that. And I just thought it was so damn nice that he would do that. So I can't appreciate people saying he's arrogant. I've walked with him, I've seen him stop talking with me and go over and talk with some kids, up and down Broad Street. One day there was a kid in a wheelchair, and Bill went over and started pushing the wheelchair, asking him where he wanted to go. Now maybe you might say he did that because I was there, but I don't think so. That's Bill."

That was Bill, every week on TV. In showing life with the Huxtable family, he showed a great deal about his own real life reactions around the house, from cute to conservative, from confused to curmudgeonly to comical. The audience picked up on him so strongly that the show was actually getting bigger ratings when it went into reruns in the spring! Cosby's number-one rated show helped make NBC an overall ratings winner. "I want it known it was me who saved NBC!" Cos joked. Most insiders believed it was no joke at all.

Describing his vindication as an advocate of family TV, Cosby called his success "a major, major step, not just for the American people but for those who control what goes on the air. The truth is in the numbers, and this helps straighten out nonbelievers concerning what an American audience will watch."

Cosby brought many of his friends on the show in that first year, including Clarence Williams III, Lena Horne and Tony Orlando. Orlando's episode was supposed to be a spinoff for another series.

One of the most affecting episodes in the first season was the one that brought Sheldon Leonard back before the cameras. He played the hospital's administrator who gives Dr. Huxtable an award.

The speech to Dr. Huxtable was more a speech from Sheldon Leonard to Bill Cosby. He said he hired minorities "because they had talent." He said, "About twenty years ago I recruited a young doc named Heathcliff Huxtable. He was a diamond in the rough . . . but to prove how good my judgment is in people, he has turned out to be extraordinary . . . he brings to his patients a degree of empathy and compassion that is very hard to match."

Then a joke to knock the edge off: "His dedication to this hospital is so great that, whenever business in the maternity ward slowed down, his wife came in pregnant."

On many TV shows, once a script is done, that's it; no changes. But according to "The Cosby Show"'s head writer and co-executive producer, John Markus, the writers were "always changing things, trying to make them better and better." The actors read the lines, then the writers made changes, "adding and taking away." Lines were altered up to the final taping, even beyond. If Cos felt that during performance, another line might work better, he would go with the feeling.

While the highlight in most episodes was usually Cosby in some kind of solo moment of mime or monologue, the writers didn't leave the script blank and pencil in: "Bill does his thing." According to Markus, the writers worked hard to provide a few minutes of monologue material: "We would write the monologue and Bill would read it at the rehearsal. Sometimes he would pretty much toss it and ad-lib one. There was a healthy competitiveness between writer and star." In fact, it wasn't just the monologue or solo parts that would get tossed: "If Bill didn't think we did it right he'd throw the script out and we'd start again."

Bill kept firm control on the writing staff. He knew what he wanted for the show and what he didn't want. It grew out of his stand-up routines. Bill had long been working on bits from the father's stern viewpoint and on this sitcom, the father would certainly know best. John Markus recalled, "The underlying concept was that these kids are gonna ruin us because they're idiots."

Added to that was Bill's admonition, "No conflict. No jokes." What he meant was no artificial and corny sitcom plots and no scripts peppered with wisecrack insults. Markus remembers, "We were forced to write human behavior, and that was very difficult. We had to be careful about messages. If any message gets spoonfed to an audience they'll turn on you like crazy. You can't pull it off unless the actors are believable. Bill had a way of combining serious issues with humor. On the show it was never "our" kids who got into serious trouble, it would be *other* kids."

An example of that was the show in which Theo was caught with marijuana. The show gave Cos the opportunity to gruffly state his opposition to drugs "while you're in this house . . . after you leave this house . . . and when you're seventy-five and we're dead!" But the light touch was that it wasn't Theo's pot; a *friend* had stashed it in one of the kid's books. In this and many other episodes, the Cosby kids were thereby allowed to remain good role models and strong characters.

"The Cosby Show" went through a triple polishing process. First there were the rehearsals. On these long days, everyone worked hard, even the youngest Cosby kids. They had a schedule that included three hours of school a day. Then they had their rehearsing. Their average day began at ten in the morning and finished at six in the evening.

Their rehearsals mostly involved memorizing their lines and finding their "marks" (knowing where to move when the camera was following). They didn't do a lot of actual line-reading with Bill. According to one of the writers, Matt Williams, "Bill didn't like to rehearse a lot with kids. The more you rehearse the more they start *acting*. The kids were under rehearsed so they didn't know what Bill was going to do."

This helped the director get very authentic reactions, whether it was shock over a moment of very real-looking Cosby admonition, or smirks as Bill tempered a morality lesson with funny faces or a sudden ad-lib of comic logic. Matt Williams knew in writing scripts for the show, "words on paper just aren't enough. Bill would put topspin on what was written." There was no doubt that the scripts, as good as they were, would not have been "classic" if the lead was Flip Wilson or virtually anyone other than Cos.

There was double and then triple polishing when the show was taped *twice* on Thursday evenings.

Each half-hour episode took about two weeks to write, a week to rehearse, and four hours to film. Four cameras were used, all running at the same time. That allowed the director to pick from a wide variety of angles and edit the show while it was being taped. The best takes from the two shows were edited together for the one complete episode.

"The Cosby Show" was the hottest ticket in New York and both tapings played to a packed studio audience. The audience would file in about an hour before actual taping began. They were "warmed up" with the help of a stand-up comic hired for the occasion, and then generally were treated to one of the latest episodes yet to be aired. This would be followed by a question-answer session done by one of the writers, the producer, or Cosby himself.

One week it was John Markus answering the questions:

"Who's Dr. William H. Cosby, Jr.?"

"That's Bill!"

"I have a photo, can I get Bill to autograph it?"

"That's . . . tough . . . because of all the work we have to do. I'm afraid we don't have time."

"How many shows do you do a year?"

"We do twenty-five shows."

"Where is the house they use when they film Cliff coming home?"

"That was done on the East Side of Manhattan someplace. The Huxtables live in Brooklyn, but it could be anyplace in the boroughs."

During lulls in shooting, usually caused by a technical problem or two, Bill would sometimes amble over to the audience and continue the question-and-answer session.

"In that scene where you were eating scrambled eggs, was that real food?"

"We always use real food. When I was on 'I Spy,' there was a scene that called for me to eat some Japanese food. Now I *love* Japanese food, so I ate a lot of it. Then we had to do the scene over. I was already stuffed, but I had to continue eating until we got the scene right. I didn't feel too good later."

"Do you really drink Coke?"

"Yes!"

The audience was seated in front of a large stage that held three main sets. In the left corner was the bedroom. In the center, a spacious kitchen. And to the right, the complete Huxtable living room. Of course, when people climbed upstairs to the second-floor bedrooms, they had to stop. There *was* no upstairs. The hallway and the children's rooms were actually at stage right, almost out of sight of the studio audience.

When a scene took place in Theo's bedroom, audience members had to watch it on the television monitors that were hung from the ceiling. It was the best that could be done; the building had not been set up to be a theater, but as a honeycombed sound stage where individual scenes could be shot quickly and economically.

The cameras would slide across the floor from set to set. Each scene was usually written to be short, from two to five minutes, starting with a character entering the living room or kitchen, and finishing when the character left. Doing short sequences let the actors refresh themselves and restudy the script. There were no "idiot cards" around. The actors had to know their lines.

Of course, even after a week's rehearsal, sometimes a line would be a problem. Most every week there was a good outtake or two. When the show began, six-year-old Keshia had the most problems. When she delivered a cute line she sometimes couldn't help but smile along with the audience, giggling when they laughed.

When she got an attack of the giggles, Cos was very much in character. He'd grab hold of her and pretend to throttle her, telling the audience in mock-exasperation, "We're going to lose a kid after this shooting, so you all explain to your neighbors why the kid died!"

In a scene between Bill and Malcolm Jamal Warner, an alarm clock was supposed to go off, waking the boy up. Bill hovered at his son's bedside, waiting for the alarm clock to buzz. He smiled. He waited. His smile got sillier and sillier, stretching broadly across his face. Finally he broke up and said, "Let's start again. The clock's broken on the first take!"

When the audience was a part of a flub like that, the laughter would be even louder when the scene finally was done right. Viewers at home might have thought the audience was responding to prompting lights on the set, or applause signs, or that the laughter had been added via some kind of canned soundtrack. But the laughs were genuine. In one scene, Malcolm was supposed to glide past Cosby, but instead bumped into a chair and stumbled. When he did it over again and managed to bypass the chair, there was some appreciative laughter that the home audience could not have understood.

Sometimes the laughter continued well after the scene was shot, with Bill ad-libbing nonsense just for the crew and the audience. After a breakfast sequence, Cos and the crew were about to shift to the living room set. Suddenly, Cos rushed back, swooped down and swiped a bowl of cereal off the breakfast table. His eyes went large, then he grinned impishly and started eating big spoonfuls of cereal, guarding the bowl and trotting far away from the giggling cast members, and little Keshia, who was trying to grab her bowl back.

With the short taping sequences interrupted by changes of costume, technical checks, and changing camera angles, the cast would often sit around in the living room quietly reading their scripts over, looking just like a family sharing the Sunday paper. They'd go over particular points together, sometimes breaking up over some spontaneous gag.

With time to kill, Cos would often wander around the set, very much the informal host, sharing a word or two with a crew member or asking about a technical point. Most of the time he was neither conspicuously "on" trying to force laughter, nor the other extreme, grimly "off" and bored. He was as casual as any worker in an average office, talking to co-workers, taking an interest in all phases of the work but not letting himself get too wound up. He was not one to constantly interject advice and opinion. He let his staff do the work they were trained to do.

While waiting for a scene to be set, Bill would sometimes walk past the lights and pause in the darkness near the first row of the studio audience. "It's nice and cool back here," he'd explain. Then he'd move back before the cameras.

There was no way of knowing when the irrepressible gremlin in Cos would slip out. Preparing for a scene in the bedroom, the technicians killed the hot, bright lights in the kitchen set and the living room set. When Cosby came back from a costume change in the make-up room backstage, he entered the dark stage.

He began to stumble through the living room in his long nightgown calling out, "I can't see back here!" Then he began to howl like a Halloween ghost, moving slowly through the eerie empty set, moving toward the brightly lit bedroom bellowing "Whoooo aah-woo" in a deep, low, funereal voice.

The audience began to giggle as the somnambulist spirit lumbered through the darkness of the living room and kitchen sets. But once he got into the bedroom, abruptly the ghostly siren went off and Cos became all business, taking his place near the bed and waiting for his cue.

Dr. Cosby always seemed to know when enough was enough. He disciplined himself and the rest of the cast. When the breakups began to get out of hand, he'd mock-glower and say, "Come on, we want to get home before Saturday!" Sometimes he'd shout an all-business "Let's get it together" to bring everyone back to professional reality.

In the first season especially, the young cast members picked up a great deal from Bill. It was "like learning from a master," Lisa Bonet said. She and the others would often come to Bill with a professional problem and even some personal ones.

Some of the kids in the cast routinely called him Dad, while others called him just plain Bill. The Huxtable kids all met their real-life Cosby counterparts in visits to Cosby's home in Amherst or his townhouse in Manhattan. The kids got along pretty well, although comparisons were sometimes inappropriate. For example, Cosby's son Ennis stood about six-four while Malcolm was five-six. When they played basketball together, it was no contest.

As it turned out, many of the traits assigned to the Huxtable clan would come directly from real-life experiences. Cosby's son Ennis was discovered to have dyslexia and trouble achieving high grades in school. This later became a key episode of "The Cosby Show."

Well into the first season, Malcolm said, "It's still coming to me that I'm working with *the* Bill Cosby, the same Bill Cosby who has been around for twenty years. He has a nice personality. He's funny. He acts like a parent and a friend."

The two went on a "father-and-son" trip to Atlantic City, where Malcolm saw Bill perform his stand-up show. Bill and Malcolm had a lot in common, especially the way they behaved in public school. Malcolm was now being tutored, but he admitted that if he were in a classroom situation, he'd be like Bill at that age: "I'd probably be one of the students the teacher would ask to be quiet."

Many of the shows during the first season were about the son, Theo

Huxtable, and clearly based on Cosby's childhood and his experiences with Ennis. The first truly memorable moment on "The Cosby Show" was a father-and son-confrontation. Theo's grades were going down and he was ready to chuck school and go out and become an ordinary worker. "Maybe I was meant to be a regular person," he told Dr. Huxtable. "Maybe you should accept me and love me as I am because I'm your son."

It was a touching moment. A sincere moment.

"Theo," Dr. Huxtable said, with all the earnestness he could muster, "that's the dumbest thing I've ever heard in my whole life!"

The audience roared. And Bill went on to deliver a funny lecture on the importance of money and a job with a future. The episode sent a message out. "The Cosby Show" would indeed be honest, true, and sentimental—but it was also going to hard-headed and realistic and funny.

In another episode, Theo was behaving like other yuppie-influenced kids. He went out and bought a ninety-five-dollar "status" shirt. It took a half hour for him to learn that status comes from inside.

The real-life Cosby kids had to learn the same lessons, and it was sometimes difficult for them. After all, they'd see Bill pick up car number fifteen, or go out to an auction to buy a $125,000 antique chair or a $95,000 set of Tiffany flatware. But Cos taught them what value is all about, in both material things and intangibles. They knew that they'd inherit a lot of money when they grew up (Cosby's yearly income back then was estimated at between seven and ten million dollars) but Cos remained firm: they wouldn't get it if they didn't complete their education.

In one episode, Cos intimated that it wouldn't take an A average to get all that gravy. When Theo got a B-plus on a paper and worried that it wasn't good enough, his father said, "An A is just a grade. The important thing is that you applied yourself."

In other shows, Bill was able to work in some classic moments from his stand-up act. It must have been a kick for Cos to tell his TV son the same thing he said his Dad had told him years ago: "I'm your father. I brought you into this world, I'll take you out of it!"

Occasionally a writer would ask for a little background on Bill's real-life Dad. Bill didn't dwell on the painful recollections. Instead he recalled the good things. Although his father wasn't around much, when he was, he'd often take little Cos for a special treat, like a Duke Ellington concert. It was touching to realize that Bill's father had wanted to be a pharmacist but couldn't afford to continue his studies. Now, here was Cosby playing Dr. Huxtable.

Sometimes a critic would complain that the "average black family" couldn't be dining on fine foods and enjoying the lifestyle of the Huxtable clan, implying that Cosby himself must've come from an unusually privileged household. Yeah, Bill admitted, sometimes his family dined well: "We had filet, lobster thermidor, great stuff." That was because his mom was able to bring home table scraps from the rich people she worked for. It was nice for Bill and his brothers, "but sometimes we had to cut around the bite marks."

From the beginning episodes of the show involved questions of parental trust and communication. In the episode when Theo was accused of smoking marijuana, and denied it, Dr. Huxtable said, "You are some things, some good, some bad, but you are not a liar."

Sometimes there was a reversal. Instead of art imitating life and Cosby episodes being drawn from real experiences, things on the show had an impact on Bill's actual family. In one script Sondra was getting set for a sojourn to Paris. This was especially exciting to . . . Erika Cosby. "Hey Dad," she said, "how about sending your *real* daughter to France?" Cos thought about it for a moment and . . . *voilà*. The entire Cosby clan was set for a two-week summer vacation in Europe.

Of course, household communication could get comically strained at times. The dialogue in the Huxtable household was always realistically similar to real life. Theo to his father:

"Dad, Denise is hogging the bathroom."

"Use the one downstairs."

"But that's the guest bathroom."

"Well, pretend you don't live here!"

Cosby prided himself on slice-of-life humor that seemed to come right out of anyone's home. Like the little vignette when Heathcliff quizzes daughter Vanessa, and his wife decides to join in as well.

Cliff: "Did you practice the clarinet?"

Vanessa (feigning innocence): "You didn't make me."

Clair: Will you tell your daughter how important this is?

Cliff (to Clair): "You planning on leaving town right away? The girl is standing right there! *You* tell her!"

The writers quickly began to catch on to the Cosby style. The early episodes of the show had only a few weak moments of sitcom-style unbelievability. Like the episode in which an Oriental husband, after seeing a film on the birth of a baby, fainted dead away every time Dr. Huxtable mentioned "labor pains" or "the film." More often the warm, natural humor flowed, as Cliff tried to guess his birthday surprise, or his kids tried to find ways of wheedling a secret out of him. Some "slice of life" episodes had little payoff, just the satisfaction of seeing a family handle life's little problems. Both fathers and daughters could relate to Dr. Huxtable's gentle but stinging comments in trying to keep some control in the house. Before Denise goes out on a date, the doctor grumbles, "How ugly is he? Who's his parole officer?" And after checking out his daughter's tight pants: "No! Blood can't get up to your head!"

Bill didn't want the scripts to get too explicit about dating problems or to let the camera linger too long in the Huxtable bedroom. While there wasn't much sex on "The Cosby Show," he said, "Hopefully, you know, there's some sex behind the scenes! But unlike the night-time soaps, the camera doesn't go into the bedroom and under the sheets. But hey, I don't want to sound like a prude. I'm not against that. Not all shows should be like ours. I just happen to be a little old and perhaps a bit too pudgy to be doing hot and heavy love scenes!"

Now that he was in his late forties, Cosby's face seemed to be more mobile and expressive than ever before, and some mild scenes around the dinner table or living room sofa were livened up by brow-furrowing scowls, worry-eyed perplexed looks, and blameless grins. Many a scene was saved by a reaction shot from Cosby, especially when dealing with his youngest kids.

"He's not only a great comedian," Phylicia Rashad (Dr. Huxtable's wife, Clair, on the show) said, "he's a great actor."

The relationship between Clair and Cliff Huxtable mirrored Cosby's life with Camille. One episode, about the couple trying to get away from their kids for the weekend, echoed the real-life joy Bill and Camille had when they spent a rare Easter by themselves.

"Oh, that was juicy," Bill said at the time. "That's a fine Easter, man. Or Passover or whatever it was. We were havin' a ball that weekend. It was quiet. We just stood in the room and said, 'Listen to this. This is the sound of our children not being here.'"

On television, Clair Huxtable portrayed an independent woman. Camille is the same way. Cosby encouraged her to go to graduate school, and even flying school. Cos says, "I know my wife, and I get in the plane with her, but . . . she's sort of bossy . . . in the plane, you know, and she uses that to get me to do things that I would say no to. So it isn't fair the way she uses that plane. She'll get me up there and if there's a little turbulence she'll say, 'I'm the only one who knows what's going on up here and there's something I'd like to talk to you about.' And she really makes me believe she really doesn't mind going down in this thing."

Camille encouraged Bill during the tough phases of "The Cosby Show" 's development and Cos has always been quick to praise her: "That lady has stood so solidly with me all these years. Whenever the time comes when one of us needs the other's support, that support is there, and it's real because we love each other. And we'll say, 'Thanks a lot for that. I really needed it.' I don't come home at night expecting Camille to be there to rub my back, but I do try to be there to rub hers whenever she needs it. These are the things that make our marriage work."

Phylicia Rashad had many of Camille's attributes. In the first years of the show, she had not yet married Ahmad Rashad, so she was billed as Phylicia Ayers-Allen. She was a single mother, working hard to raise her young son properly. Like Camille, she was often described as cool, classy, and well-educated. Coincidentally, both women have fathers who are in the medical profession. Phylicia's mother is Vivian Ayers, a writer who was nominated for a Pulitzer Prizer as the author of *Spice of Dawns*. One reason the show worked in its portrayal of upper-middle-class blacks was because quite a few of the show's stars were just that.

The first year, Phylicia remarked, "It's wonderful working with Bill because he's always looking out for everyone." She quickly learned something else: "He's the most intelligent silly person I've ever met."

She could point to any number of incidents over the years that illustrated what she meant. One was the day young Keshia had to do a leap into the air. The little girl was terrified. When she finally summoned the courage to try the jump, she tumbled over and smacked her head against the floor.

People ran forward as the girl began to cry, but it was wise Cos who got her attention. When he saw that she was all right, he flung himself down on the floor and pretended that he, too, had gotten hurt just by deliberately falling down. His tantrum of woeful cries got the girl giggling gleefully.

There were moments like that on the show itself, and everyone who watches it, rerun after rerun, has their favorites. For Phylicia, the comedy still rings true because "it's based on human behavior, not one-liners. There's so much love in it, so much truth in it; there's so much heart in the writing, directing, and the performance. It seems people enjoy seeing the best part of themselves in it."

Camille would usually be at the tapings. The studio audience often recognized her, but that was easy. Who else would Cos suddenly walk off the stage to talk to and kiss? While she was not one for the spotlight, she did appear, indirectly, in front of a national audience. When Bill hosted a special on the reopening of the Apollo Theater in the spring of 1985, he wore a photo T-shirt with a picture of her on it and the words CAMILLE'S HUSBAND.

Every day he wears a bracelet with those very same words on it. Sometimes on the show it can be spotted, glinting on his right wrist.

"The Cosby Show" received eight Emmy nominations for the first season. Of course, Bill wasn't up for one. Along with another television veteran, the late Michael Landon, he had deliberately removed himself from the competition, feeling it was time to let someone else benefit from the honor. Phylicia Rashad was nominated for best actress in a comedy series. Coincidentally, her sister, Debbie Allen, was nominated for best actress in a dramatic series for her work in "Fame."

It didn't take long for all three networks to try for Emmy-winning sitcoms using the Cosby formula. One of the first shows that tried to duplicate "The Cosby Show" was "Charlie and Company," starring Flip Wilson. Out of the limelight even longer than Cosby had been, Wilson figured his sitcom was going to be even better. He knocked Cosby: "Cosby's family is bourgeois; we're an average black family. . . . I don't think Cosby has as much depth as I do."

Wilson was right. His show had enough depth to plummet to the ratings cellar. Another "warm, family-oriented" sitcom began a more successful run. This was "Growing Pains," but painful when compared to "The Cosby Show." *Newsweek* called it "icky." Each year it seemed that a few new shows tried to climb on the "wholesome" bandwagon. Cosby didn't mind. He welcomed more quality television. He was saddened when a show that offered quality and good taste (he specifically mentioned "Frank's Place") was taken off the air.

There was no question about the status of "The Cosby Show." It was now number one in the ratings, having been one of the few shows in television history to work its way up to the top spot in its very first season.

The second season began early for the Cosby staff. While television viewers would not see the new shows until late September and even October, taping began in the heat of the New York summer, on August 9. Beginning the second season, Cosby stepped out between scenes to address the audience.

"Ladies and gentlemen," he began slowly and soberly, "on behalf of the cast, the crew, the producers, the director, the assistant, we are very happy to be back.

"The second season means an awful lot to us, especially because of where we are in the ratings. We didn't know where we would be last year. However, this does not give us any particular, uh, rest spot. We have to continue to give you the quality you ask for."

The audience was hushed by the dead seriousness of Cosby's measured speech. "We certainly hope *this* particular show will give you a feeling that 'The Cosby Show' is going to be as good, perhaps even better than last year. This episode of course is about the first day of school. I'm sure all of you can identify with these children having a problem getting out of bed. So if anyone asks about 'The Cosby Show' this year, you just tell 'em we're working even harder to make this the kind of program that you can sit and watch with your children, with your parents, and enjoy."

The slow cadence, the earnest expression on Bill's face did not change. "And then before you go to bed," he continued, "have a good discussion about how much you love each other, and understand and get along with each other . . . regardless of the fact that they're your parents or your children!" The audience began to laugh and giggle.

"You can get a good discussion from both sides. Thank you very much. We will try and keep you entertained during the breaks."

Cosby turned around and noticed Tempestt Bledsoe entering the living room set, dressed in a conspicuously fancy dress. Cos chuckled and said, "This year you will notice our own actress here, Tempestt Bledsoe, carrying on with some fashion!"

The girl smiled as the audience laughed. Cos, his voice low in conspiratorial glee, added, "And this year we have something new with Vanessa, her character. The breast fairies have arrived! And she doesn't know where she's going or what she's doing. She just knows she has certain feelings about her body and herself, and this will be a good year. . . ."

Someone called for Bill, the cameras got ready, and the audience burst into applause before hushing themselves in anticipation of the funny scenes to follow.

And they followed for another season, and another, and another.

Lisa Bonet had returned to the show for the second season wearing an entirely new hairstyle. She'd cut it short over the summer, slim on the sides and bushy over the forehead. This had *not* been cleared by NBC, and could have been a major disaster. Television viewers like their favorites to look familiar every week, almost to the point where they wear a "uniform" in every episode. "He's teasing me," Lisa said of Cos, "But his wife has short hair, so I think he likes it."

The crew began to like it a lot less when Lisa demonstrated further "star" behavior. Things seemed to be restored to normal when she was "spun off" into her own show, "A Different World." It was there that she discovered the full consequences of responsibility, and of being in the spotlight. She would soon develop an even greater respect for Bill, and the way he had been able to handle all the pressures.

While Lisa became a favorite of the tabloids, who followed her around to take pictures of her latest partying outfits and to wonder what outrageous things she was planning for her career, "The Cosby Show" continued onward, Bill keeping the show at number one in the ratings, and keeping himself at number one of the "TVQ" survey that rated stars in terms of "familiarity and likability."

In fact, Bill had the highest ratings in the twenty years of the survey, far outdistancing Clint Eastwood, Alan Alda, Tom Selleck, and Carol Burnett. His appeal, of course, helped him land commercials for everything from Jell-O to Kodak. But it also helped "The Cosby Show" charge more for commercials than any other show on the air.

When the show first arrived, NBC was charging $110,000 for a thirty-second spot. By the second season, the price went up to $200,000 (surpassing "60 Minutes," which was charging $190,000). By the 1990s, "The Cosby Show" was costing sponsors $400,000 for thirty seconds. In the first year, the cost to NBC to produce an *entire episode* was $450,000.

Cos continued to get raves, even from such unlikely personalities as Howard Cosell. When Cosell decided to leave Monday Night Football, he considered only one man worthy of taking his place: "That's right, Bill Cosby! He'd really shake things up, make people notice . . . he knows what he's talking about. He's a brilliant communicator, witty, knowledgeable, and vastly entertaining!"

But Bill wanted to stay with his own show, and to tackle each new year of sitcom situations and moments of education and learning. He worked closely with his friend and advisor, psychiatrist Dr. Alvin Poussaint, now the associate dean of student affairs at Harvard Medical School. Together they planned out ways of incorporating educational facts into an entertainment show.

By phone from Massachusetts, Dr. Poussaint discussed how his partnership with Bill worked. Often, as it was with this interview, the discussion was by phone: "Sometimes the writers called me to ask a specific question. Bill had a rule. Even though it's comedy, your information must be correct. So the writers can't say that Rudy has a temperature of 112, just to get a laugh. You see? You have to keep it within reality. You would say 101. Not 105. A lot of kids at that point would have convulsions. There's the risk some parents would watch the show and think they could let it go till it reached that level. You can't mislead or misdirect people."

There was a certain amount of glamour to Dr. Poussaint's job, but it was only as glamorous as any other job in medicine. "I was a consultant," he said evenly, "it's like medicine. They can listen to you and not do what you want." It was up to the writers to decide if a broken toe for Clair sounded funnier than a twisted ankle, but when it came to figuring out how the injury occurred, "or if it's a question of medical fact, they listened. If someone was sick and they gave him medicine, I checked the script to make sure it was the correct dosage." Scenes in operating rooms or hospitals, or even light discussion between Dr. Huxtable and his son-in-law Elvin in med school all had to be carefully checked for accuracy.

Most important were the almost subliminal attempts at educating viewers by example. "The show always gave a lot of information about nutrition," Dr. Poussaint said. "For example, Cliff was supposed to be on a low-fat, low-salt diet because of his age and trying to avoid heart disease. So there was a better chance of seeing chicken on the dinner table than steak. See? So all those things were part of it."

Over the years Dr. Cliff Huxtable had to offer patients advice on pregnancy and childbirth. He had to be able to explain complex medical problems quickly and, in most cases, with a little touch of humor. One of the best examples of that was the time little Rudy had the flu. "In the show he discussed how the bacteria got into her system and how the virus gave her a fever. That was a nice little lesson on infectious diseases. We discussed all of it, and I had to make sure that whatever he said, even humorously, was basically correct."

Cosby received an award from the American Medical Association for the positive way Dr. Huxtable was presented on television. Bill gave the honor to Dr. Poussaint, who arrived to give the acceptance speech.

For many viewers, "The Cosby Show" was not only a comedy tradition every week, it was an educational lesson in relationships, in how to deal with people, even in how to handle little medical emergencies around the house. Over the years the Huxtable family grew and changed and faced new problems and created new solutions. It had become such a tradition, viewers hoped it would never end.

Chapter Twenty

A fter the first edition of this book was published in 1986, Bill put out a book of his own. It wasn't an autobiography, it was *Fatherhood*, his first collection of comical essays and routines. While this biography of Bill was a Literary Guild selection and was serialized on the front pages of newspapers around the country, *Fatherhood* proved an even bigger hit, selling over two million copies.

When he promoted it on Phil Donahue's television show, Phil read some segments from *Fatherhood*. But then he wanted to know more about something he'd read in *this* book.

Phil and Bill were discussing God and morality. Cosby was finishing up his answer:

"I don't have to go to a human being and have them tell me what Jesus said or what God said. I've made many many mistakes in my life, and making many, many more, but I do believe there are times, and the best time is when your fellow human beings get a feeling from you and you get a feeling from them. Selfishness plays a large, large role in our lives and many times we do things to see if we can get away with it. The more power you have, the more you have to control yourself in terms of using and abusing people. And I think that there is a supreme being, but I also think it is our job to be as sensible as we can, and not as selfish. Think twice and then go on with what you believe in."

Phil nodded and asked, "Are you sorry that you punched Tommy Smothers in the face?"

Bill's eyebrows rose. He paused and finally answered, "There's no apology necessary, and I will not apologize to him for it. And I think Tommy understands me better now."

The audience giggled. Phil asked, "He knows why you punched him in the face?"

"He absolutely does, he's well aware of why it happened."

"But you won't tell us why?"

"No, it's none of your business."

"Can you talk to him? If you met him today you'd say hello?"

"I would *not* talk to him. There's no reason for me to talk to him."

"Where's this forgiveness from the Bible and all this good stuff?"

"Same place that I get when I don't hit him again! Once again, see, if I talked to Tommy, then I wouldn't be for real. What would I have to say to him if I don't like him? Now if Tommy made some changes, then that would be fine."

It seemed rather odd that both Bill and the Smothers Brothers, who had delighted young fans with so many albums of humor about childhood, were now involved in what had been a schoolyard-style fracas. No doubt most of the adults in Donahue's audience had grown up enjoying both mens' recreations of naive, childlike behavior. But Bill refused to be naive when it came to making up with Tommy.

Bill assumed his slowest and most deliberate professorial tone. He announced, "There's a difference between having *faith* and having *hope.* I don't have any *faith* in Tommy Smothers. I have *hope.*"

Tommy seemed to shrug off the "rivalry."

"Cosby and I had a running disagreement from just about the time we met each other," Tommy said. He didn't seem angry about it. He was just stating a fact. "He had this kind of arrogant attitude . . . I kind of razzed him; where was his position during the sixties? You saw no position from Cosby. And I would call him on it."

"Dick Gregory took a position," Dick Smothers pointed out.

Tommy nodded and added, "Cosby was quiet on civil rights issues, like Sammy Davis, Jr., as far as making a stand, and at the time I was very volatile and thought everybody should take a stand."

"But you know," Dick said, "everybody has a right to take a stand or not take a stand." He grinned as he said to Tommy, "But when you're really involved you get a little shrill."

Some veterans of the "Tonight" show recalled that when Bill was hosting, and Tommy and Dick were among the guests, Tommy made some on-air references to Cosby's "rude" attitude toward some of his guests. He'd told Bill that he didn't think he'd "handled it well." This rankled Bill considerably.

"But it was little things," Dick continued. "Tommy would get the better of Cos when we did "Tonight" shows together; not just ad-libs, but by playing off attitude and character. [Cosby throwing the punch] was just a misunderstanding, the wrong time and the wrong place." He turned to Tommy with a smile and said, "It was the culmination of about fifteen years of you getting on Cosby's case!"

"You're exactly right. I didn't know his show had been canceled that day. I'd seen it. I loved it. I said, 'Hey, congratulations on your show.' And he said, 'That's the last straw.' "

And then came the big surprise.

"Surprise? It was a sucker punch! It was a low-class . . ."

"Tommy!" Dick called out, just as if this were a comedy routine, "You're going a little too far!" Dick added, "A lot of people think he's a very kind and considerate person. It's just chemistry."

Tom said in all seriousness, "I have a great respect for Cosby." But he couldn't resist playfully starting up again. "I'd never let Cosby one-up us. We were on his show once and he wore those big boots, just to be taller!"

"That's enough!" Dick insisted. "He's gonna be president some day and we won't be invited to the Black House!"

While Bill was still considering himself the injured party, it was obvious that the brothers could look back on it with humor.

Less humorous was the quiet rivalry between Cos and Harry Belafonte, one-time film co-stars. Usually considered in the same breath in liberal discussions as "role models" for young blacks, in the nineties the two veteran black entertainers began clashing over who was really the better role model.

Belafonte was critical when Bill allowed "The Cosby Show" to be syndicated to South Africa. Bill felt it was important to show a positive, functional middle-class American black family to South Africans. He believed he was preserving the boycott against South Africa's apartheid policy in other ways—such as by not performing there in person. Bill also felt that South Africans would get it when he referred to his grandchildren on the show—named Winnie and Nelson. Still, Belafonte angered Cos by calling him "a major violator of the boycott."

The more serious part of the feud occurred when both expressed interest in making a film about Nelson Mandela. This was a complicated proposition, especially when there were rifts between Nelson and his wife, Winnie, and it was difficult to be sure if one or both needed to be consulted on any "official" project. Adding to the tangle, Winnie had been friendly with both Belafonte and Camille Cosby, evidently giving them both an "exclusive."

Harry called up Bill and tried to straighten the matter out. Cos didn't want to get in the middle of it. "My wife has the rights," he told Harry, "you have to deal with her." This irked Harry, especially since he and Camille hadn't gotten along that well, going back to the sixties.

"Look," Harry said, "it's a legal matter, and I have the rights. We have to work this out, and if we don't, we'll have to turn it over to our lawyers."

Cosby pondered that for a moment, and answered, "Well, call your best shot."

The feud eventually turned into a lawsuit and when it ended, it seemed that Belafonte had won. He announced that Sidney Poitier (who had directed Cos and Belafonte decades ago) would star as Mandela. But it seemed that the old ties with Poitier were just as shaky as the ones with Cosby. Poitier signed a deal with Showtime for a Mandela movie and once that happened, Belafonte's project collapsed.

Over the years, Cosby's usually managed to keep rifts with fellow performers from exploding into tabloid headlines. If anybody was going to read something about him, he hoped it would be something from one of his books.

As the years rolled by and "The Cosby Show" retained the number-one spot, Bill remained number one in the bookstores, too, turning out a series of best-selling titles. Rather than autobiography, each was a series of essays. He covered aging, marriage, childhood, whatever he wanted to talk about.

Bill writes books the way he creates his monologues. For monologues, he writes down ideas on a yellow legal pad: "I get an idea of about three sentences that I feel good about and I begin to write and

rewrite. I don't go to comedy clubs or try it out on friends and relatives. I put it on its feet by sliding some of it in at concerts after people have laughed for fifteen minutes. Each night I make notes and
rewrite. Some of what's added is from writing while in front of the
audience, and then I extend it the next time. You have to get as many
unfunny things out as possible. Finally there's a point where I say to
myself, 'There's no more I can put in.' Then it's ready."

For the books, some of these routines are then transferred to the
printed page with the help of his long-time ghost writer, Ralph
Schoenstein. The books also contain material that went from yellow
legal pad directly to typing paper; thoughtful or involved material that
Bill felt wouldn't be "funny, ha ha" on stage, but would raise a smile
when read: "written pieces that could not be performed but are interesting and funny thoughts."

Many critics praised Cosby's way with an anecdote, his ability to
be a storyteller both in concert and on the printed page. "My storytelling," Bill says, comes not only from a love of the printed words of
Mark Twain, but from "Samuel Russell Cosby, Sr., my paternal grandfather, and William, my father." Grandfather Sam not only told funny
stories, he was a funny character, even as an old, old man confined to a
wheelchair:

"My grandfather at age ninety-eight had a birthday party. My
Aunt Clara brought the cake out, with all the candles, and said blow
it out. They cut off both his legs, he had no teeth, shirt collar with a
little small neck in it, and he's sitting there, and she said, 'Blow the
candles out, Daddy.' And he went, 'They're out.' And they didn't go
out. And Aunt Clara said, 'Daddy, you're ninety-eight, how does it feel
to be ninety-eight?' And he said, 'It wasn't worth the wait.'

"As a kid I watched this man. He told stories. My father did, too,
but not to me, mostly to my mother. Between the two I learned how
to tell a story. I always loved comedy, on the radio before television. . . .
I listened to Jack Benny, I listened to Jimmy Durante, I listened to
Arthur Godfrey but only for the comedian . . . then television came,
The [Colgate] Comedy Hour. Then I fell in love with a man named
Buster Keaton. Odd that a storyteller would fall in love with a man
who does silent films, but Buster's work in storytelling was so won-
derful and funny, to this day he is my main hero. Did you ever see *Mad
Mad Mad Mad World*? Those two or three seconds that Buster does

with the car—no words, just body, and you understand and laugh and it's gone, and you fell on the floor."

In 1987 Bill published *Time Flies,* loaded with routines about aging. He wrote that he was no longer the athlete he once was. He was now "a quarter-miler whose son now says, 'Dad, I just can't run the quarter with you anymore unless I bring something to read.' "

In 1989 he released *Love and Marriage.* It gave some little glimpses into real life at the Cosby house. As it turned out, even Camille could get a bit tired of the ponderously pontificating Bill:

"The argument I dislike most is the one in which Camille just suddenly walks away from me and I forget my next line. When she returns, I can either vamp until I remember what I was talking about or I can start a new fight about her halftime break.

'That was really lovely to just walk out that way,' I once told her.

'I thought I'd so some shopping while you were trying to find your point,' she said."

From *Fatherhood* to *Childhood,* Cos had great success with books and his show remained number one. It was human nature, of course, to want even more success. He had the books and TV, but what about films? Unfortunately, Bill's films brought snickers, not laughter, from critics. Both *Leonard Part 6* and *Ghost Dad* were box office failures.

On a scale from one to four, the *New York Post* gave *Leonard Part 6* no stars and called it "silly, inane, sick, stupid, embarrassing" and then became downright critical. What could be made of a movie that somehow managed to combine an armored Porsche, ballet shoes, killer bees and lobsters, dishwasher detergent, hamburgers, hot dogs, and a ride on an ostrich? Why was Cos playing an ex-CIA agent now running a restaurant, who must battle a vegetarian murderess who raises killer rainbow trout? Why did Cos, usually such a wholesome character, play someone who had an affair with a nineteen-year-old while his own twenty-year-old daughter appeared in nude plays while sleeping with the show's sixty-six-year-old director? What was so funny about being pelted with foodstuffs? And why the "blatant, annoying plugs for Coca-Cola, which just happens to own Columbia Pictures?"

Cosby wasn't too surprised about the negative reviews. He had already realized that the movie was a bomb. *Post* reviewer V. A. Musetto duly noted, "Cosby, who also is listed as producer, refused to attend its lavish benefit premiere at the New York Hilton the other night. One gossip item even had Cosby offering Columbia $10 million in cash and $10 million in endorsement time if they would destroy the movie."

Columbia was going through a lot of problems when Cosby arrived to make *Leonard Part 6.* The head of the studio at the time was David Puttnam. He wouldn't be there long, but he was there long enough to, from Cosby's point of view, throw a few monkey wrenches into the proceedings.

"I learned a lot from *Leonard Part 6,*" Cosby told writer Bart Mills. "First of all, I learned I have to fight for Bill Cosby. If you buy Bill Cosby, then the only way you get the real Bill Cosby is with Bill Cosby doing it. You have to work with him, not against him."

For *Ghost Dad* Bill was reunited with his old friend and director, Sidney Poitier. Instead of a crazy spy script, the story was about family values. Cosby really thought that he had a winner and bragged about it on TV talk shows. He insisted that he had figured out what the problems were after doing *Leonard Part 6* and assured fans that they would enjoy themselves if they gave him one more chance and went to see *Ghost Dad.*

Ghost Dad was going to have some of the family charm of "The Cosby Show" but the movie magic and special effects of *Topper* and *Ghost,* with Cos playing a spirit coming back to earth to help his kids.

Roger Ebert reviewed it: *"Ghost Dad* is a desperately unfunny film, a strained, contrived construction that left me shaking my head. How does Bill Cosby, so capable on television, get himself into movie disaster zones like this one . . . how half-baked and lamebrained the screenplay is. . . . He overacts in the most painful and unconvincing way . . . was there nobody on the set to help him find the right note?"

The *New York Times* began, "There once was a time when Bill Cosby was a very funny man . . ." and the review didn't get better.

The *New York Post* said that at the movie theater, "high schoolers began booing and making rude comments at the screen before The Cos had run through his bag of tricks . . . Cosby has honed and perfected a kinder, gentler humor that at this point is almost a parody of itself. . . . Unfortunately, if the only black film role models today's kids have to choose between are Bill Cosby and Eddie Murphy, who can blame them for going with Murphy, who screws the system that screws people like him, and has fun doing it. Murphy, the antithesis of everything Cosby stands for, has broken boundaries of language and taste. Kids like that."

The feud between Murphy and Cosby had been going on for years. Murphy had always been quick to point out Richard Pryor as a big influence, lesser praise going to Cos. While Murphy had appreciated that Cosby maintained a great role model for most everyone, he couldn't resist working up a Cosby imitation that was less than flattering. In one comedy routine Murphy insisted that wet blanket Bill called him up to complain about obscenities in his act. In recreating the moment, his impression of Cosby was devastating.

In a June 1990 appearance on "Larry King Live," Cos finally answered back publicly: "In his act he says I chastised him for cursing, which is not true. I chastised him because I had heard from enough people as I followed him on the road that Eddie was telling audiences, whenever he got upset with them, how much money he made. I said that isn't the right thing to do."

Cosby's judgement proved correct. Murphy didn't know the right thing to do on stage and while his stand-up career began in spectacular fashion, after a while fans and critics got bored when they got cursing and posturing instead of more solid routines. Eddie Murphy would abandon stand-up for movies while he still had a reputation.

Eddie was just another stand-up without staying power. Meanwhile, despite all trends, Bill Cosby kept right on going. He continued to maintain a lucrative schedule of stand-up dates, never abandoning them despite his grueling TV schedule. While Johnny Carson was loudly applauded for putting together thirty years of the "Tonight" show, Bill Cosby quietly achieved a landmark in the history of stand-up. He became the only stand-up comedian to consistently play the top concert venues and produce comedy albums for thirty years.

At an appearance at the Las Vegas Hilton, Bill was delighted to learn that Muhammad Ali was in the audience. He asked for the house lights to be turned up so Ali could take a bow. When nothing happened, Cosby announced, "Nothing's more redundant than a black person standing up in the dark!"

Chapter Twenty-One

Into the nineties, many noticed that Bill was becoming much more vocal on racial issues. It seemed to start when his TV show was in the powerful number-one position. The first incident had come in the second season, when Cosby fought with NBC over an "Abolish Apartheid" sign on Theo's bedroom door. NBC objected. Cosby said, "There may be two sides to apartheid in Archie Bunker's house, but it's impossible that the Huxtables would be on any side but one." He added, "if they want the sign down, there will be no show."

Now, Cosby began speaking his mind on almost any issue. For decades, he'd rarely made a public declaration concerning politics or show business. He now seemed to have a public opinion on most anything. When Pee Wee Herman (Paul Reubens) was arrested in an X-rated Florida movie theater for doing what everyone else was doing in there (watching the film single-handed), Cosby immediately rallied to his defense.

"I'm a concerned citizen," Cos declared. "When I see injustice, prejudice, or anything dishonest or unfair, I get upset. I feel the need to speak out. If Paul's guilty, he'll be judged by the legal system, and pay his debt, but the media's blowing the thing out of proportion."

Cosby also came to the defense of seventy-year-old sportscaster, gambler, and oddsmaker Jimmy "The Greek" Snyder. Jimmy had theorized to a reporter why there were so many blacks in sports: "It all goes back to the Civil War when the slave owner would breed his big black to his big woman so that he would have a big black kid."

The outrage was instantaneous and Jimmy was tossed off the air. Black leaders cheered. The "politically correct" thing to do, for most every commentator, black or white, was to condemn Jimmy the Greek. But Bill Cosby had a different point of view and he would not remain silent about it. It became front-page news when he declared that Jimmy the Greek be forgiven.

"It's not that I think he's a wonderful guy," Bill said. "We don't hang out together, but these hangings that are going on don't make us better human beings. On the eve of celebrating Martin Luther King Day, we should be more forgiving."

Cosby added that firing Jimmy was just a way for the network to "get the heat off" quickly.

Cosby believed the "quick fix" was not going to change things, because it wasn't educating anyone. Jimmy the Greek's statement was uttered more out of ignorance than racism. But it was easier to fire him than to try to educate him (and those who secretly agreed with him) and explain why this theory that seemed so logical to him was so wrong.

Bill believed that education was the answer, and he put his money where his mouth was. He gave $20 million to Spelman College.

The amount was so staggering that the news was broadcast all over the world. But it was only one of many donations that Bill made to charity.

There was the $1.3 million that was divided between Fisk University, Florida A&M University, Howard University, and Shaw University. There was $325,000 to Central State University. In 1989 Cosby raised $100,000 via two concerts in Harrah's Tahoe so that the Red Cross could supply relief to earthquake victims in northern California.

He donated time for the causes that were important to him. He couldn't just "throw money" at the problems of the world, and he knew it. Eluding photographers and reporters when he had to, one of America's most famous men would suddenly disappear, turning up quietly at the children's ward of hospitals, giving them video tapes, autographed photos, and hope.

"The Cosby Show" continued to be a forum for Bill's views on education and family. It was also a place where professional respects were being paid.

Over the years, Cosby continued to show his loyalty and support to old friends. Cosby brought Robert Culp back as "Scott Kelly" (a reference to the characters on "I Spy"), suddenly Cliff's "oldest friend from the navy." The episode was nothing much. What seemed like a serious theme, Kelly's quadruple bypass surgery, was dismissed with a quick joke from Dr. Huxtable: "You shoulda told me. I could've done it for half price." It was just a slice-of-life episode mostly concerned with a slice of pizza, forbidden on Scott Kelly's diet, and Cliff Huxstable's too. They never did get to eat it (with potato chips mashed on top), due less to their own discipline than their scolding wives.

The episode was just a pleasant half hour, but it meant a lot more to Robert Culp. The same was true of many other shows. Sammy Davis, Jr., was in poor health when he made his memorable appearance on "The Cosby Show," and so was Danny Kaye, who managed one last effervescent moment for his fans. The great humor of jazz stars Dizzy Gillespie and Joe Williams was brought to a whole new audience through Bill's show. As he had done with his first sitcom, when Lillian Randolph, Moms Mabley, and Mantan Moreland got another chance in the spotlight, Cos made sure there were opportunities for performers who had been waiting a long time for a fresh chance.

Sometimes a fresh chance did no good. After leaving "The Cosby Show" for the spinoff "A Different World," Lisa Bonet made headlines for her love life, for her opinions, and for her nude scenes in a new movie. She developed a reputation for being difficult and after many a disaster chronicled in the tabloids, left "A Different World" and resurfaced on "The Cosby Show" in 1988. And then she was gone again, her departure wearily ascribed to "creative differences." Her marriage went under and her career cooled down almost to the point of hibernation.

Same fans couldn't understand how Lisa, "one of the family" on "The Cosby Show," could run into such troubles when there was that "perfect" father figure around for advice and support, Bill Cosby. But there was a limit to what Cos could do with someone who was not his daughter.

Then came another shock. There was a limit to what Cos could do *with* one of his own daughters. One of Bill's own children, his daughter Erinn, was making headlines. Rebellious and difficult, she had dismayed her father with her choice of boyfriends and with a partying lifestyle that led to excess and disgrace.

In 1989, after over two decades projecting the image of a fair and just father, a man able to lead a family through any crisis, Cosby had to painfully admit that he was having problems with errant daughter Erinn. She had to make some mistakes and find out for herself. One night, she did.

Erinn had met many celebrities in her time, but it was something special when she joined up with Mike Tyson's partying entourage at a nightclub. The music kept pounding and Mike began insisting, "Come back to my place."

Before too long, Erinn was in a limousine with Mike. They shut the door on the pulsating lights and the milling sidewalk throng that had gathered to get a glimpse of him. The city streets were still crowded with people, but as they drove away, Erinn saw the teeming city and its thousands of brightly lit apartment windows disappear into the dark, flat, bleak suburban landscape of New Jersey. As the city lights faded in the distance, with only a passing headlight to brighten the desolate gloom, Erinn realized it was getting past one in the morning, and maybe she had gone a little too far.

There were two maids on duty in the lonely Tyson mansion. The soft-spoken boxer casually began to show Erinn around the place. She walked into one room and heard a door lock behind her. She recalled:

"He just came at me. All I know is I was on the ground, struggling. He was groping me and I was on my stomach, and he had a hand over my mouth."

Erinn said that she struggled furiously to get loose. Tyson, 220 pounds of heavyweight muscle, couldn't quite get a grip on Erinn as the girl writhed and ducked to get away. She kept moving and kept screaming, until she heard someone knocking on the door.

It was one of the maids. According to Erinn, this interruption evidently was enough to stop Tyson.

"I was in shock," she said. "Everything happened so quickly. I wanted to get out of the house. . . . I told my parents."

Bill Cosby assessed the situation and decided the best plan for Erinn was to go into therapy, which she did. He also demanded that Tyson get therapy as well, for at least a year.

It only took two weeks before Erinn and Tyson met up again. It was in another nightclub. Erinn was out partying and Tyson was on the prowl. When he saw Cosby's daughter, his eyes narrowed. He moved forward, the crowd pulling out of his way on all sides.

He didn't have any apologies to make to her. He had one question. Why had she made him look bad to one of his idols, one of the men he admired most: Bill Cosby?

Nothing seemed able to stop Mike Tyson. Before long, he ended up in prison, convicted on a rape charge.

The only way to get Tyson under control was for him to do some time.

But for Erinn, that same logic applied. She was out of control and she needed to chill out. She did a stint in a drug rehabilitation center at Edgehill Hospital in Newport, Rhode Island.

When Cos got back to work on his TV show in September 1989, Erinn was ready to check out of the hospital. But she didn't check back in at the Cosby home. She was determined to go out on her own, and the tabloids caught up with her, embarrassing both father and daughter with their headlines.

"The problem isn't alcohol or drugs," Bill said. "It's behavioral. She's very stubborn. It's going to take her hitting rock bottom, where she's totally exhausted and at that point where she can't fight anymore. We're estranged."

Erinn's problems seemed to have gone from bad to worse. She admitted that at fourteen she first secretly took a drink. She moved on to drugs, and when she was nineteen, was spending $200 a day on cocaine.

With an out-of-control situation, Cosby was sounding like any anguished father, his anger rising above his frustration:

"She's never held down a job, never kept an apartment for more than six months. She uses her boyfriends. She wants the finer things but she can't stand anybody else's dirt."

Cosby declared: "We have four children—I mean five children. And the other four happen to be just fantastic people. Not only to us, but to themselves. They're enjoying the fact that education is important to them. They're out there learning, enjoying, and challenging themselves. One out of my five children has a problem, and that one is getting the most attention . . . we don't want any more publicity about her because all it does is sell publications for people who are really not interested in helping at all."

Erinn began to work at solving some of her problems. "Looking back," she said, "I can't believe how Dad managed to go on with his show every week, portraying America's favorite father" while suffering "the agony of having a daughter like me causing so much pain."

The tabloids had become an increasing nuisance for Cos. They were hunting for dirt on his family, on him personally, and if they couldn't find any, they could always alarm fans into buying newspapers by intimating that he was going to leave the show, or that he was suffering from some mystery ailment or other. One tabloid headlined "Brave Bill Cosby Fights to Save His Sight," and insisted "he has already lost most of the sight in one eye" to glaucoma. They headlined a quote from Bill which was actually taken out of context from one of his comedy routines: "At age fifty things are breaking down in my body." "The outlook for Cosby is not good," the paper moaned, adding, "Blacks do not respond to treatment as readily as whites."

The outlook for Cosby personally was actually much brighter than it was professionally. At the turn of the 1990s, the cycle that had embraced "family values" was coming to an end. The dream years of prosperity and the Reagan White House were gone, replaced by inflation, unemployment, and discontent. Skinhead racism and anti-white rap songs were in the headlines. The number-one show in America was not "The Cosby Show" anymore, with its image of hope and optimism. It was "Roseanne," a program of blue-collar reality fronted by a star who made headlines for a variety of selfish and uncouth indulgences.

She was joined by cynical sitcoms about dysfunctional families, scripts loaded with deliberately crude humor and hostility. "Married . . . with Children" was a new hit, and so was the cartoon show "The Simpsons," a fad sensation. With a fiendish sense of anti-establishment glee, the upstart Fox Network decided to move their big hit cartoon from Sunday nights to Thursday nights opposite the paragon of (once again) *old-fashioned* virtues, Bill Cosby.

Cosby found himself in the same position as an aging heavyweight champion. A knockout sensation once, after three or four years he was being accused of having grown complacent. After five or six years, he was aging, getting heavy around the middle, getting by on reputation and old tricks. And now? And now, a light-heavyweight was moving up to challenge him and the oddsmakers were figuring that he didn't have the skills and reflexes to hold on to his title.

Critics jumped on Cosby almost as they had done during the first season. They insisted "The Cosby Show" was unrealistic, and they welcomed the reality of sassy cartoon characters like Bart and Homer Simpson.

A few critics saw through all this. David Bianculli in the *New York*

Post wrote that "The Cosby Show" presented positive role models "not just for black families, but for all families. And that's what's so infuriating about the talk about 'The Cosby Show' not being realistic or representative or 'black' enough. Nobody ever accused Danny Thomas, in 'Make Room for Daddy' of not being representative of most Lebanese people. And did anyone ever complain about 'Designing Women' that most white women don't live that way?"

A pair of professors from the University of Massachusetts published "Enlightened Racism: Audiences, 'The Cosby Show,' and the Myth of the American Dream," declaring that the affluent Huxtable family was desensitizing white people to the real problems of blacks. Funding for the project had come from William Cosby, Ph.D.

Considering the ingratitude of the media, and the insult of their charges, Bill took "The Simpsons" challenge with remarkable good humor.

In the fall of 1990, he told interviewers that it was silly for a grown man to defend himself against a cartoon character. He vowed to continue his show, his way: "It just isn't in me to alter what I'm doing below my commitment to education and aiding better family understanding. On 'All in the Family,' Archie Bunker never learned, never apologized. The Huxtables learn, they apologize. And yet you hear the loud voices saying that these people are too perfect."

Bill was confident that the America that had embraced his show and applauded his family values in the eighties would not become disillusioned in the nineties. But critics were annoyed that "The Cosby Show" was cutesier than ever. With Keshia Knight-Pulliam too grown up, Raven-Symone joined the cast, becoming the new darling for wide-eyed Jell-O pudding takes and wise-beyond-her-years chirps. Critics put down Cosby's soft and cuddly show in favor of the new "cutting edge" in comedy as exemplified by "The Simpsons" and the outrageous "Married . . . with Children."

Cosby said, "The mean-spirited and cruel think this is 'the edge' and their excuse is, that's the way people are today. But why should we be entertained by that?"

While "The Simpsons" promised a variety of outrages for the next season's battle with him, Cosby was looking to see what new statements he could make.

Having begun his show with an all-male staff of three writers, he now hired four women. The *New York Times* reported on scripts that would take on women's issues: "episodes about the first menstrual period of his character's daughter Rudy and about the pressure on a new character, a teenage girl, to have sex with her boyfriend." Another script attacked the male concept of a bachelor party, and Cosby applauded it for putting a finger "on what's demeaning and what is not . . . I felt that women could not only check, as in chess, what the male writers were writing, but could color things in a way that the men never could have thought of."

"The Cosby Show" did not win many new viewers with this strategy and before long, Bill was admitting: "I think some of the stories have offended some viewers, but I thought it was important for us to break down some of the foolishness that goes with stereotypes of the female in this country."

The show still had one major thing going for it: it still had Bill Cosby. As numbing or preachy as some episodes might have seemed, and as confusing as it might have been to follow the various marriages and births and new characters that were threading their way through the episodes, there was still Bill. There were still his moments of studious sincerity and super-silliness.

The show was still "family" for a lot of people, and it was fun to watch the old family members Keshia, Malcolm, and Tempestt grow. It was fun to see Phylicia remain forever youthful, warm, and elegant.

There had been a big off-camera change, of course. At the start of the show, she was Phylicia Ayers-Allen. Now she was married to Ahmad Rashad.

During a kissing scene on the show, Bill stopped and called out to director Jay Sandrich, "Jay! She just doesn't kiss the same since she got married!"

Another time, Clair and Cliff Huxtable were about to get cozy. Phylicia began to read her lines: "We could get under the covers," she said with a sexy lilt, "and snuggle and take all night."

Cos: "And Ahmad won't be there?"

After a while Bill stopped teasing Phylicia over the marriage. She was now pregnant, and there was even more to joke about!

As Phylicia's condition became more visible, she had to be written out of some everyday scenes that would involve her walking around the apartment. Sometimes the director would try a trick or two to camouflage the pregnancy.

Once, when Phylicia had to walk into the kitchen to talk to Cliff, there were two big bags of groceries conveniently placed on the table in front of her.

During rehearsals of that scene, Cosby loudly exclaimed, "Anybody have any idea why these bags are here?"

Then he took the bags away and pointed at Phylicia's protruding middle. He announced, "Next week we're gonna have a car in here!"

As Phylicia and the crew broke up, Cos complained, "Ahmad Rashad will no longer come on this set and ruin my show!"

As it turned out, nothing could really ruin Bill's show. Not even the competition from "The Simpsons." In September 1991, NBC paid a reported $2 million per episode to get another year of "The Cosby Show." "We're still there, after all that bombardment," Bill enthused. He admitted that he had learned some lessons, too: "We were sort of tripling up on the reinforcing of certain moral aspects in trying to teach values . . . we're recovered from that and obviously I know a lot more now than I did then."

The old heavyweight champ had gone the distance. The ratings weren't as high as they once had been, but it was "The Simpsons" barely scraping into the Top Forty while Cosby remained in the Top Ten. It was a tough struggle for the champ, but he had done it. And he had done it with humor, as in the Halloween episode of the show that featured a Bart Simpson costume for a gag.

When it came to gags, sometimes Bill was on the receiving end. Like one from an unlikely source—a wiseguy kid in Boston named Conan O'Brien. As Conan remembers it:

"When I was going to school me and a couple of friends decided, 'we want to meet Bill Cosby.' So we made up an award. We just made up an award and we wrote him a letter and said, 'You've won this award, come and accept it. . . .'

"We went out and bought a bowling trophy and sawed off the little balls. Seriously. It looked like a guy who was striding purposefully. . . . We just called it 'The Excellence Award.' It was for excellence . . . it comes time, somebody has to pick up Bill Cosby at the airport. . . . I said I'll go pick him up at the airport. *Now* I know when a celebrity is gonna get picked up, you send a limo. That's what you do. What I did, I said don't worry, I'll get him. I go to my dad's house, who also lives in Boston, and I picked up the family car, which was a 1976 Ford station wagon with wood paneling. True story. My dad bought this car second hand from a motel in Maine. It still had the logo of the motel on the side. Yeah, it was like 'The Pine Lodge Motel' and it had a painting of a pine tree on the side.

"So I drive there, I'm dressed like a slob; I think I'll change later. I drive to the part of the airport where the Lear Jets land. And I go there and a Lear Jet lands, Bill Cosby gets off with a tuxedo, and an entourage, they're all in tuxedos. And I'm like: 'Hey guys, over here! Yeah, right here!' and I lead them over to the crappy car. And I open the door, and they look at it but they get in nicely, and they cram into the back and their knees are stuck and I'm driving along. Bill Cosby isn't saying anything. And then he looks down. I'd forgot to clean the car. He looks down and he picks up a Big Mac container and wrapper and everything and just holds it up to me and says, 'I believe this is yours. . . .' "

Cosby was duly awarded the "bowling trophy for excellence." As Conan recalls it, "He wasn't that mad about it . . . there's no way I'll ever get him as a guest. . . ." Indeed, the favorite talk show for Cos through the nineties would be hosted by David Letterman, not Conan O'Brien.

Cos had made it through even with competition from himself! In 1988 Cosby made headlines when his show was first sold for syndication—at the unheard of price of over $500 million. By now, many viewers were regularly watching "The Cosby Show" reruns every night. Even so, they hadn't grown tired of it, and were still watching the new weekly episodes unfold.

The ratings battle between "The Cosby Show" and "The Simpsons" had been watched with great interest even by people who watched neither show. Sociologists checked the ratings to see how the country was feeling about its future. It was clear that while the ratings showed a faith in the values of "The Cosby Show," the success of the cartoon pointed to a nation feeling a certain amount of hostile, Simpson-styled cynicism.

Cosby admitted: "Bart and his family are in fact sharing the same problems that people are sharing all over the country. They cannot feel they are in control of their lives anymore. A kid like Bart who is—or was—very popular, with even black kids walking around with him on their T-shirts, you can see that he was speaking out against society. He is anti-social.

"When Bart first came out, *USA Today* had a story with somebody who said, 'I don't want to watch "Cosby" because I get a headache because I learn too much.' And I said, 'Bravo.' I know that I've lost that person, but by the same token obviously that person has gotten the message."

Cosby had sent a lot of messages. His show had been in the Top Ten for most of its eight-year run, and now that he had staved off "The Simpsons," it was time to retire with dignity and pride.

Even the President of the United States doesn't stay in office beyond eight years.

When "The Cosby Show" ended its run, many gave it a fond farewell. In *TV Guide,* Coretta Scott King wrote of her personal respect for Cosby:

"Bill Cosby has been an electronic guest in my home since 1965 when my husband, Martin Luther King, Jr., and I became fans of his hit series 'I Spy.' . . . We soon became aware of his genius for comedy as one after another of his record albums climbed the charts, providing us with welcome relief from the intense struggles of the civil rights movement . . . but I didn't fully appreciate his extraordinary personal decency until my husband was assassinated in 1968 and Bill and his 'I Spy' co-star, Robert Culp, came to my home to pay their respects."

She wrote that "The Cosby Show" was Bill's most influential achievement, "for no other program of the last decade has had a more lasting and far-reaching impact on television and the nation. 'The Cosby Show' has set the highest standard for TV programming about family life. At a time when American families have been disintegrating at an alarming rate, Bill and his excellent cast and staff have taught viewers so much about the importance of strong, caring parents, about the values of honesty and openness in family communications that seem to be lacking in too many homes today. . . . [It] provided a refreshing alternative to the mindless violence of so much programming about family conflicts, with its constant barrage of insults.

"On 'The Cosby Show,' conflicts were resolved not with hurt and humiliation, but with truth, love, and forgiveness, tempered by a sense of humor, the way it should be done in real life. Such highly visible models for family healing are desperately needed in this era of epidemic child and spouse abuse. . . . As Bill Cosby closes another chapter of his distinguished career, the nation owes him a great debt. . . ."

Many thought back to their favorite episodes of the show. Some of the cast members had favorites, too. Malcolm Jamal-Warner directed and hosted a special that preceded the final episode. Called "The Last Laugh: Memories of 'The Cosby Show,' " it featured highlights and interviews. Malcolm said that his favorite moment was the time Theo was taught to sing the blues by Dr. Huxtable. Tempestt Bledsoe mentioned the episode in which her character sneaks down to Baltimore to attend a concert. Cosby recalled that his favorite episode arrived at Thanksgiving time: "I dedicated it to Buster Keaton. It was Thanksgiving and Cliff had to go out over and over to get eggs, and spices, and Cliff kept going out in the rain, dripping wet with that long face."

Speculation was high over how "The Cosby Show" would end. David Letterman read "The Top Ten Rejected Plots for the Final Episode of 'The Cosby Show.' " Among them:

After prosecuting Gotti, Clair gets whacked.

Whole group settles down to view a tape of *Ghost Dad.*

Family learns that Cliff's colorful sweaters have given them radiation poisoning.

Rudy gets in trouble when she tells her father "Jell-O sucks."

Alien creature explodes from Theo's stomach and eats everyone.

A farewell episode can be preachy and dramatic ("M*A*S*H") or it can be all soppy hugs and tears ("The Mary Tyler Moore Show"). But for "The Cosby Show," it was business as usual. Because with a family, life goes on. The episode was about Theo's graduation and offered just one flashback, a look at the very first episode when it seemed that Theo was going to drop out of school completely. All the Cosby trademarks were back, from a cute scene with a child (Cos keeping Raven-Symone from reaching the door just by holding on to the back of her shirt) to little lessons in life (Clair to Cliff: "Children like it when you tell them the truth.")

There was inspired silliness as little kids were told that graduation day mortarboard hats were originally used in olden times as snack tables, with the tassel designed to sweep away the crumbs. Phylicia Rashad brought a tear to the eye just by her earnest reading of the line, "My baby's graduating from college." And education? It was still the only show on television that could quote Einstein and get away with it. Because "imagination is more important than knowledge." "The Cosby Show" always had both.

The two leads on the show were firm in their admiration for each other. Phylicia Rashad said of Bill, "He taught us so much about spontaneity. And oftentimes he would whisper things in our ears, things we should do during the taping and they'd turn out so great and he'd never take credit for it. He'd get annoyed if we gave him credit for it." Bill said, "Eight years and we never had an argument . . . she was absolutely spiritually wonderful."

Chapter Twenty-Two

The night of the 208th, last episode, there was a strange irony in the air. Before "The Cosby Show" was aired, news broadcasts described rioting in Los Angeles and crimes of racism, hate, and murder. After "The Cosby Show," the late night news had the horrifying and frustrating pictures of a city under siege from itself.

In the *New York Daily News,* the column from TV critic Kay Gardella headlined: "Goodbye to a great one. Cosby exit no surprise: a laugh-filled winner." But the big headlines in the paper that day read: "Rioters take streets."

Over the next nights, there was more misery on the TV news shows. Viewers could have used more programs that offered the alternatives of kindness, education, and understanding.

In lamenting the end of "The Cosby Show," *Newsday* noted the large hole that was being left behind: "And now, instead of Cosby as the premiere black-oriented show, we have a bunch of second-rate black comedies with near-stereotypical characters, the kinds of programs Cosby himself has publicly criticized."

At a Television Academy Hall of Fame dinner, it was a solemn Bill Cosby who told the media, "I thought I had given you something with 'The Cosby Show.' But I see that you've learned nothing." He wondered aloud why so many shows had stereotypical teens with their hats on backwards, women playing nothing but hookers or victims, violence before every commercial break.

In interview after interview, Cosby complained to anyone who'd listen and, more importantly, to those who refused to listen. On "Good Morning America" he pointed out the new trend in black sitcoms:

"Just because you see black people in sitcoms it doesn't mean it's going to be honest. We have to watch out for the images that they're putting out. Some of these things just wind up being minstrel shows. I know there are network people who ask for 'hands on hips, shake yo' head, mo' def, everybody put the hat on backwards, everybody walk the hip walk' and they all center around what I call minstrel show characters. The only thing is you don't have to put the makeup on now. . . .

"Many comedy writers, the only God they have is comedy and they will kill to get the joke, so they really don't have taste in terms of what is the image of this particular person; what is the honesty?"

On Arsenio Hall's show, Bill was once again ready to confront the stereotypes, even if some in the audience were part of it, hats backwards and hooting raucously with hands in the air.

"You seem to have a problem with images," the young host said. Cosby answered, " 'The Cosby Show' came on and we were there for eight years. We were making a statement about who we are as Americans. Not the full scope of it, but certainly we didn't want to be seen as one note. Now anything after that, after 'The Cosby Show,' the step should go up. But today, what producers and writers are trying for is one note. You've got to have more than that. You have a family, you have aunts and uncles. If you look at these sitcoms, I don't know how many of your family and friends you can see there. Night after night you're being hit with a bunch of people you wouldn't want working next to you and you wouldn't want in your house!

"It's just not fair, there's no level of intelligence. And there's intelligent humor to be had instead of the 'drive by' image, you see. I said to a person one time when I was having a problem with the script, I said, 'You don't have respect for these people. I'm saying, you don't have respect for the characters you're writing.' If a person has dropped out of junior high school, it is not to say this is an ignorant, Stepin Fetchit, Uncle Tom type of character. Because the person is not a college graduate. It's not to say they can't string two sentences together or not be disrupted because a lady walked by.

"African Americans. Americans, that's the important thing, that's who we are. You can't say to me I'm acting white because I'm wearing a suit and tie and I graduated from college. You can't say that. If you listen to these people, the ones in power, it's absolutely mindboggling the way they think. First of all they blame everything on the Midwest: 'The people in the Midwest don't know anything about this and they're not going to really respond to it.' You've got Northwestern University, University of Chicago, and these people are not hip enough to know anything?

"So the important thing is: I want them to raise that level. I want to see people I know. Who are funny. And they say it in an intelligent manner. Many times broken English, many times ultra hip, but certainly not the same note. And the 'drive by' is what they see when they're driving by and that's the image.

"Its not *all* Caucasian Americans. One of the important things that James Baldwin said, he said before the Africans came here, or were brought here, there was no such thing as the White Person. It was was Spanish, French, Italian. You were English, Scottish, Welsh, Russian. . . . When Africans were brought here, everybody became white. So there was a white man, tne red man, the black man, and then, this terrible color they called the Asians. The United States of America: I was born here, my parents were born here, my grandparents were born here. This is what I am. All of a sudden I'm not supposed to have a suit? If I'm not supposed to have a suit, you're not allowed to put your hat on backwards. You got to listen to Connie Francis all the time. . . ."

The networks didn't seem to be listening to Cosby. The new season produced few quality sitcoms and more stereotypical shows. Without "The Cosby Show" for a lead-in, "A Different World" plummeted from the top ten, belly-flopping down to number sixty-one. On October 23, 1992, Cosby's agent, Norman Brokaw, met with NBC executives. No, Bill wasn't interested in putting a new sitcom together. He was concerned about *all* the sitcoms on the schedule. And the adventure shows and drama series, too.

He wanted to change what he was seeing.

He wanted to *buy* NBC!

The shock waves rippled through the entertainment world.

Cosby, worth an estimated $300 million, could not hope to buy the network himself. General Electric bought NBC from RCA in 1986 for $6.4 billion. But with the help of some key investors, he figured he could come close to a reasonable buyout figure.

While nothing came of the idea, Cosby's message came through clearly. There had to be some changes in the way television executives were thinking.

Some members of the media as well as the public were put off by Cosby's opinionated lectures and speeches. Their attitude was that actors shouldn't speak out because they aren't experts, just *actors*. And comedians? Comedians are supposed to be funny; it's unsettling to see them frowning and thoughtful. Why, it's almost a betrayal—we come to them to be entertained, they're supposed to make us smile.

When Cosby called attention to causes he felt strongly about, there was always the double edge—supporters proud of the way he was using his fame, detractors insisting he was just "abusing" his fame. On one subject, Cosby was always ready for debate and discussion: education. The three letters that allowed him that license weren't NBC but Ph.D.

In a piece for *Ebony* magazine he reiterated that nothing could be more important than a good education. He gave a speech that he hoped would be read by all fathers to their sons:

"Getting an education is no longer an option . . . it is a need. If we wait to keep hoping for money to suddenly appear and improve conditions at your school, you will die uneducated. I'll do what I can as your father to help you. This includes meeting with your teachers and protesting when there is injustice. However, you as the student must do your part and achieve education *by any means necessary*. When Malcolm used these words, he didn't mean just holding a gun by the window. Without education there will be no empowerment for our people.

"Do not let yourself be overwhelmed! If you are wise and strong enough to survive the threatening atmosphere of the streets, then channel that same energy into thriving in the same atmosphere at your school. . . . Part of the problem stems from self-inflicted exclusion. This includes using and selling drugs, and a need for the quick fix and instant gratification in a society where patience and hard work are a must for survival. You shouldn't speak of death for yourself at such an early age. Your strength and courage are proved by your willingness to learn and change the law. Breaking the law and chanting 'kill me' defines a mental shortcoming and changes nothing. . . .

"The older you get, the more you hear about the disillusionment and who's to blame for your school's situation. Soon your friends will begin to drop out. . . . I'm saying to you, my son, empower *by any means necessary* with a book instead of a gun. If you say you want me to give you something, surely I can get a book for $12 much easier than a pair of $150 sneakers or a gold chain."

Bill Cosby, "educator and philanthropist," continued to speak out for his causes. Bill Cosby, "entertainer," now had to go about finding a new audience and a new show.

After all those sitcom years, he decided to try a new venture anchored in reality. He decided to try the quiz show format of "You Bet Your Life" because it would give him a chance to bring real people to television, even if only as "contestants." After eight years of memorizing scripts and supervising each episode, here was a way for Cos to relax and still exercise his ad-libbing and his sense of fun and be totally honest with his comedy.

Groucho Marx's original version was on NBC from 1950 to 1961. Buddy Hackett's syndicated revival was on and off in 1980. It seemed like the time was right to try again. Bill reasoned, "People say things that a writer could never have faith in getting a laugh, that an actor or actress could never see the laugh in. But the laughs are there and they're genuine and real."

The show began taping in Philadelphia with only a few minor changes in concept from the original series. Groucho's white "secret word" duck was now a black goose. Bill decided to go with a female announcer/sidekick. The questions were a bit easier than on the old show, but as Bill pointed out, "We don't mean to be 'Jeopardy,' our questions will never reach 'Jeopardy' status."

It wasn't long before the show had its own "highlight" moments, like the time Bill interviewed a pregnant woman:

"How many months are you?"

"I'm 32 weeks."

"How many *months* are you!"

"I don't know."

"Would you like to sit down?"

"No, I'm fine. Plenty of time. You're a doctor, anyway, aren't you?"

Another time, Cos interviewed a woman who worked in a condom factory, testing the rubbers.

"So are they on a conveyer belt?" Bill asked.

"A form comes down. You put the condom on the form and it goes around to be electrically tested."

"How big is the form? I would think that some of the forms should vary."

"They're all about the same size."

"No, they're *not* all the same size! And you're testing? What else? Your job is . . ."

"'To make sure the girls are watching their work."

"You're making sure the girls are watching their work? As opposed to what? Playing at work?"

"Absolutely!"

"Well, it's a good job and it's an honest job. You've probably saved a lot of people. Yes indeed. . . ."

Cos was never as caustic as Groucho, at least not with the contestants. But when people filed into the Philadelphia studio, most of them never having seen a TV show being taped before, he made sure to lay down the law to them. At least, in a comic way.

"The thing that gets me," he said, "is that they don't seem to understand that the quiz part is for the people on stage. It's not for them! So they're whispering and trying to guess the questions. Sometimes I've got to stop the taping and I go out into the audience and I tell them something.

"I tell them: *you* are *not* going to win! And what's worse, you may prevent these people from winning! So please, please, please, do not yell the answers out!"

"You Bet Your Life" was the sure bet of the season. Even now, critics aren't sure just why it didn't take off with instant high ratings. *Newsday*'s Marvin Kitman wrote, "I thought it was pretty good. Then again, I didn't watch it past the first episodes I reviewed, even though it was on every night of the week for months." Many viewers simply were hooked on the competing quiz shows "Wheel of Fortune" and "Jeopardy." And there were reruns of sitcoms like "Married . . . with Children."

While Bill explored new options, other members of "The Cosby Show" cast also began to experiment with new directions. Tempestt Bledsoe gave a shot at the stage, acting in an Off-Broadway show called *From the Mississippi Delta*. She continued her education, taking courses in finance at NYU. When she first began them, Cosby rearranged the taping schedule so that it wouldn't interfere with her work. During the great "talk show glut" of 1994–95, Tempestt had her own program. The response was generally favorable to her youth-oriented show and, unlike many guest-baiting stars, she managed to put up the kind of thoughtful, responsible front one expected from her schooling under Cosby.

Keshia Knight-Pulliam returned to high school, hoping to become a pediatrician.

Of the older daughters on Cosby's show, Lisa Bonet, divorced from Lenny Kravitz, had her hands full raising her daughter, Zoe, and taking occasional acting roles. Sabrina LeBeauf appeared as Rosalind in an outdoor version of *As You Like It.* In addition to Shakespeare, she champions a vegetarian lifestyle and works for PETA, People for the Ethical Treatment of Animals.

Like her television husband Cosby, Phylicia Rashad has dedicated herself to philanthropic causes. In December 1995 she became an honorary spokesperson for the American Diabetes Association. Especially concerned with an outreach program targeted toward black women over fifty-five, she declared, "African Americans need to understand how serious diabetes is and that by eating healthy, exercising, and taking the right medicine they can help prevent diabetes' devastating complications."

At the same time Cosby was premiering "You Bet Your Life," Malcolm Jamal-Warner, now twenty-two, began playing a youth counselor on his new show, "Here and Now."

He described starting work on it as "kind of strange at first. . . . 'The Cosby Show' was like college. 'Here and Now' is graduate school." He said that the end of "The Cosby Show," including the last episode, was not a wrenching experience: "Everybody wants us to say it was a tear-filled moment, but we spent the last ten shows counting down. After eight years we were all very happy when we got to the end, even though one of the rare things about our show is that everyone honestly liked each other."

Like his old show, the new one was going to have something positive to say. "This is as real as you can get in a situation comedy," he insisted. "We do get to deal with issues that plague young people every day, but at the same time we have to come to a conclusion at the end of the half hour."

He added that compared to Theo, his new character was definitely going to be "more hip, more street-wise. . . . People have this misconception because I grew up in television that I come from this wealthy background," just as some didn't realize that Bill Cosby had come from the projects in Philadelphia.

Unfortunately, the style of "The Cosby Show" was hard to duplicate and, to some degree, after so many years the "audience pendulum" of interest was swinging away from that steady diet of well-intentioned family shows with a message. Like the rest of the Cosby kids, Malcolm found it tough to immediately find a new, workable identity as an actor.

As a celebrity, he could still make the circuit and appear in guest-star roles as well as such events as a 1996 golf tournament raising $43,000 for the International Sickle Cell Foundation. Among the participants in that event in the Bahamas: O.J. Simpson and his daughter Arnelle. In the summer of 1996, while Cos was preparing his new show to much fanfare on CBS, Malcolm and actor Eddie Griffin put together episodes of their own sitcom. The result, "Malcolm and Eddie" would premiere to some good notices on the UPN network, several weeks before Cosby's new sitcom arrived.

While some were clearly missing "The Cosby Show," on "Good Morning America," Cosby reiterated that he didn't miss it as much as the fans: "No. I was ready to go. I didn't have anything else. Some of it was biographical and I really caught up with myself. Cliff went past me! He had grandchildren and I really didn't know what to say anymore. And the house was loaded with an awful lot of people, and children had changed. And television was changing . . . and then the demands began to come where the censorship was stretching more and more and more and people were asking for things to come out that I really didn't want to do. So it was time to move on . . . let somebody else do those jokes."

Reruns of "The Cosby Show" continued to do well in various evening time slots, with many educators glad to see it broadcast in the morning or afternoon where it could influence families with young children at home. Laurence Steinberg, a professor of psychology at Temple University, said that the reruns, five times a day, could help reinforce the Cosby method of parenting:

"Cosby's warm, affectionate, and relatively strict, but it's a strictness that is reasoned and reasonable, based on the belief that what children need from their parents is guidance and training. . . . From an early age, these kids know they are loved. This gives them a secure emotional foundation to work from."

Meanwhile, Cosby had to find a new foundation for success. Reflecting on the demise of his game show, Cosby had to admit that the "game" part was embarrassingly "horrendous . . . the people were funny, but they couldn't do the quiz. Ask 'em 'what color is an orange' and they didn't know."

Cosby's old friend Sheldon Leonard had a new idea: 'I Spy' in TV movie form, featuring Bill, Robert Culp, and "their children," who would spin off and become the new, hip black and white spy combo for the nineties. Leonard happily told reporters, "The story is finished, and Bill likes it. There have been some changes with these two guys over the years, but some of the basic things about their friendship have remained the same, which is as it should be." Even before Bill began finishing up the last episodes of "You Bet Your Life," CBS jumped in to give the go-ahead to the project.

NBC was really missing "The Cosby Show." The loss of their most popular sitcom, coupled with the final drip from their barroom comedy, "Cheers," left them with a lot less muscle in The Top Ten. The loss of David Letterman to CBS put a serious dent in their domination of the late night hours. In February 1993 the new West Coast president of the network, Don Ohlmeyer, announced that he had firmed up a deal that would bring Cosby back from CBS. After finishing the CBS project, Cos would begin filming a made-for-TV movie for NBC.

The idea was to produce a "light mystery," one that could eventually become a new series. Cos and NBC agreed that it would be better to fine-tune the detective character in a film, perhaps as many as four over the course of a year, and then consider a weekly hour. Dick Van Dyke was proceeding that way with his TV movies as a sleuthing doctor, and NBC was able to hold on to Raymond Burr by allowing him a less demanding, informally scheduled bunch of Perry Mason movies.

"We're certainly hoping that Bill Cosby will be ready to do the hourly show in 1994," Ohlmeyer said.

In 1994, despite the disaster of "You Bet Your Life," Cos was in the enviable position of having two made-for-TV movies going and an open invitation for a new series.

For those wanting a break from the Winter Olympics, Cosby premiered *I Spy Returns,* generally considered an above-average TV movie. The real drawing card was seeing, after so many sitcom years, the more heroic side of Cos. Fans nostalgic enough to recall the chemistry between Robert Culp and Bill Cosby were also not disappointed.

For Robert Culp, the days on the set of the new movie were just like old times. He remembered how he and Bill were always joking: "When I walked into the studio in the morning, whatever he was wearing, if I liked it better than what I had on, I'd say 'Oh, man, that is a great jacket.' Or 'terrific sweater,' and he would have to take it off and give it to me. And it was mine forever. And vice versa. He would walk in and he would say, 'Oh God, that's the greatest shirt I ever saw.' And I'd have to take it off then and give it to him. I don't know where this gag came from but it got so expensive we had to quit."

The reunion between Cosby, Culp, and producer Sheldon Leonard led to some memories of the good "old, old" days. That was when Culp was dabbling in writing, and Cosby was just hoping to land a guest-spot on one of Leonard's TV series, "The Dick Van Dyke Show."

Cosby had actually been brought down to the show's set for an informal "visit." As Dick Van Dyke recalled, "He did a bit for us about Noah and the Ark. Right there on the set. We were all on the floor, laughing. He acted out the whole thing—I think he must've done his entire act for us." Everyone agreed that this was a guy with tremendous potential, but oddly enough, while a few other talented black actors did appear on the show (Greg Morris and Godfrey Cambridge), no episode materialized that would showcase Cosby.

In the old days, Culp would jokingly say, "I'm the star of the series, your job is to carry me!" Now, even though Cosby was clearly the draw, Culp was still allowed top billing. Otherwise, there was complete equality as usual. Culp and Cosby had the same screen time and the same importance to the plot, although the opening offered up some interesting twists on the fortunes of the two characters.

Just what *had* Kelly and Scott been doing for the past, oh, *thirty* years?

Kelly Robinson (Robert Culp) remained with the government's "Special Services Agency," moving from agent to a desk job as the head of field operations.

Alexander Scott, however, in keeping with Cosby's efforts to promote education whenever possible, had retired years ago to become a college professor specializing in Romance languages.

When Kelly requests his old partner to come to Washington, Scott reluctantly grabs his old government ID card and his gun. He's changed just a little bit as he shows his photo ID to Kelly's receptionist.

"Long assignment?" she wonders.

"Sick leave," says Scott.

One might expect the two old partners to be happily reunited after all these decades, but instead of shaking hands, Scott smiles and levels his ex-buddy with one left-handed punch.

"Get up! Get up," he shouts. "You recruited my daughter! Unless you UN-recruit her, I'm gonna break your face."

Yes, cool Scotty's daughter is now a secret agent like her dad. He only recently discovered this fact because "she's slick, just like me." He'd thought she was away at medical school.

Scott is about to rip up the office but stops just as he's about to destroy a statue. "That's a real African piece," he marvels. "Genuine!"

Now that the real hostilities are over, it's time for the friendly hostilities to begin. The old Culp-Cosby banter returns as the duo fuss with each other, trading insults and put-ons.

"You have that happy Buddha look," Kelly tells his only slightly paunchy pal.

"Is that a hairpiece," Scott deadpans.

"No, it is *not* a hairpiece," Kelly replies with an Oliver Hardy sense of pique.

As it turns out, not only is Scott's daughter Nicole (Salli Richardson) in the service, so is Kelly's son's Bennett (George Newbern). They're about to go out together—on their first assignment. The idea of a son of Kelly Robinson immediately makes Scott suspicious.

"He has your genes? And your horniness?"

The two fathers decide to shadow their progeny and make sure that they don't get into trouble. The kids seem to have a simple job. They merely have to act as bodyguards for a scientist and his wife about to defect to America.

Of course, in true "I Spy" tradition, where race is never mentioned, everyone ignores the fact that the kids will be "incognito" as an interracial honeymooning couple—in Vienna. While Scott and Kelly never consider that this alone will make the kids' job of inconspicuously shadowing their quarry difficult, they do constantly worry that their children are simply too inexperienced to do their job without attracting attention. They're just too green for the job, not too black and white.

While the story itself is adequate, and the plot twists enough to keep anyone from channel surfing, the main draw through the next ninety minutes are the moments of bickering between Cos and Culp, the neatly timed byplay of two buddies:

"You are your famous intuition."

"You always trusted my intuition before."

"That was then."

"I'm smarter now."

"I wish I could say the same."

Even the old hipster lingo is back, with Culp sternly telling his friend, "That was snively craven."

The two dads are generally more of a nuisance than a help in this comedy-thriller (a running gag has them caught, stripped naked, and tied to chairs) but they're still the show. Any ideas that a "Generation X" version of "I Spy" could be spun from the film died a quicker death than the movie's bad guys.

John J. O'Connor in the *New York Times* spoke for most critics when he called the little flick "not a good career move for either actor. But 'Returns' does manage to tap back into the ingratiatingly offbeat humor of the original series."

In the real world, Cosby found himself on the wrong side of the law—or rather, the target of an assault lawsuit. At stake was three million dollars. Richard Corkery, a chunky, middle-aged photographer for the *Daily News* was a veteran who never seemed too awed by the celebs he followed. He amused fellow paparazzi with down-to-earth wisecracks as they all waited in stuffy ballrooms or on cold, drizzly streets hoping to get a clear shot at a star's coming or going.

Somehow, with all the jostling that goes with the territory, he felt that Cosby played a little too rough at an awards ceremony back in June 1992. Finally, in August 1994, the case was resolved. Cosby admitted that he "touched" the photographer, but hardly rattled the guy's film cans.

The jury didn't give the photographer the three million he demanded. They awarded him one dollar for assault, one dollar for battery. And since Cosby was deemed only 10 percent responsible for the incident, he only had to pay twenty cents.

Was Cosby pleased?

Of course not: "Ten percent is my fault and ninety percent is their fault, and they win? What is that, the new math?"

The innocent would get off and the crooks would be 100 percent guilty on "The Cosby Mysteries."

Ironically, the made-for-TV *The Cosby Mysteries* premiered the night of January 31, 1994, four days before CBS got around to screening *I Spy Returns*.

He played "Guy Hanks" (the name taken from his father-in-law.) The character was intended to be as believable as the ones used by Cosby's contemporaries: Andy Griffith's Matlock and Dick Van Dyke's Dr. Mark Sloan. Certainly, if these guys, both light comedians in the sixties, could be taken semi-seriously, why not he?

Looking back on it, Cosby seemed to do everything right. His character on the show was definitely someone viewers could watch every week. There was nothing "unbelievable" about Guy Hanks, nothing that would be a stretch for the real man Bill Cosby.

Guy Hanks might have to use a gun as he deals with New York thugs?

Cosby has walked the streets of New York City carrying a .25 semi-automatic; he's among many celebrities licensed to own a weapon.

Guy Hanks won a lottery and doesn't have to work because he's wealthy?

Cosby has a lot of money, period.

Guy Hanks has a keen insight into human nature, a thoughtful disposition, and a good education?

Ditto, Cos.

About the only thing that Hanks and Cosby didn't share was the part of town they called home. Cosby's townhouse is on the Upper East Side of Manhattan. Guy Hanks, despite his wealth, has no plans for moving out of 610 West 110th Street, an area that mixes tenements and drug dealers with local college kids, pensioners, and the middle class. Technically Hanks couldn't live at "610" West 110th even if he wanted to. A building at that address would be somewhere in the Hudson River.

The feelings were positive as Cosby debuted his first TV appearance as Hanks. "Murder She Wrote" was still one of the most popular shows on TV, and Cosby's co-producer William Link was a producer for that show, as well as Jim Hutton's stylish "Ellery Queen" series and Peter Falk's comedy-drama hit "Columbo."

Right from the start, the first "Cosby Mystery" showed that Bill was not going to play a humorless character. He tracks down a criminal who hides in a men's room stall. Ignoring the danger of being alone with an armed thug, he calls out through the door, "You're gonna be there long?" And as the tension mounts: "Be sure you flush before you come outta there."

Even while the gunman has a bead on Cos, the cool one can't help but make deadpan jokes. He looks into an empty stall and declares in funky exasperation, "Why is it men will not flush when they're finished? Look at it. . . ." A beat later: "There's a whole newspaper in there!" Rest assured, Cos would never resort to grossness for a laugh. After getting the gunman to surrender, Cosby makes sure he learns an important lesson: never touch the flush handle with your hand, kick it with your shoe!

Throughout this, and the subsequent series, there would be jokes made at Cosby's expense, usually a poke in the ribs over his middle-aged spread. As Lynn Whitfield says in the movie, "There is no reason for a man your age to have a body like that!"

Cosby shot the movie on location in New York and included a few New York touches, like Fox's U-Bet syrup as the ingredient of choice in his egg creams: "If you don't have *this,* you don't have a real egg cream." He paid special attention to the soundtrack, enlisting The Mingus Dynasty Band to play the music—which he co-wrote with Craig Handy. In one scene he comically tried to learn to play the clarinet—from a sadly disillusioned instructor played by the show's co-creator, William Link.

There was plenty of room for other in-jokes. In one scene the retired Cosby asked about some of his colleagues down at the 15th Precinct:

"Ohlmeyer?" "Desk duty." "Littlefield?" "Lock-up." "Brokaw?" "Morgue."

The first two names referred to NBC executives Don Ohlmeyer and Warren Littlefield. The last, Cosby's agent, Norman Brokaw.

Instead of a Brooklyn theater, filming for the show took place on the streets of the city. Wherever he went, Cosby took pains to wave to fans and keep onlookers happy. Unlike many production crews that blocked off streets and tyrannized residents by refusing to let them in and out of their own apartments even during long lulls in filming, the Cosby staff made sure to treat everyone with respect.

Sometimes Bill offered more than an autograph or an impromptu dance step. After he filmed some shots of the brownstones in Hamilton Heights, he sent the local Convent Avenue Neighborhood Association a bonus check for $1,000.

For indoor scenes, Cosby and his crew worked out of a huge warehouse near the Hudson River. Cosby was, as usual, attentive to all details of the production, but not such a tough boss that there wasn't room for fun. "There's a very high silly quotient in every member of this cast," said James Naughton, who played Guy Hanks's friend and link to the police force, Detective Sully.

While most stars make sure to plug their shows at every opportunity, it isn't that important to Cosby and his "very high silly quotient." One night he was supposed to appear on David Letterman's show to talk up *The Cosby Mysteries*. In the previous segment, Dave pulled a typical stunt, seeing if a passing cab driver could be persuaded to stop, get out, and come into the theater to hear a few jokes. Bill was so amused by this, he wanted to play, too.

So instead of telling folks why they should watch his new show, Cos strode out of the theater, a mobile cameraman struggling to keep up with him. Cos emerged on the street to hail a cab driver, a perplexed Turkish immigrant named Buke Kadikiran. The young cabbie couldn't believe he had been hailed by Bill Cosby himself—and that Bill was telling him to simply leave his cab parked at the curb and come be a part of the show. The driver was afraid somebody would steal the car, but a grinning "It'll be all right" from Cos reassured him.

Letterman asked the driver a few questions—and then Cosby began to ask questions, too. Bill was having so much fun he didn't mind relinquishing the spotlight. When it was time for a commercial, Bill was still feeling playful. Once more he decided he'd rather goof with the audience than answer a single question. He asked for a ladder so he could greet the seldom-seen folks in the balcony. As the crowd roared, a very rickety-looking ladder was hastily being assembled. As a pair of stagehands leaned it up against the balcony and tried to steady it, Letterman caught up to Bill and pressed his mouth close to Bill's ear, literally pleading with him not to do something so dangerous.

Bill was having too much fun to listen to the warning; he gleefully clambered up the unsteady rungs. One false step and he'd plunge about five feet down onto audience members below . . . now ten feet, now fifteen . . . but Bill made it, shaking hands with the cheering throng around him.

The stunts were a comedy highlight for the Letterman show, moments of silly inspiration. Cos wasn't thinking that he could have a serious fall from that ladder. Nor, evidently, was he thinking that with or without promotion, "The Cosby Mysteries" was headed for a fall. The warning signs were there.

An unfunny thing happened to "The Cosby Mysteries" on the way to becoming a series. The cycle for nonviolent sleuth shows featuring older stars had run its course. Even updates to include youthful co-stars hadn't helped Gene Barry ("Burke's Law") and Dick Van Dyke ("Diagnosis: Murder") from languishing in the forties and fifties of the ratings, along with viewers the same age. Network execs, never too happy with shows that can't attract free-spending thirty-somethings, grumbled their disappointment as Cosby failed to put up the big numbers.

Some critics reviewing the show seemed more annoyed with the entire mystery genre than Cosby himself. Jeff Jarvis of *TV Guide* complained, "What is it about mysteries and age? When stars get older . . . it seems they all want a mystery show. It's true of viewers, too: I don't know a soul my parents' age who doesn't love these shows . . . I just find it dull . . . I used to be the world's greatest fan of his sitcom until he got to be a preachy know-it-all . . . What I see is a star who couldn't think of something better to do."

Bill took his cancellation philosophically. "I must not have been delivering what the audience wanted, at least not enough," he said. He was proud to have put together "a quality show" and wouldn't cast the blame on the network: "NBC gave more than enough in terms of confidence and money." As to the immediate future, he said, "Well, I certainly can't go back to 'You Bet Your Life'!"

NBC had been saved by "The Cosby Show." They didn't get anywhere with "The Cosby Mysteries." Bill quipped, "we're even."

A year down the road, and even "Murder She Wrote" would disappear from the schedule after posting numbers hardly better than Cosby's.

For Bill, the most important thing to do after filming had stopped was—stop eating. The catered food on the set of "The Cosby Mysteries," and the nervous-eating that also was endemic to working on a high pressure show, had caused Cos to paunch out to 240 pounds. That was at least forty pounds over his acceptable middle-aged limit.

˙ A paunchy two-time loser was not a positive image; but it was not something that Cosby seemed to dwell on. And this was fortunate, since for every positive sign urging him forward and appreciating his achievements, there seemed to always be a dig in the other direction.

In April 1996 New York radio station WPLJ ran an Easter contest. The idea was for a star to call in, representing a charity organization. "The biggest star" that called would win a Volkswagen Rabbit for his or her favorite charity. Penny Marshall called. Johnny Depp called. Brad Pitt called. Courteney Cox called. And Bill Cosby called.

The Volkswagen Rabbit was duly sent—to the charity selected by Brad Pitt, "the biggest star." Bigger than Cosby? According to who? "Our listeners," the show's producer insisted.

Chapter Twenty-Three

A lthough he'd had two losers in a row, nobody was writing off Bill
Cosby. In a March 1995 piece on "TV's Ten Most Powerful Stars,"
Bill was still considered an awesome force: "All he has to do is snap his
fingers and he'll get any show he wants on the air next year."

Even without a TV series, Bill's schedule was still as hectic as ever,
filled with charity appearances as well as comedy concerts. Just a few
dates from his calendar:

June 1995: Bill mc's a benefit concert at Lincoln Center in New
York that raises over half a million dollars for their jazz program.

August 1995: Bill lends his support to a charity tennis event in
New York raising money in the name of Arthur Ashe, who died after
contracting AIDS from a blood transfusion during a medical operation.
He declared, "AIDS is in the same position as polio was, and tubercu-
losis and cancer, when I was growing up in the forties and fifties. People still want to keep it hush-hush. People still have prejudices about
it." On Robert Dole, who had returned fund-raising money when he
discovered it was from a group of gay Republicans, Cosby said, "The
last person you can embarrass is a politician."

On the lighter side, he takes to the court in a doubles match with
Billie Jean King. She admits, "He's a really good tennis player. Serves

great." And a good sport: he barely gives a comic scowl when she deliberately bounces one of her serves off his rump.

October 1995: Cosby is the big draw at a tribute to saxophone great Frank Foster. Cosby even plays a big of sax himself, leading Foster to call out, "Get that Bill Clinton thing off the stage!"

As for comedy concerts, Bill was still dropping by Las Vegas for some weekends of fun. The climate for stand-up was back to "politically incorrect" humor. When asked about that term, Professor Cosby was prepared to ruminate:

"When you have people saying 'It's okay to not be politically correct,' what are you saying? What is to not be politically correct? To not think that you may offend people. . . . To not think about other people's feelings—male, female, whatever. In your dog. A fellow called me the other day, he said, 'I just bought a puppy.' I said, 'What are you gonna do with it?' 'cause he's single and he works every day. I said, 'You know, that's not fair to the puppy, to leave it at home.' And he said, 'Yeah, you're right, but I love the puppy so much.' I said, 'But where's the responsibility?' And that's the key thing."

Cos remained "correct" on stage and off. Clint Holmes found that out when he became Cosby's opening act at Caesar's Palace. The country singer walked away admiring the big comedy star's humility.

The featured performer usually isn't too pleased if his "warm-up" does well, but after Clint got a standing ovation, Cosby applauded him. "So," he told the crowd, "you stood in line to see Dr. Huxtable and Clint Holmes ripped your faces off!" He knew what to do about that. When he got off stage, he told the theater manager, "Take Mr. Holmes's things and put them in my dressing room and put my things in his. I want you to double his pay. Take it out of mine, because this is what he's worth."

From coast to coast, Bill was appearing in concerts, at schools, at charity events, wherever and whenever he felt he could do some good. One place he didn't go was "The Million Man March" in the fall of 1995.

He heard people muttering "Is he going to march? Was he at the march?" He told his publicist, "Ask them if *they* were at the march. And did they find me?"

On CBS's "Morning Show," Cosby said, "I heard some wonderful things reported by the television. There was a professor, a Harvard professor, and he said he walked around and must've stepped on a hundred feet and nobody said hey! People were shaking hands, talking to and with each other. The spirit of this, I'm sure when they come back, and there's some people they have to face, the neighborhood, those who are not interested in anything but their own agenda—this is where the *real* battle begins. We've often seen it many times, but this time the spirit is very, very strong."

By March of 1996, Cosby had indeed fulfilled *TV Guide*'s prediction. He was ready to start production on a new series. (He probably could've financed his own show on his own network. *Forbes* magazine once estimated that with his investments, endorsements, and the third share he gets from "The Cosby Show" reruns, Bill pulls in about $60 million a year, ahead of Oprah Winfrey's $40 million and Michael Jackson's $30 million.)

Word had it that Cosby's deal was worth a million dollars an episode. Industry insiders felt that, perhaps, it could come to that if the show was a hit and rerun revenue was added in. But given Cosby's lack of recent success, and the salary levels of the average big sitcom star (Kelsey Grammer's $250,000 per episode), most priced him closer to $200,000 per episode.

Whatever the price, CBS was glad to get Cos.

The network had lost a lot of ground within one season. Once invincible shows like "Murder She Wrote" and "60 Minutes" were chopped down in the ratings by younger and more vigorous competition. David Letterman's reign as number-one late night comedian was long over, leaving him to literally bellow at his audience and repeat himself in delirium.

While the trend had been to find stand-up comics and build a familiar series around them, the odds of succeeding with a Brett Butler were tempered by the greater failure of a Margaret Cho. In 1996 executives were reconsidering proven winners like Bill Cosby and Ted Danson—building fresh series around familiar faces.

CBS executive Leslie Moonves went with "Ol' Cos" to star in a new sitcom for the fall of 1996—committing to at least forty-four episodes and relying on him to start off CBS's Monday night line-up, one of their better-rated evenings.

The feeling was that whatever had gone wrong with the mystery show and the quiz series, Cosby was a sure thing in the sitcom format.

CBS executives in New York could see for themselves that "The Cosby Show" in reruns was still a phenomenon. On New York's WWOR-TV, the show was airing an astonishing four episodes a day. From eleven to noon and from two to three, it was all Cos, and from three to four Cosby alumna Tempestt Bledsoe starred on her own talk show.

At a press conference, Moonves announced, "This is a giant step in the rebuilding of CBS. There aren't enough adjectives to accurately describe my delight at Bill's decision to do a sitcom for us. He is, quite simply, in a league all his own."

Cos, sporting a Dizzy Gillespie-like tuft of hair under his bottom lip (he was filming *Jack* at the time), declared that CBS was "the place that offered us the most attractive contract. Not only with dollars, but with people. . . . It's also a family feeling here."

The "family" had to be a little disconcerted when *Jack,* opening in August 1996, was not the big hit most had expected from a Robin Williams movie directed by Francis Ford Coppola. The film could have added some needed luster to Cosby's image, erasing memories of his recent losing streak on television. But once again, movie success eluded him.

Not that it was his fault. He played a tutor for childish Jack (Robin Williams), a boy whose physical body has suddenly aged to forty-something dimensions. His small role was greeted with amusement, but the rest of the film was not so well received. It was pulled from the Venice Film Festival, an early sign of disaster. It was called "utterly predictable," by the *New York Times.* The *Times* didn't want "a sloppy wallow in cheap sentiment" and the *Chicago Tribune's* Gene Siskel simply found the whole thing "tiresome." The *New York Post* headlined "Hit the Road, 'Jack'" and called the film "a tedious stinker."

Back at the Brooklyn studio that was serving as 1539 Blake Street, home of Hilton Lucas (a.k.a. Bill Cosby), the summer continued to see revisions and improvements in the series as it headed for its fall premiere. CBS seemed relieved that the show was being helmed by the Carsey-Werner production team. They'd produced "The Cosby Show."

The main question was how closely the series would resemble the show it was based on, a British comedy called "One Foot in the Grave." There was still some cachet in Americanizing a British series. Critics remembered how "Steptoe and Son" spawned "Sanford and Son," and

"Till Death Do Us Part" produced "All in the Family." The main character of "One Foot in the Grave" was almost as salty as the abrasive leads in the earlier British shows. Cosby himself described the new role as being "Archie Bunker without the racism and sexism. He's . . . a curmudgeon, a correctable fool . . . it's impossible to embarrass him."

It was a little embarrassing when the initial script wasn't too amusing. Cosby found that audiences turned off to the overly stern and nasty personality of the character he was playing. Fans didn't want to see Cosby as old, retired, and grumbly. In fact, they didn't want to think of him having one foot in the grave. So the show would be titled "Cosby," and the character warmed up to be more like Bill.

The immediate casualty was writer Richard Day, who fumed that "Cosby took a dark, interesting show and turned it into something bland. . . . Of all the stars I worked with—Roseanne, Garry Shandling, Cybill Shepherd—I had the worst experience with Cosby."

As various staffers and execs saw it, Cosby's personality had to be softened and made more in keeping with his image. The almost feuding relationship between Cos and TV wife, Telma Hopkins, could not continue. In fact, it was felt, the new Cos probably wouldn't be married to someone that adversarial. Exit Hopkins, reenter Phylicia Rashad.

The reteaming of Cosby and Rashad was good news for fans. One of the first reactions from the public came from an anonymous woman who collared Bill on the street: "You know what the woman told me? She said, 'I'm happy that Phylicia is with you because I think if I had seen you with a different wife, I would've thought that the two of you were divorced and that wouldn't have been nice.' "

But as with any break-up, even with a "television only" man and wife, there was some acrimony behind the scenes. While Hopkins chose not to comment on what had to be a tremendously disappointing turn of events, the tabloids began rumbling that the firing was all Cosby's idea. Cosby sent out a statement through his publicist: "I did not fire Telma Hopkins. It was not my idea to replace Telma with Phylicia Rashad. This was the decision of the other producers. These producers are my partners. I trust their judgment and I do not make every decision regarding my show."

"A pilot is a work in progress," Cosby said. Of the outcome, he said, "I'm not predicting that I'll be number one because I don't know how to make a number-one show. I can try and make a funny show." And even then, he added, "there are too many instrinsics that go with it." But ultimately he said, he'd make any moves necessary to make the show a success. That meant changing wives on the show—or even booting himself off the air: "With my ego, if this show is not good, if it is low in the ratings, then I don't want to cost CBS any more money!"

Another cast member was fired. Again, Cos insisted that there was nothing he could do: "Audra McDonald, who won a Tony on Broadway, they didn't write anything funny for her, so they said, 'She's not funny' and they let her go . . . the writers only knew how to write for me."

Trying again, a more recognizable star was signed up, a woman who already had a comic persona that the writers could work with: droll, urbane Madeline Kahn. She quickly earned an affectionate nickname from Cosby: "Space." It came from the spacey way she would stare, pondering compliments, advice, or virtually anything said to her. Madeline and Phylicia would play co-owners of a flower shop. Cos, of course, was "one foot in the grave" with no job, having been laid off by his airline company.

As the staff worked on the show, Cos tried to strike a balance between what the British show's curmudgeonly star could get away with and what would be suitable for him. He says, "The English fellow in that show would be dead in America. I mean, some of the things this guy did. For instance, there was one script where this woman walks by his house and she's drinking something and she throws the can on his lawn. He picks it up and he yells at her, then he follows this woman to her home, and gets the contents of a trash can and dumps it through her mail slot. Now in America, you could get away with that halfway through, before somebody would come out and you wouldn't live anymore! I kept saying to the writers, you can't do this in America."

A lot was riding on the premiere of "Cosby." CBS was calling their line-up that night "Big Comedy Monday" and were counting on him to lead the way. Cos was nervous, too. The first show selected for airing was not, in his opinion, the funniest.

Still, for those expecting merely "The Cosby Show" without the kids, there was plenty of comedy—some of it definitely stronger than the old show. In the premiere episode, Cosby tries to get his car fixed and suffers through a Latino mechanic who can't speak English—and his Irish boss who has an impenetrable brogue. He lets his weary face register the aggravation—and there's no Ph.D.-inspired minute urging tolerance of multiculturalism afterward.

Later, Cosby decides he can take care of a pet turtle. But when he starts burning leaves in the backyard, the turtle becomes part of the fire. There was nothing "happy" about Cosby carrying a charred, almost unrecognizable shell into the kitchen to water it down. Somehow the turtle survives. The only point to all of this (since the weak script dropped the topic shortly after) seemed to be that in this version of Cosby, even household pets aren't safe from comedy.

In the next few episodes, the new Cosby was curmudgeonly toward one tottering old lady ("She's going so slow she'll have to speed up to stop!") and accidentally smacked another one over the head, leaving her unconscious. A running joke seemed to be his wife's sultry walks upstairs to the bedroom—and his muttered declarations of still being ready, willing, and able to service her. Another was his playful teasing of Madeline Kahn, asking her, "Do you love me?" Each time, her answer was a different baleful putdown. And when it came to insulting one-liners, even Cosby got into the act now and then. Describing how he had to run all the way to a job interview: "I was shaky, sweaty, incoherent—the man thought I was James Brown."

The new Cosby was like the old Cosby in two important ways—he was still lovable. And he was once again a hit. He cracked the Top Five, just behind "Home Improvement" and well ahead of "Frasier," "Mad about You," and "NFL Football." When the competition, "The Jeff Foxworthy Show," premiered a week after "Cosby," viewers weren't interested. The second "Cosby" episode scored at 14.9 rating and grabbed 24 percent of the audience watching TV. Only fifteen percent were watching Foxworthy.

Just as he had "caught the wave," coming up with a family show at a time when there was a new baby boom and renewed commitments to family values, Cosby was now speaking to the large segment of "downsized" America, out of work or worried about losing their jobs. He was speaking to the large segment of retired America, and the predominant segment of the population that were now fifty-something and wondering how to deal with it. Cos was dealing with it—with feistiness *and* humor.

With new movie possibilities and a new sitcom filming in New York, Cosby expressed gratitude for having a "full plate" in front of him again, along with jazz concerts, book offers, and stand-up.

Cosby knows that whatever he does, there will be people interested in his point of view and ready to give him a chance. "I feel as though the love I have to give to people is appreciated," he admits. "I just want to give more and more and more."

Personally, Cosby has a happy home and he has Camille: "My life now is a very, very happy one. It's a happiness of being deeply connected, of knowing that there is someone I can trust completely, and that the one I trust is the one I love. I also know that the one she loves is definitely one she can trust. It is immeasurable, the wisdom she has given me. With her strength and help, I can only become better . . . and I want to . . . because I want her to be proud of me."

Cosby has reason to feel pride in all he has accomplished, in all the laughter and love and understanding he has brought to audiences. The involvement between audience and artist is mutual. He is one of America's most beloved entertainers.

"I love work," he says. "I enjoy the fact that I can get involved in new projects. I don't want to retire just because I have money."

Bill Cosby wants to do more because, as he says, "I'm emotionally involved with *life.*"

"He Was My Hero"

This book was literally at the printing plant when Ennis Cosby was shot to death in Los Angeles early in the morning of January 16, 1997. The official news did not reach Bill until he was at work on the "Cosby" set in Astoria, Queens. He was called away to take a phone call. As the cast and crew waited, Bill heard the unexpected voice of a Los Angeles police officer.

"I have the worst news to tell you, and I'm very sorry," said Police Commander Tim McBride.

As Bill uttered, "Oh my God," McBride helped the grieving father over the shock. The heartache was something McBride understood all too well: in 1979, McBride's sixteen-year-old daughter had been killed in a hit-and-run accident.

Bill, joined by two staffers, was driven to his 71st Street townhouse. He walked alone to his front door, where a dozen reporters and photographers stood waiting. He was wearing the same kind of cap he wore on the show, a puffy, faded brown snap-brim. He had on a yellow shirt buttoned to the collar, a sweater, and a brown topcoat that was loosely gathered by its belt. Carrying a brown briefcase and looking like any tired man on his way home, he held his keys in his right hand and prepared to get past the crowd as quickly as possible.

They made way for him. The first reporter to ask a question got a somber shake of the head from Bill as he walked past. Cosby was weary but composed, and he paused very briefly to say into the nearest of the microphones held out to him these four words about Ennis: "He was my hero."

Then he quietly closed the barred glass door, looking faintly apologetic that he simply could not say more.

The statement issued by the Cosby family was almost as brief. In the 30-degree air outside the Astoria studio in Queens, spokesman Gerardo Cruz read the official Cosby family response, his voice breaking with emotion: "We have every confidence in the LAPD. Our hearts go out to each and every family to whom such an incident has occurred. This is a life experience that is truly difficult to share."

Stunned fans arriving at the studio saw a sign posted on the door: "The 'Cosby' tapings for today, January 16th, have been CANCELED. We apologize for any inconvenience. All ticket holders will receive tickets for a later show date."

Ennis had been on his way to visit friends that night. He was driving through affluent suburban West Los Angeles near Sepulveda Pass. He pulled off the freeway at the Skirball Center Drive exit. This was a desolate stretch of road. It was around 1:15 A.M. when he used his cellular phone to call one of the people he was to meet, a forty-seven-year-old woman. He explained that he had a flat tire and needed help.

Commander McBride noted that by the time his friend arrived, "he had already put on the spare tire. The car was jacked up and lug nuts were on the ground." Ennis had put on his emergency blinkers as well.

When the woman pulled up at 1:30, she saw Ennis Cosby lying dead, the victim of a single bullet fired by a white male now making his getaway.

Camera crews were quick to arrive on the scene and helicopters buzzed overhead. As the distraught woman stood in the glare of camera lights, detectives were already trying to make sense of this sudden act of violence in a city that had seen more than enough meaningless highway shootings as well as racially motivated mayhem. Did the murderer know it was Bill Cosby's son? Was it a car jacking?

Commander McBride gave a cautious assessment: "It's unknown whether he was being followed at this time or not. I think that's a good probability. But it may have been a chance opportunity that somebody took, robbery being a positive motive. . . . This is really a low-crime area. This is a high-rent district. You have to assume the suspect wasn't up here wandering the street on foot."

Ennis was driving a $130,000 Mercedes 600 Series sports car. McBride speculated, "Somebody just saw this nice car and said, 'There's some money here, a nice car, maybe I can get some of that.' "

The initial shock over Ennis Cosby's shooting turned into an outpouring of sympathy for Bill. News reporters didn't hide their sadness, acknowledging that Bill was such a beloved figure that most everyone felt he was "a member of the family." Fans left flowers at the Cosby townhouse in an expression of sympathy for a man who had given nothing but warmth, love, and happiness to millions.

This was not the time for tabloid journalism. Gory footage of the crime scene was shot by a local TV station's helicopter, and a close-up of young Cosby's body was aired nationwide on CNN at 2 o'clock in the afternoon, just as the story was breaking. Hundreds of angry calls lit up the switchboard. Within a half hour, CNN anchorwoman Bobbie Battista apologized: "There was some tape that aired that showed a close-up of Ennis Cosby, and it was inappropriate to air that. We apologize for that, and to his family as well."

The shockwaves of grief richoceted around the country. It was similar to the grief and bewilderment over John Lennon's assassination and other crimes that seemed to portend a world gone wrong and innocence defiled. On a KABC call-in radio show that day, a distraught woman said, "I can't stop crying. I feel like this world is too hard for me to live in." On Tom Snyder's call-in TV show that night, a caller suddenly asked guest Alan Alda to make some optimistic sense of a world where there seemed to be more and more violence—and more of the good dying young.

"I'm as at sea as anybody is," he said. "As a consumer of this culture, I wonder about it, too; is it a more violent time than it was before? I think I agree that it is . . . it seems harsher. Everything seems harsher. Traffic is harsher. Comedy is harsher. . . . I'm picking on trivial things but . . . twenty years ago they didn't shoot at you from the other car . . . it's terrible. I was thinking earlier that this terrible tragedy [is] shared by the whole country. [Bill Cosby] is so loved by the whole country, it is as though it happened to a family down the street. . . . Maybe that will have some impact at least. Maybe we'll all be a little less tolerant of the casual violence that we see. Who knows, I hope that there's some positive fallout like that, but everybody is feeling it."

"He was my hero," Bill had said, and now a nation knew why. Twenty-seven-year-old Ennis, a 1992 graduate of Morehouse College, received his master's degree at Columbia University Teacher's College in 1995. This was a wonderful turnaround from the son Bill had described in his book *Fatherhood*:

"... Whenever you asked him how he was doing in school, he always said, with simple eloquence, 'No problem.'

"And, of course, his answer made sense: there was no problem, no confusion about how he was doing. He had failed everything; and what he hadn't failed, he hadn't taken yet."

Now Ennis was working on his doctorate at Columbia. During the winter break he was in California, not for a vacation but to tutor students with learning difficulties. Ennis had triumphed over his own dyslexia (the subject of a memorable "Cosby Show" episode with Malcolm-Jamal Warner) and had demonstrated the same commitment to education as his father. Cosby had been anticipating Ennis's return to New York. He was due back home in just a few days, the 21st, the day after Martin Luther King, Jr., Day.

Speaking for himself, for his network, and for millions around the country and around the world, Dan Rather said on the evening news of January 16: "For those of us who work at CBS, Bill Cosby isn't just an entertainer, but a treasured colleague, a member of our team who for many of us comes closer to being a member of our own family—partly because he's given the country so much. Our hearts, thoughts, and prayers go out to him tonight, to his wife, and to his daughters."

Cosby Credits

Comedy and Spoken Word Albums

Bill Cosby Is a Very Funny Fellow . . . Right! (Warner Bros. W 1518)

Bill's first album includes "Noah and the Ark," his recreation of a dutiful if doubting Noah wondering why he's following a mysterious god's baffling instructions. After all, "what's a cubit?" Also on the album are quickies: "Toss of the Coin," "A Nut in Every Car," "Hoof and Mouth," "Superman," "The Difference between Men and Women," and his cute TV commercial about a pro athlete so dumb that he's amazed that "little tiny hairs" grow out of his face—and that a razor and shaving cream strop them off.

The first bit Cos ever did on the "Tonight" show is here, his report on "Karate." To be good, one must practice until you get a "big slab of callus on your hand. It makes your hand look like a foot. Don't laugh. This is good. Keep your hand in your pocket for nine days, then when somebody attacks you, you take a swing at 'em and even if you miss, the smell'll kill 'em."

I Started Out as a Child (Warner Bros. W 1567)

Bill's first childhood reminiscences appear on this 1964 album as he tells short anecdotes about the day he first put on "sneakers" and what it was like to play street football with great plays like this one:

"Arnie, go down ten steps, and cut left behind the black Chevy. Philbert, you run down to my house and wait in the living room. Cosby, you go down to 3rd Street, catch the J bus, have him open the doors at 19th Street—I'll take it to ya."

There's an embryonic version of his classic "TV Football" routine and some memorable quickies on a wide range of topics: a beautifully deadpan look at "The Neanderthal Man" who eats bushes and tries to kill a saber-toothed tiger, some rare sick comedy on "Rigor Mortis" (burial at sea), and a bit on a drunken Lone Ranger.

There's a movie parody ("The Wolfman" going to a barber shop) a dash of sex (the gorilla who can't mate in "Seattle") and a hefty helping of wry downbeat satire (a vignette about people so cool they ignore a man with a pet rhinoceros).

In his gentle way, he even got away with a Nichols and May type bit on funerals:

"They see ya, in the casket, stoned away, nothin' but a rigor mortis face there. And they come out and say, 'Didn't he look like himself?' Which is sickening. If you put yourself in bed like that, they'd say, 'He's dead!' " He imagines hooking up a tape recorder so that the deceased would not only look lifelike, but talk to the mourners: "Hi. How've you been? Don't I look like myself?"

Why Is There Air? (Warner Bros. W 1567)

Cosby's first two albums did not sell particularly well, but this one, coming around the time of "I Spy" on television, was the breakthrough. The album offers his hilarious slapstick recreation of college football and a game against "Hofstra."

It's his story about "the nut squad, these are guys that can play, but they're afraid, they don't wanna go out there . . . they put their helmets on sideways lookin' out through the earhole . . . guy with a scuba outfit, snow shoe, and an ice skate." When the nut squad of Temple University is called upon to play the ferocious Hofstra squad, it's eight minutes of pandemonium ("Kamikazee play—Cosby up the middle, the whole team off the field!") and absolute torment: "Do not touch certain areas of your bodies . . . while you're out there on the football field."

Other cuts include: "Driving in San Francisco," "$75 Car," jock straps and "Personal Hygiene," and an anecdote about taking Midol to cure "The Toothache." He adds to his repertoire of childhood bits with "Kindergarten."

Wonderfulness (Warner Bros. W 1634)

The first three albums Cosby made were not overtly rooted in childhood. This one marks Cosby as "the guy who does all those bits about being a kid." The highlight is his recreation of "The Chicken Heart," the radio drama that frightened him so badly as a child that he smeared Jell-O all over the floor to keep the monster away. Another famous routine is "Tonsils," about a childhood trip to the hospital. He wonders why adults put dangerous contraptions like monkey bars into "The Playground," what kind of weird "Lumps" lurk in Cream of Wheat, and what the joy of "Go Carts" is all about.

He describes getting even with his mom: "I put mashed potatoes in the bottom of my sleepers . . . look, a dead rat! She'd faint dead away." Only one cut is off the childhood subject, and that's a brief anecdote about "I Spy" producer Sheldon Leonard vacationing at "Niagara Falls."

Revenge (Warner Bros. WS 1691)

Cosby has evolved an entire childhood gang by this time, and this album is of special interest to those who like those "gang" stories. This album offers the debut of Fat Albert, a "two-thousand-pound" heavyweight who makes the ground shake during the playing of "Buck Buck." A highlight is the horror-comedy of going home over the spooky "9th Street Bridge," and the wonderful title cut, where Cosby, furious over being hit with a slushball by Junior Barnes, plots to keep a snowball in his refrigerator and ambush his nemesis in the middle of the summer.

Other cuts include "Two Brothers," "Two Daughters," "Planes," "Cool Covers," "Smoking," and "Wives."

To Russell My Brother Whom I Slept With (Warner Bros. WS 1734)

The progression in Cosby's comedies about childhood reached a peak with the twenty-six-minute title cut. It's loaded with brotherly recognition comedy. When Bill has to share the same bed with Russell he shouts, "I don't want you touchin' my body because you're not really my brother anyway. You know I'm older than you and actually you were not born here you were brought here by the police . . . they said, 'take care of this boy until he starts lying.' And I'm gonna tell the police that you have *lied* and you'll go back to jail." The album also includes some discussion of his young daughters ("The Losers") plus "Baseball," "Conflict," and "The Apple."

200 MPH (Warner Bros. WS 1757)

A change of pace, the title cut is a leisurely twenty-two-minute rap about driving sports cars, complete with an audience participation segment where Volkswagen owners receive derisive jeers. Car fanciers will be especially amused. The mild album includes "Dogs and Cats" plus a brief discussion of "Mother's Day" and "Father's Day." Another highlight is a report on his "Grandfather," who taught him to smoke cigars "to keep the worms away."

It's True, It's True (Warner Bros. WS 1770)

Cosby was comfortable enough to move away from set routines to free form, and this album sports a loose fourteen-minute segment where he recounts anecdotes about his visit to Japan during the making of "I Spy." The title of the album is explained in his "Foreign Countries" routine. Does Japan really have nude bathing? "Its true!" Cos squeals with delight, "It's true!"

An early crossover album, Cosby switches from stories from a child's point of view to more mature material for the Vegas crowd. He describes "The American Gambler," does a mild bit on trying unsuccessfully to find "Spanish Fly" in Spain, and describes the time he went to the "Burlesque Shows," only to be perplexed by what he saw: "Why do men go into a place and watch a lady take her clothes off? That's sick. If you're hungry, you don't watch a guy cook a steak! You move away from it!"

Bill Cosby Radio Program (Serial Number 1568)

Cos tried to syndicate a kid-oriented radio show in 1968. Radio stations got a record featuring a few minutes of sketch material and song. This "sampler" record of two complete shows and a variety of individual bits, released primarily to radio stations and publicists, is the most easily attainable of the short-lived series. Most of the comedy is similar to the things Cosby did on TV variety shows of the day. Along the way Cos offers a few Soupy Sales-type words of wisdom: "Charity begins at home. Lend me a dime, mom!"

8:15 12:15 (Tetragrammaton TD 5100)

Cosby was a part owner in the ill-fated Tetragrammaton label. His two-album set is Vegas oriented, with a lot of casually paced free form ad-libbing to the ringsiders and humor about gambling and golf: "You got the ball. You had it right there. Then . . . you hit it away! And then . . . you go and walk after it again! It's a dumb game!"

A memorable highlight is his advice on never challenging "Worse." "You know who's out there? Worse. Worse is out there. Yeah, worse follows everybody . . . don't ever say, 'Things couldn't get worse.' Worse is rough. He followed me over to the baccarat table. Sat down with me. And I said, 'Oh man, things can't get worse.' And he said '*Worse!*'

"I know one time, I was down to my last two hundred dollars. I mean, not to my name, but I lost all I could sign for. And I said, 'I'm gonna win somethin'. It can't get worse!' I went over to the roulette wheel . . . covered the table. I mean covered the table! Red and black. . . . I'm gonna win something before I go to sleep. And the guy spun the ball and it fell on the floor."

Bill Cosby: Sports (UNI 73006, reissued as MCA 552)

Bill's debut for Uni Records in the early seventies was in a sports-oriented album with bits on basketball, baseball, track and field, etc. It had a gatefold cover and inside pictures of Bill from his Temple University days hurling the javelin and hurtling over the high jump bar. Cuts include "Football," "Baseball," "Track and Field," "Mile Relay," "High Jump," and "Bill Cosby Goes to a Football Game."

Though Cosby actually was a star athlete, he describes some less than heroic moments. He remembers being benched most of the time. His football coach calls him from the bench:

"I jumped up, I said I was ready to go! I'm gonna score out there! And he said, 'Gimme your jersey.' I said, 'What?' He said, 'Gimme your jersey. Johnson just ripped his jersey.' So I gave him my jersey. It was twenty degrees below zero out there. And I sat down again, my skin stuck to the metal bench, and then I started to root for my jersey! I said 'Go ahead, jersey, get a TD!' And my jersey scored! Then I started to root for Johnson's pants. I was afraid that was next!"

Live at Madison Square Garden (UNI 73082)

Cosby is in great form before an enthusiastic New York audience. He hasn't spun a really memorable anecdote in a while, and "Handball at the Y" fills the gap nicely. It's the kind of comical story that can be heard over and over as Bill registers grouchy irritation and glaringly deadpan frustration over losing to an ancient old man who simply knows exactly where to stand to hit the ball back where Bill can't get to it.

There's also an embarrassing, hilarious true story of Cosby's visit to Ray Charles's room. In addition, before a child-filed audience, he offers some cute stories about animals (a chicken who wonders why other animals give birth to live creatures and all she gets is an egg) and, of course, many observations on parents versus kids: "Ennis and His Two Sisters," "Bill Takes his Daughters to the Zoo," and "His First Baby."

When I Was a Kid (Uni 73100, reissued as MCA 169)

One of Cosby's lesser efforts, there's a six-minute routine on his childhood hernia—and Fat Albert shouting "Hey hey hey, Hey hey hey" every time Cos tries to lift something.

Another very long routine describes watching Buck Jones movies. Cosby's memory is fine—but he's forgotten to add humor and broad hyperbole. He describes how cool Buck Jones was: "He kept chewing gum in his pocket, and whenever he got angry, and he was getting ready to hit ya, he'd reach into his pocket and get his gum. . . ."

There are brief meetings with "My Brother Russell," and some meditations on "Dogs," "Frogs," and "Snakes and Alligators."

For Adults Only (Uni 73112, reissued as MCA 553)

Circa 1972 Cosby was facing a kind of crisis in his stand-up. He had used up a large well of childhood comedy and the subject was getting a bit stale, especially for adults in nightclubs. He was also now a parent with many kids running around—and prone to see things from an adult's viewpoint.

He describes his frustration in coping with young girls who try to emulate him—by standing up to use the toilet. And he indulges in some of the most risqué humor of his career in order to win back a mature following. He describes visiting a hotel where there's a "Mirror Over My Bed":

"I was uneasy going to sleep. When I sleep I toss and turn and when I woke up I thought I saw a naked skydiver coming at me."

Still, Cos manages to tastefully avoid any bad words or too-nasty description:

"But I don't know what it's there for. I really don't. You gonna shave in bed? What the hell you gonna watch? All I know is from the way I . . . umm, errrr, you get a broken neck tryin' to watch . . . and Camille's a virgin Catholic, I know she ain't peekin'!"

Other cuts on the album ("Bill Cosby Fights Back," "Be Good to Your Wives," "Masculinity at Its Finest") are for "adult's only" only because they talk about husband versus wife, not parent versus child.

Inside the Mind of Bill Cosby (Uni 73139, reissued as MCA 554)

This one was released around the time of his unsuccessful variety show. Cos does a routine on "The Invention of Basketball" that recalls Bob Newhart in style. According to Bill, the game began when two men started to toss a ball into a trash can. He wonders about chitlins in "The Lower Tract": "That's pig intestines! That includes the lower tract—ain't no food down in that area. Chitlins . . . I think somebody misspelled that word." Most of the album is devoted to mild, conversational domestic comedy involving "Froofie the Dog," "Slow Class," "Bedroom Slippers," and "Bill's Marriage."

Fat Albert (MCA 333)

Cosby's 1973 release balances "Fat Albert" routines on one side and more conversational bits on the other. "Fernet Branca," a nine-minute recollection of dining in Italy (on whole barbecued sparrow) points the way to a style Cosby would develop over the next decade: a leisurely kind of "ramble" where there are fewer jokes but enough humor in the telling to make the end result memorable and satisfying. Cos simply describes ordering his meal, his repulsion at eating it, and his misery in trying to deal with gas pains—with the help of a potent Italian liquor.

Another long routine on the album recreates an argument between teenage Bill and his father over using the car. Bill's used the car and left the gas tank empty. His father shouts, "Don't start cryin', I'm gonna knock you out anyway . . . I brought you into this world I'll take you out. . . ." And at the end, he forces Bill to walk eight blocks to a gas station, come back with gas, put gas in the car, and then stand in front of the car: "then I'm gonna run over you!"

On the lighter side, pun intended, there's a rare bit of racial humor. Cos reports that his brother Russell had almost pink skin when he was born: "So I took him home—and put him in the oven." If that wasn't bad enough, there's also a routine here on trying to flush his brother down the toilet.

My Father Confused Me, What Must I Do? (Capitol ST 11590)

Coming four years after the 1973 "Fat Albert" disc, Cosby's new stand-up album, is a triumphant comeback. He does nine minutes on "The Dentist," one of the best routines on the profession.

Cos draws a bizarre picture of his runny-nosed daughter, whose shimmering face makes her look like "the Glazed Donut Monster." He takes aim at the drug culture, lampooning pot smokers unable to handle simple reality—something like seeing a hamburger grilled and eaten. Wide eyed and frantic, Cos cries, "The dude took a piece of round meat! And threw it on the grill! Then he turned it over! It had black stripes on it! I said 'Far out!' And the dude ate it! I can't deal with it!"

Cuts include "The FCC and Mothers," "Mothers Enunciate," "Mothers Will Hit You for Nothing," "Marriage and Duties," "Fathers Are the Funniest People," "New Husbands Kill Things" and "The Lizard and the Mouse." In one bit he describes parental clichés of violence, like "I will knock your brains out."

"That's horrible, man. She's gonna hit you in the head and your brains are gonna fall out on the floor! I always wonder what would've happened if I went to the store, got some calves' brains, and when she hit me threw 'em on the floor . . . pow! Knowin' my mother she'd say, 'Pick those brains up and put them back in your head and don't let your brains fall out of your head again! Or I will knock you into the middle of next week!'

"Please do, 'cause I'm having a rough time this week."

Bill's Best Friend (Capitol ST 11731)

The nine-minute "Roland and the Roller Coaster" describes a boy who can turn his eyelids inside out and curse cool ("Gad dang!"). Cosby is still a grand story teller as he describes his battle with "Chinese Mustard," his voice changing while he's trying to impress a teenage date, and the problem of wet dreams during "Puberty":

"The first time it ever happened I got scared, man . . . I looked at it, I didn't know what it was. I said, 'Uh oh, I ate too much corn bread last night.' I wasn't about to show it to my mother . . . so I rolled up the sheets and went down to the laundromat, did my own sheets, man. Five o'clock in the morning, nine twelve-year-olds down there doin' their sheets too, man. After that day I'd get out of school . . . I'd be back in bed again . . . yes indeed, three glasses of water and a picture of Dorothy Dandridge and I was on my way!"

There are cautionary tales on "Illegal Drugs" and "People Who Drink" as well as "Famous People" and "Let's Make a Deal."

Bill Cosby Himself (Motown ML 6026)

Some of the material here is duplicated from his first Capitol album. Cos talks about "The Dentist" again, but covers some new ground, demonstrating his vocal dexterity as he imitates various dental tools and drills, and does a hilarious dribbling effect pretending to have novocained lips.

He has a few parental words on drugs:

"What is it about cocaine that makes it so wonderful?"

"Well, it intensifies your personality."

"Yes, but what if you're an asshole?"

He describes the chaos in his household now that the kids have grown up. They seem to answer every question with "I don't know." They fight over taking a shower ("Same Thing Happens Every Night") and he becomes so frazzled he ends up letting them have "Chocolate Cake for Breakfast." Fatherly Cos realizes, "Parents are not interested in justice—they want quiet." He wonders about these kids who obviously suffer from "Brain Damage." His answer: "Kill the Boy."

Bill Cosby/Hardheaded Boys (Nicetown NT 1001)

In 1985 a Philadelphia record company discovered the documentary Cosby filmed at Graterford Prison in 1972. A look at prison life complete with interviews with convicts, Cosby did some stand-up for the prisoners as well. These moments are clipped out, yielding only eighteen minutes of Cosby. The rest of the record is taken up by a rap group called "Double Force" singing tunes about ghetto life and "Hardheaded Boys."

For the cons, Cos briefly touches on his own hardships: his mother working, father gone, the family just one step ahead of eviction. He adds, "No matter how big you get you still have to answer to somebody."

The question-and-answer segments are not too different from talk show material. The cons ask him to name his favorite fighters (Muhammad Ali is "a funny cat" but the greatest is Ray Robinson) and his favorite friends (Cos names Henry Silva and Clarence Williams III). In an obviously dated bit, he declares that he'll never write a book "because I can do it on film and on records a lot quicker, and you can get my feeling. The written word to me is fine but it leaves too much to the reader—once you hear something, and hear me say it, the sound is there, the attitude, you can feel it."

Those of You with or without Children, You'll Understand (Geffen GHS 24104)

Cosby was never more in demand than he was in 1986 at the height of his new-found fame thanks to his number-one TV series. He broke records with a series of engagements at Radio City Music Hall (and repeated the feat in 1987) and was a sellout whenever he had time to play the resort circuit. He's very much the "old professor" on this one, talking in measured tones, pontificating grandly on life and family. There's a comic lecture on the Bible, noting the human nature of mankind.

He says, "Man invented an automobile. Called it fantastic. God did a tree—said it was good. The wheels fell off the car . . . the tree's still up: Good."

Adam and Eve were not as well mannered as the animals. "God didn't have to say to the kitty cat, 'Don't go into the ocean, you can't swim' . . . everyone behaved. But look at Eve: 'Don't eat the forbidden fruit.' 'Where is it!' 'It's over there. Don't eat it.' Right!"

There are some obvious parallels between this Bible bit and the one on Cosby's very first album issued over twenty years earlier. As

Cosby puts it, "If God had all this trouble, what makes you think you're gonna walk through this thing unscathed?"

The second half of the album elaborately describes Bill's problems with his grown-up kids. Bill's son is given instructions on the use of condoms:

"I pulled out this packet. I said, 'See these, son? The next time you go out on a date, I want you to put one of those on. As a matter of fact, before you leave this house . . . I want you to put it on. As a matter of fact, before you go out that door I want to see it on!' "

After Hours (CSL Ltd. CC 1001)

A cassette tape released in 1987, "After Hours" was recorded live at Lake Tahoe and and features some general audience bantering ("What did you have for dinner? What are you looking at him, for? Weren't you there when you were eating? A what? A vodka seven? No vegetables?").

Oh Baby (Geffen GEFD 24428)

Cos offers fifty minutes of anecdotal storytelling on this 1991 release. It's divided into two parts. One long routine is "Skiing" and certainly will amuse ski buffs. The other long routine is the title track, "Oh Baby." It meanders through six minutes on urination technique in the dark bedroom bathroom versus a bright public men's room, and ends up looking at the various ways love changes after five, fifteen, and more years of marriage. In a technical throwback to his very first album, Cos uses a catchphrase as a running gag. Back then, in the "Noah" routine, it was "Right!" Here, it's "Oh Baby," an ironic and deadpan repetition of what was a heartfelt cry of young love on the old love ballad "Ain't No Mountain High Enough." As Cos points out, there's a difference between a young lover ready to climb the highest mountain and what really goes on:

"There will come a time in your marriage when you and your wife, both people, begin to change. And in that change there will be things that you're not going to do for her anymore. And there will be things that she is not going to do for you anymore . . . there are things I'm not doin' anymore. Not because I can't. But because I don't want to . . . 'ain't no mountain high enough to keep me from gettin' to you, oh baby.' Back then I would climb in the winter up 18,000 feet. Oh baby.

And I don't know when the change occurred, whether it was the fifth year or the fifteenth, but I know today if somebody came up to me and said, 'Mr. Cosby, your wife is up on top of the mountain; said for you to come and get her,' first thing I'd say is, 'What the hell is she doin' up there?' Then I'd call my son: 'Go on up there and get your mother . . . oh baby!' "

Compilation Albums

Warner Bros. issued *The Best of Bill Cosby* featuring "Noah and the Ark," "Revenge," "Lone Ranger," "Street Football," and others. *Volume 2* included "Dogs and Cats," "Hofstra," "Karate," "The Apple," "Toss of the Coin," and more. Later they offered a more complete two-disc set called *Cosby Classics/Cosby and the Kids.*

MCA put out a two-record set culled from his Uni/MCA years called *Bill.* It features "Handball at the Y," "Fernet Branca," "Wallie Wallie," "My Dad's Car," "Froofie the Dog," Survival," "Buck Jones," "Bill Cosby Fights Back," "Basketball," "Masculinity at Its Finest," and others. A CD from MCA, "At His Best," includes "Froofie the Dog," "Football," "Grover Henson Feels Forgotten," "Track and Field High Jump," "Fat Albert Got a Hernie," and some tracks from the "Adults Only" album.

Music Albums

Bill released his first "straight" album in 1968. Titled *Silver Throat Sings* (Warner Bros. 1709) it was a rocking soul disc that included a cut written by Cosby himself ("Doncha Know"). Other cuts included the Wonder-Cosby composition "Little Ole Man" plus: "Mojo Workout," "I Got a Woman," "Big Boss Man," "Tell Me You Love Me," and others.

The followup was *Hooray For the Salvation Army Band* (Warner 7 Arts 1728) that was a lot looser and featured humorously exaggerated treatments of soul classics "Hold On! I'm Comin'" and "Reach Out I'll Be There." He also covered "I Can't Get No Satisfaction," "Sunny," and "Sgt. Pepper's Lonely Hearts Club Band." Cuts written or co-written by Cosby: "Funky North Philly," "Ursalena," "Time Brings About a Change," "Stop Look and Listen," and "Hooray for the Salvation Army Band."

Around 1970 Bill issued *Bill Cosby Presents Badfoot Brown and the Bunions Bradford Funeral and Marching Band* (UNI 73080). Temporarily retiring his vocal chords, Bill offered jazz jamming instead. The first side contains the fifteen-minute "Martin's Funeral," a musical interpretation of Bill's feelings attending services for Dr. King. Side two is a twenty-minute jam called "Hybish Shybish." Music composed by Bill Cosby.

A second album, also titled *Bill Cosby Presents Badfoot Brown and the Bunions Bradford Funeral and Marching Band* (Sussex/Buddah SXBS 7024), was issued in 1972. It offered more jazz instrumental jams. On the bizarre fifteen-minute "Abuse," Cos raps out some anti-drug lines: "Goodbye, drug pusher, goodbye, with your bag of death and agony and pain. You'll have to find somebody not as smart!" Since the music is way beyond a child's taste, it seems more directed to adults. Especially jazz musicians? A highlight is "I Love You, Camille," a haunting, melodious cut blending African percussion and sax riffs. Two cuts, "The Blues" and "Mouth of the Fish," are sung by Stu Gardner. All selections written by Bill Cosby.

In 1974, Silver Throat came back, but as a baritone. No longer straining for the high notes, insisted the album *At Last Bill Cosby Really Sings* (Partee PBS 2405). There are some sizzling instrumentals and vocals here, with several cuts written by Bill Cosby and Stu Gardner: "It's Strange," "Dance of the Frozen Lion," "Take Your Time," "Train To Memphis," "Kiss Me," "No One Can Love The Way You Do." Cos wrote another cut on his own, "Dedicated to Phyliss."

Bill Cosby Is Not Himself These Days, Rat Own, Rat Own, Rat Own (Capitol ST 11530) was a breakthrough album of cuts that satirized popular R&B and funk stars.

It was a bold move for Cosby, who hadn't released a successful music album in ten years ("Little Ole' Man" from *Silver Throat Sings* cracked The Top Ten). In fact, he hadn't had a successful comedy album in five years, and had been without a record label for three.

"Yes Yes Yes," a parody of Barry White's butterfat balladeering, made the charts. Cosby uses a deep, intimate baritone to speak words of . . . love?

"I wowna ask ya a question, darlin' . . . last night baby, did you go through my pockets? Rat own, rat own . . . wowna ask you another question, baby . . . did you bash the side of my car, baby?"

The song is a ballad about the miseries of married life. When he sings about the joys of love, it's equally ridiculous. He croons, "My love is so deep for you, you can't find it." He insists one lady "could look good anywhere . . . standing up in a garbage truck." Other soul stars take their lumps, too, notably James Brown, during Cosby's screaming "I Luv Myself Better than I Luv Myself." Other cuts include "Ben," "You're Driving Me Crazy" and "Chick on the Side."

Disco Bill (Capitol ST 11683) offers more of the same. Some cuts by the team of Cosby and Gardner have better titles than lyrics: "What Ya Think 'bout Lickin' My Chicken" and "Boogie on Your Face." They also wrote "Rudy," "That's How I Met Your Mother," "What's in a Slang," "Section #9," and "A Simple Love Affair." Cosby gets sole credit for the soulful "Nasty Birthday."

Cos has been involved on several jazz projects. He produced and arranged an album called *For the Cos of Jazz* (Capitol) featuring the First Cousins Jazz Ensemble. He wrote the original liner notes for 1972's *Charlie Mingus and Friends*. Of course, he was involved in the TV soundtrack album for "The Cosby Show" (Columbia CK 40270, CK 40704). He supervised two jazz CDs for Verve, *Where You Lay Your Head* (Verve 8419301) and *My Appreciation* (Verve 847812), the latter gathering great jazz musicians to play his favorite pieces by Duke Ellington, Miles Davis, Thelonius Monk, and . . . in the case of "Camille" and "3rd Avenue Jog," Bill Cosby.

Other Albums

In addition to his own comedy and music albums, Bill Cosby appears on *Diana: The Original TV Soundtrack* (Motown). The Diana Ross TV special originally aired in 1971. His 1972 appearance before *The Con-*

gressional Black Caucus was released on Motown's documentary label, Black Forum.

For the original cast album of The Electric Company (Warner Bros.) he talk-sings two funky humor cuts, "Downright Uptight" ("You dragged me down, baby, I'm downright uptight 'cause of you!") and "Jelly Belly" ("nice and fat, where it's at!"). He also teaches kids about "Double E." For *Bill Cosby Talks to Kids about Drugs* (MCA) he offers advice and songs. Cosby's children's albums include *Creativity, Starring Fat Albert* (Kid Stuff KS 021), *Fat Albert's Halloween* (Kid Stuff KS 029), and *Fat Albert Rock 'n' Roll Disco* (Kid Stuff KSS 094).

Emmy Awards for Television

1966

Outstanding Performance by an Actor in a Leading Role in a Dramatic Series, "I Spy" (NBC).

1967

Outstanding Performance by an Actor in a Leading Role in a Dramatic Series, "I Spy" (NBC).

1968

Outstanding Performance by an Actor in a Leading Role in a Dramatic Series, "I Spy" (NBC).

1969

"The Bill Cosby Special" (NBC).

1970

Nomination: Outstanding Musical or Variety Program, "The Second Bill Cosby Special" (NBC).
Nomination: Outstanding Performance by an Actor in a Leading Role in a Comedy Series (NBC; he lost to William Windom).
Nomination: Outstanding New Series, "The Bill Cosby Show" (NBC, lost to "Room 222").
Nomination: Outstanding Comedy Series, "The Bill Cosby Show" (NBC, lost to "My World and Welcome To It").

1975

Nomination: Outstanding Individual Achievement in Children's Programming, "Highlights of the Ringling Brothers Barnum & Bailey Circus" (NBC, lost to Elinor Bunin).

1981

Outstanding Individual Achievement in Children's Programming, "The Secret," episode of "The New Fat Albert Show" (CBS).

1985

Bill requested his name be removed from Best Actor consideration to give others a chance for exposure and honors. "The Cosby Show" won three Emmy Awards in the first year alone: Outstanding Comedy Series, Outstanding Writing in a Comedy Series, and Outstanding Directing in a Comedy Series.

Grammy Awards for Recordings

(All awards and nominations, unless otherwise noted, are for Best Comedy Album).

1963: Nomination: *Bill Cosby Is a Very Funny Fellow . . . Right!* (he lost to Allan Sherman)

1964: *I Started Out as a Child*

1965: *Why Is There Air?*

1966: *Wonderfulness*

1967: *Revenge*

1968: *To Russell My Brother Whom I Slept With*

1969: *Bill Cosby: Sports*

1970: Nomination: *Live at Madison Square Garden* (he lost to Flip Wilson)

Nomination: *Grover Henson Feels Forgotten* (lost, in the Spoken Word category, to a recorded speech by Dr. Martin Luther King, Jr.)

1971: Best Recording for Children: *Bill Cosby Talks to Kids about Drugs*

Nomination: *When I was A Kid* (he lost to Lily Tomlin)

1972: Best Recording for Children: "The Electric Company"

1973: Nomination: *Fat Albert* (he lost to Cheech and Chong)

1976: Nomination: *Bill Cosby Is Not Himself These Days, Rat Own, Rat Own, Rat Own* (he lost to Richard Pryor)

1986: Nomination: *Hardheaded Boys,* in the Best Spoken Word category

1986: Those of You with or without Children, You'll Understand

Bill Cosby has four "gold" albums to his credit: *Revenge, 200 MPH, To Russell My Brother, and Those of You with or without Children, You'll Understand,* and five "platinum" albums: *Bill Cosby Is a Very Funny Fellow . . . Right!, I Started Out as a Child, Why Is There Air?, Wonderfulness,* and *The Best of Bill Cosby.*

Television Series

"I Spy" (NBC, September 15, 1965–September 2, 1968). Bill Cosby as secret agent Alexander Scott, Robert Culp as secret agent Kelly Robinson.

"The Bill Cosby Show" (NBC, September 14, 1969–August 31, 1971). Bill Cosby as Chester "Chet" Kincaid, with supporting players appearing on an informal basis: Lillian Randolph (first year) and Beah Richards (second year) as Chet's mother, Fred Pinkard as Chet's father, Lee Weaver as Brian Kincaid, Olga James as Verna Kincaid, Sid McCoy as Principal Langford, and Joyce Bulifant as guidance counselor Mrs. Peterson.

"The Electric Company" (PBS, 1971–1976). Guest stars included Bill Cosby, Rita Moreno, Lee Chamberlin, Jim Boyd, Morgan Freeman, Hattie Winston, Judy Graubart, Skip Hinnant, and Irene Cara.

"Fat Albert and the Cosby Kids" (CBS, premiered September 9, 1972). Bill Cosby as himself, Fat Albert and others. Additional voices by Jan Crawford, Gerald Edwards, Eric Suter, Erika Carroll, Michael Lee Gray, Keith Allen, and Lane Vaux. Title changed in fall 1979 to "The New Fat Albert Show."

"The New Bill Cosby Show" (CBS, September 11, 1972–May 7, 1973). Starring Bill Cosby. Regulars included Foster Brooks, the Donald McKayle Dancers, and Quincy Jones conducting the orchestra.

"COS" (ABC, September 19, 1976–October 31, 1976). Starring Bill Cosby. Regulars included Jeff Altman, Buzzy Linhart, Tim Thomerson, Marion Ramsey, Willie Bobo, and Charlie Callas.

"The Cosby Show" (NBC, September 20, 1984–April 30, 1992). Bill Cosby as Heathcliff Huxtable. The original cast: Phylicia Rashad as his wife Clair, Sabrina LeBeauf as Sondra, Lisa Bonet as Denise, Malcolm Jamal-Warner as Theo, Tempestt Bledsoe as Vanessa, and Keshia Knight Pulliam as Rudy. Later regulars: Raven-Symone as Olivia, Earle Hyman and Joe Williams as the grandfathers, and Geoffrey Owen as Elvin.

"You Bet Your Life" (syndicated quiz show, premiering in various markets in September 1992. It ran for less than a year.)

"The Cosby Mysteries" (NBC, September 21, 1994–April 12, 1995). Bill Cosby as Guy Hanks, with Rita Moreno as Angie, James

Naughton as Detective Sully, Dante Beze as Dante, and Lynn Whitfield as Barbara.

"Cosby" (CBS, premiered September 16, 1996), Cosby as Hilton Lucas, featuring the return of Phylicia Rashad as his wife, and support from Madeline Kahn and Doug E. Doug.

Movies and Videocassettes

To All My Friends On Shore (1972). Bill Cosby, Gloria Foster, Dennis Hines, Ray Mason, and Dennis Pate star in this made-for-television drama. A struggling father, trying to make a life for his family, learns of his son's incurable illness.

Man and Boy (1972) with Bill Cosby as Caleb, Gloria Foster as his wife, George Spell as his son. Including: Douglas Turner Ward, Yaphet Kotto, Henry Silva, Dub Taylor, Leif Erickson, and John Anderson. A family Western, the action centers on a father and son's adventures protecting their homestead and tracking down the man who stole their horse.

Hickey and Boggs (1972) with Bill Cosby as Al Hickey, Robert Culp as Frank Boggs, and Rosalind Cash as Nyona Boggs. Including: Vincent Gardenia, Louis Moreno, Ron Henrique, Robert Mandan, and Lou Frizzell. Bill and Bob play a pair of rundown detectives trying to recover $400,000 in stolen money. Robert Culp directed the film.

Uptown Saturday Night (1974) with Bill Cosby as Wardell Franklin, Sidney Poitier as Steve Jackson, Rosalind Cash as Sarah Jackson, Ketty Lester as Irma Franklin, Lee Chamberlin as Madame Zenobia, Calvin Lockhart as Silky Slim, and Harry Belafonte as Geechie Dan. Including: Richard Pryor, Flip Wilson, Roscoe Lee Brown, and Harold Nicholas. A factory worker and cab driver go after gangsters who made off with a wallet containing a fifty-thousand-dollar lottery ticket. The first of three movies directed by Sidney Poitier.

Let's Do It Again (1975) with Bill Cosby as Bill Foster, Sidney Poitier as Clyde Williams, Lee Chamberlin as Dee Dee Williams, Denise Nicholas as Beth Foster, Calvin Lockhart as Biggie Smalls, John Amos as Kansas City Mack, Ossie Davis as Elder Johnson, Jimmie Walker as Bootney Farnsworth. Using hypnosis, two lodge brothers try to fix a fight and save their community center.

Mother, Jugs and Speed (1976) with Bill Cosby as Mother Tucker, Raquel Welch as Jennifer "Jugs" Jurgens, Harvey Keitel as Speed, Allen Garfield as Harry Fishbine, Larry Hagman as Murdoch, and Milt Kamen as Barney. Including: Dick Butkus, L.Q. Jones, Bruce Davison, Valerie Curtin and Toni Basil. A "M*A*S*H" on wheels: life in the fast lane with a high-living ambulance squad.

A Piece of the Action (1977) with Bill Cosby as Dave Anderson, Sidney Poitier as Manny Durrell, James Earl Jones as Joshua Blake, and Denise Nicholas as Lilah French. Including Hope Clarke, Titos Vandis, Marc Lawrence, and Jason Evers. It takes two (Bill and Sidney) to help a social worker reach young street kids.

California Suite (1978) with Bill Cosby as Dr. Willis Panama, Richard Pryor as Dr. Chauncey Gump, Gloria Gifford as Lola Gump, and Sheila Frazier as Bettina Panama. And starring in the film's other segments, Alan Alda, Jane Fonda, Walter Matthau, Elaine May, Maggie Smith, and Michael Caine. Among the vignettes covering the lives of couples in a swanky hotel, Cos and Pryor play two doctors encountering a variety of slapstick misfortunes and miseries.

Top Secret (1978) with Bill Cosby, Gloria Foster, and Tracy Reed. In a salute to the days of "I Spy" (Sheldon Leonard has a small role), Cosby plays a secret agent handling a caper in Italy. This was Cosby's second made-for-television movie.

The Devil and Max Devlin (1981) with Bill Cosby as Barney Satan, Elliot Gould as Max Devlin, Susan Anspach as Penny Hart, Adam Rich as Toby Hart, Julie Budd as Stella Summers, Sonny Shroyer as Big Billy Hunniker. Featuring Ronnie Schell, Julie Parrish, and

Charles Shamata. A shifty landlord strikes a dying bargain: he can stay alive he if delivers three souls to the devil.

Bill Cosby Himself (1983). Bill's solo performance film, written and directed by Bill Cosby himself.

Bill Cosby: 49 (1987). A shorter performance movie, Bill's concert turned up often on cable TV and was quickly issued on videocassette.

Leonard Part 6 (1987). Featuring Bill Cosby as Leonard, Tom Courtenay, Joe Don Baker, Gloria Foster, and Moses Gunn. Ex-agent Cosby comes out of retirement when some of his spy pals are being killed by a pack of wild animals, the dirty work of super-villainess Gloria Foster.

Ghost Dad (1990). Featuring Bill Cosby, Kimberly Russell, Denise Nicholas, Ian Bannen, Christine Ebersole, Dakin Matthews, Salim Grant, Barry Corbin, and Arnold Stang. Cosby plays a family man who dies in a cab accident and comes back to help his three kids. The film reunited him with director Sidney Poitier.

The Meteor Man (1993). Robert Townsend and Marla Gibbs star in a superhero parody written and directed by Townsend. Among the guest stars (including bewigged James Earl Jones and "hit man" Luther Vandross) Bill Cosby appears as "Marvin."

I Spy Returns (1994). A made-for-TV movie starring Robert Culp and Bill Cosby. The retired Cos comes back to help Culp keep an eye on a pair of young spies out on their first caper. It's Cosby's daughter and Culp's son, who don't seem to need help from the bumbling and meddling "old guys."

The Cosby Mysteries (1994) Bill Cosby's two-hour made-for-TV movie, designed to launch his new mystery series. Featuring Alice Playten, Lynn Whitfield, and Richard Kiley. Cos is "Guy Hanks" (the name a tribute to his father-in-law) a forensics expert who has made enough money to retire—but likes the chance to play amateur sleuth.

Jack (1996). Robin Williams is the star, with Fran Drescher, Adam Zolotkin, Diane Lane, and Cosby in a cameo role as Lawrence Woodruff, tutor to Jack, the boy who has quickly aged into a man's body.

Stage

"Two Friends: Sammy and Cos" (1983)

"An Evening with Bill Cosby" (1986)

Video

In addition to videocassettes of his movies, Cosby appears in *Live at Harrah's,* a 1981 hour-long concert starring Rip Taylor, Dick Shawn and Elayne Boosler. *Arthur's Eyes* (1983) was a half-hour video from Children's Video Library. Cosby narrated the story by Marc Brown of a young boy who needs glasses. In 1990 he joined Little Richard and Milton Berle in the cartoon tribute "Happy Birthday, Bugs: Fifty Looney Years." *The Entertainers,* released in 1991, was a half-hour documentary from Public Media Video and Johnson Publishing (owners of Jet and Ebony magazines) that featured Cosby, Charles S. Dutton, and Maya Angelou describing their rise to success. There are video volumes of Fat Albert and the Cosby Kids cartoons (Thorn/EMI) and *Bill Cosby's Picture Pages* (Walt Disney Video).

Books By Bill Cosby

Fat Albert's Survival Kid (Windmill Books/E. P. Dutton, 1973)
    A little full-color hardcover, the book features Fat Albert cartoons

illustrating dozens of sayings and streetwise proverbs, like: "A friend is somebody who doesn't mug you," "If at first you don't succeed, you're about average," and "You never have to explain what you don't say."

Bill Cosby's Personal Guide to Tennis Power (Random House, 1975)

Bill's 8 × 11 softcover "instruction book" offers dozens and dozens of photos illustrating the ways of holding a racket and hitting a ball while making all kinds of funny faces. As for the advice, most of it is similar to this observation: "It is a good idea to use the racket strings to hit the ball. I have tried hitting it with other parts of the racket, the rim for example, but I still believe the strings do the job best. Some of us are very possessive about our rackets. For instance, Sidney Poitier likes to use *all* of his racket when he plays. That way, he says, he gets more out of his investment."

Fatherhood (Doubleday, 1986)

Among the essays, a look at the exasperations of Father's Day:

"I am never as happy as I deserve to be on Father's Day. The problem is my presents . . . I get soap-on-a-rope . . . it is not the dumbest present you can get, but it is certainly second to a thousand yards of dental floss. Have you ever tried to wash your feet with soap-on-a-rope? You could end up with a sudsy hanging."

Or, how about when the helpful wife tries to get the kids to give a gift? And none of them has any money? "You have five children, so you give her a hundred dollars. The kids then go to the store and get two packages of underwear, each of which costs five dollars and contains three shorts. They tear them open and each kid wraps one pair of shorts for me. (The sixth pair is saved for a Salvation Army drive). Therefore, on this Father's Day, I will be walking around in new underwear and my kids will be walking around with ninety dollars change."

Time Flies (Doubleday, 1987)

Bill offers essays on aging, most of them sparked with one-liners of wit and wisdom: "The only good thing about the decline of my memory is that it has brought me closer to my mother, for she and I now forget everything at the same time." "You can teach an old dog new tricks. You just don't want to see the dog doing them." "Don't worry about senility. When it hits you, you won't know it."

Love and Marriage (Doubleday, 1989)

Bill discusses love, marriage, and all kinds of things in between, including sharing a bed: "The timeless question that no philosopher has ever been able to answer is not: Why is Atlanta in the Western Division? And it is not: Why did the Lord have to give mankind both locusts and lawyers? The unanswerable question is: Does a husband have the right to see the road to the toilet at two o'clock in the morning or does his marital vow oblige him to walk into the wall?"

Childhood (G.P. Putnam's Sons, 1991)

Cosby dedicated his book on childhood to his father, to his mother, Anna Pearl Hite Cosby (who died August 7, 1991), and to "all the people in the Richard Allen Homes." Anecdotes include the time Bill had to drink boiled cream of lizard as an asthma remedy! As always, he recreates family dialogue as if it happened yesterday. He and his father argue after Bill's been beaten up by a bully: "Bernie beat me up." "How come you let him do that?" "It wasn't my idea. He did it on his own." "Okay, now here's what I want you to do. I want you to go right back and beat him up." "He sure won't be expecting that." "Right. You'll catch him by surprise." "Yeah, he'll be surprised I wanna get killed again." ". . . If you don't go back there and beat that guy up, I'm gonna beat you up." "Why don't you just beat *him* up? Then it comes out even."